The Day the Sun Disappeared
27 November 1944

Cover art copyright © 2023 by Margaret Moxom

Maggiemoxom@aol.com

ISBN: B0C2SPYYFZ

Published by Amazon.co.uk 2023

THE FAULD EXPLOSION

At just after 1100 hours on the 27th NOVEMBER 1944, the largest explosion caused by conventional weapons in both the world wars took place at this spot when some 3,500 tons of high explosives accidently blew up.

A crater some 300 feet deep and approximately a quarter of a mile in diameter was blown into the North Staffordshire countryside.

A total of seventy people lost their lives, with eighteen bodies never being recovered.

The 21 MU RAF Fauld disaster is commemorated by this memorial which was dedicated on the 25th November 1990, some 46 years after the event. The stone, which is of fine white granite, was a gift, organised by the Commandante of the Italian Air Force Supply Depot at Novara, a sister depot of No 16 MU RAF Stafford, from the firm of CIRLA & Son, Graniti-Milano.

INTRODUCTION

The ravages of the Second World War hit the peaceful villages in the Staffordshire-Derbyshire borderlands with an awful ferocity, and had a profound impact on the whole communities.

On November 27, 1944, the biggest explosion on British soil tore through the sleepy countryside of Staffordshire.

4,000 tonnes of explosives stored in disused gypsum works underground blew up, destroying nearby farms and sending shockwaves as far as Casablanca. In the area of the explosion a 300-acre farm including people, animals, tractors, carts and buildings was completely blown away. The entire topsoil from a square mile of land went up and came back to earth up to 11 miles away. A crater the size of six football pitches, 90ft deep, was left – a pile of mud resembling a moon surface or even the battlefields of the Somme with upturned trees, dead cattle and sheep – the once green fields turned into a quagmire of barren wasteland, having huge boulders of white alabaster propelled from the mines, poking through the surface. 70 people died, with the bodies of 18 people never found. People lost their lives, their loved ones, their livelihoods and their homes.

But this was not Hiroshima or Nagasaki, it was Staffordshire. The sleepy farming village of Hanbury, 10 miles north-east of Rugeley, saw its tranquillity shattered in the most dreadful of fashions. At 11.11am on November 27, 1944, about 4,000 tons of

The Day the Sun Disappeared, 27 Nov 1944

explosives, intended for the enemy, ripped through the earth's crust.

I have included a few bits of poetry at the top of some chapters. These have been influenced by the Simon and Garfunkel song 'The Sun is Burning' about Hiroshima, and the atom bomb, and set in the same meter. It was originally written by Ian Campbell.

RAF Fauld, the depot in which the explosion occurred, the Peter Ford alabaster mines, and the reservoir used by the Peter Ford works, were completely decimated in the blast. This catastrophe changed lives forever.

Many of the houses in the nearby village of Hanbury had to be rebuilt, including the local pub, the school and village hall.

Despite the grievous injuries, enormous environmental damage and 70 deaths, the event is not widely known in the UK or even in the local area, and I feel this story should not be allowed to fade into the past as the last few people in living memory depart this earth.

There was no cover-up. They died in the biggest single explosion which ever took place in Britain, and was quite possibly the biggest unnatural explosion anywhere on earth until Hiroshima. A 416.6 ton mine which exploded under the German trenches on the Messinos Ridge on the Western Front in 1917 went into the record books. Yet, if you do not live in the area or have relatives who remember, you will not have heard of the day when between 3,500 and 4,000 tons of high explosive went off under the fields of Hanbury.

A spokesman from the Guinness Book of Records said, "It's quite extraordinary what gets overlooked in the middle of a World War. To date, while in private acknowledging that it did occur, the

The Day the Sun Disappeared, 27 Nov 1944

Guinness Book of Records has not included this biggest British explosion. It is just that, when Armageddon came to Hanbury, it was coming on a daily basis to Europe."

Everyone and every rescue force, civilian and military from Staffordshire and counties bordering it, came out to spend weeks and even months, working day and night, in an attempt to save people and try to put right the damage. Honours were bestowed on many for their valiant work. Even prisoners volunteered for land clearance and the American Air Force were magnificent in the work they carried out.

Graham Shaw at the Cock Inn, Hanbury

Also, I am most indebted to Graham Shaw, who has provided me with newspaper cuttings, photographs, letters and maps that he and his family have collected over the years, including the reports by PC Mackay, and the Inquiry statements. Graham is the grandson of Mary Cooper, who set up the temporary morgue in Hanbury. Graham has also, kindly, taken me over the area, showing me the crater.

The Day the Sun Disappeared, 27 Nov 1944

Joe Cooper

I also had the pleasure of being introduced to Joe Cooper (now 90), son of Mary Cooper and uncle to Graham Shaw, who gave me a really interesting view of life in Peter Ford's Alabaster mine and a lot of other significant facts. His father, Joseph Cooper, had been a loco driver in the mine, and was killed on the day of the explosion.

I also wish to thank Bob Minchin and his wife, Jeanne, from Tutbury Museum, who invited me to their home, to get copies of all the facts they had of the disaster. They also did research for me on PC Mackay, plus supplied me with other interesting facts.

Of interest has been David Bells, 'Staffordshire Tales of Mystery and Murder', which includes a chapter on the tragedy, and 'The Potteries at War', by Fred Leigh.

I acquired a copy of 'For a Shilling a Day' by Peter Rhodes, which has a chapter on the explosion plus the true story by Malcolm Kidd, which was not brought to light in the court inquiry.

Of great importance in writing this book has been, 'After the Dump Went Up: the Untold Story' by Mark Rowe, especially with reference to the court inquiry into the explosion and photographs. Mark Rowe kindly allowed me to use his photographs, on the request of a donation being made to a charity, which I made to Alzheimer's. I have included a chapter written by Mark Rowe.

The Day the Sun Disappeared, 27 Nov 1944

My novel is quite a gruelling book, and not to be taken in any way lightly. It has caused me great stress, at times, leading me to take a bit of time away from it - it was depressing me with the act of trying to imagine myself actually being there, but the facts are there.

I have also been in contact with people who remember or had relatives who remembered the disaster and I have added their voices.

My grateful thanks goes to Doodge Ferguson who, out of interest and the goodness of his heart, did a magnificent task of proofreading this book for me.

What more can I say, it was a catastrophe of resounding proportion, a story of a make-do-and-mend attitude by the RAF to enable the bombs to be got out in record time to try to end the war; a situation of civilians and RAF working together on the site, but not communicating with each other, leading to mistakes and short-cuts, that should never have happened.

I sincerely trust lessons have been learnt.

The Day the Sun Disappeared, 27 Nov 1944

Table of Contents

INTRODUCTION	i
CHAPTER 1	1
A REPORTER VISITS THE SITE	
CHAPTER 2	4
PC MACKAY	
CHAPTER 3	11
THE MACKAY HOME	
CHAPTER 4	21
OCTOBER 1944	21
CHAPTER 5	25
THE COCK INN, HANBURY	
CHAPTER 6	32
BURTON NOVEMBER (Olive Mackay)	
CHAPTER 7	35
UPPER CASTLE HAYES FARM	
CHAPTER 8	43
RAF FAULD	
CHAPTER 9	50
SQUADRON LEADER ANNESS	
CHAPTER 10	64

The Day the Sun Disappeared, 27 Nov 1944

HARDING FAMILY, TUTBURY	
CHAPTER 11	70
FROM VERA POYNTON	70
Now the earth has erupted	
CHAPTER 12	74
THE MACKAYS – AFTER THE EXPLOSION	
CHAPTER 13	78
PC MACKAY AT THE DISASTER	
CHAPTER 14	90
GOODWIN FARM	
CHAPTER 15	97
JIM HEATHCOTE	
CHAPTER 16	108
PETER FORD'S GYPSUM AND ALABASTER WORKS	
CHAPTER 17	115
CONTINUING THE SEARCH	
CHAPTER 18	125
JOHN COOPER	125
CHAPTER 19	138
THOMAS HUDSON	
CHAPTER 20	141

THE COCK INN, THE NEXT DAY

CHAPTER 21	154
BODY RECOVERY	
CHAPTER 22	156
WILLIAM RHODES	
CHAPTER 23	162
LEN ASHMORE	
CHAPTER 24	169
HARDING FAMILY – After the Explosion	
CHAPTER 25	173
RAF FAULD RESCUE	
CHAPTER 26	201
REPORTS OF SABOTAGE	
CHAPTER 27	207
CORPORAL ARMOURER, L.W. POYNTON	
CHAPTER 28	222
LEWIS FROW	222
CHAPTER 29	225
PETER FORD'S UNDERGROUND MINING	
CHAPTER 30	240
INTERVIEW WITH JOE COOPER	
CHAPTER 31	246

The Day the Sun Disappeared, 27 Nov 1944

    ABOVE THE AIR SHAFT
CHAPTER 32   249
    MACKAY AT THE MORGUE
CHAPTER 33   259
    Others had their stories to tell:
CHAPTER 34   267
    H J PAYNE
CHAPTER 35   271
    Story by Gary Smith – son of Nancy Smith
CHAPTER 36   274
    JAMES BRASSINGTON
CHAPTER 37   278
    PC MACKAY'S REPORT - From Day Two
CHAPTER 38   283
    REPORT OF DAMAGE CAUSED
CHAPTER 39   298
    BRIAN JOHNSON
CHAPTER 40   302
    VISIT BY THE BISHOP OF LICHFIELD
CHAPTER 41   311
    FUNERALS
CHAPTER 42   316

The Day the Sun Disappeared, 27 Nov 1944

   CORONER'S REPORT ON DEATHS
CHAPTER 43   319
   VILLAGE WAITING FOR AID
CHAPTER 44   327
   OLIVE ROSINA BOWRING
CHAPTER 45   333
   COURT OF ENQUIRY
CHAPTER 46   358
   A BIT OF LIGHT RELIEF
CHAPTER 47   361
   MEMORIES
CHAPTER 48   378
   CORONER'S ENQUIRY
CHAPTER 49   384
   CLEAR UP   384
CHAPTER 50   394
   MEMORIAL   394
CHAPTER 51   426
   AWARDS TO HEROES
CHAPTER 52   431
   30 YEARS ON – OPENING OF CLOSED DOCUMENTS.....
CHAPTER 53   435

The Day the Sun Disappeared, 27 Nov 1944

PROBE CALL ON HIDDEN BODIES	
CHAPTER 54	439
70 Year Memorial	
CHAPTER 55	442
DANGER, UNEXPLODED BOMBS	
JOHN PYE	449
MARK ROWE	456
Acknowledgements	463
Index	465
Other historical novels by the author:	a
Footsteps in the Past – John's Story –	b

The Day the Sun Disappeared, 27 Nov 1944

CHAPTER 1

A REPORTER VISITS THE SITE

A Daily Telegraph reporter visited Hanbury on Tuesday, 28th, the day after the explosion. Looking around he could see nothing that existed as it had been. "There is utter devastation both here and the whole countryside for miles around." He stood on a mass of churned earth, which had once been a road and looked at a scene that defied description. "I have seen nothing like it on the battlefield. It was as if a massive air fleet had carpeted this tiny village, its streets and its fields with bombs. All I could see were shattered buildings, some completely demolished, and everywhere giant craters." A be-medalled RAF officer spoke to me, "It looks like hell on earth had been let loose."

"When I left last night, anxious women were waiting for news of their menfolk. Good news reached some, discovering that their menfolk were assisting in the dig. Others were still waiting. Roofless houses were being patched with tarpaulins but many were homeless and had to find temporary accommodation.

The old Cock Inn was practically demolished. Above, a bed protruded crazily from the wall of a shattered bedroom. Despite its blitzing – an amazing fact which even the villagers cannot understand. A couple of the children received minor cuts, but miraculously no-one in the school, or anywhere else in the village, was seriously injured.

The Day the Sun Disappeared, 27 Nov 1944

Just yards from the Cock Inn, Ena Wetherill had just put her baby son out in his pram. She managed to snatch him to safety just seconds before the pram was crushed by boulders.

They were stunned, however, by the extent of their own misfortune. Men stood around in silent groups, gazing at the blasted walls and heaps of rubble that had once been their homes. It was useless to ask them what had happened. They simply did not know.

I spoke to one man, who was standing in a field, which suddenly erupted around him. A colossal volume of earth was flung into the air, with enough force to shatter the walls of the nearby houses. The man's nerve had gone, and all he could do was to point mutely at the craters at the spot where he once stood.

Some buildings at the dump head and two neighbouring farms have disappeared. In one instance, there is only a brick-filled hole, where a farmhouse once stood and it is not yet known how many victims have been claimed there.

Men engaged at the place said that some of their companions were 'blown to atoms'.

Police, NFS units and CD workers went into action with RAF and US Servicemen, from the entire area. Convoys of ambulance and doctors from miles around were quickly on the spot and established emergency clearing hospitals. WVS mobile canteens supplied the workers with food and hot drinks.

Villagers have been complaining that they cannot sleep because of the ceaseless roar of aeroplanes flying over to view the craters. Their nerves were shattered and they had suffered enough, without this, thinking that these aeroplanes were going to bomb them out of all existence. At times they could count as many as 100 aeroplanes wheeling and diving overhead.

In Tutbury yesterday, 28th November, street were closed as workmen pulled down a house chimney made dangerous by the blast.

This morning, the Bishop of Lichfield, Dr E S Woods, went to the village and toured the damaged area, visiting some of the people who have lost relatives. He stood aghast at the site. He slipped into one of the craters, but, though plastered with mud, he suffered no injury."

The Day the Sun Disappeared, 27 Nov 1944

CHAPTER 2

PC MACKAY

PC Mackay, although photo is one of him as a sergeant.

Just as an introduction, I am PC Albert Thomas Mackay, known to my friends and family as Tom. I report to Superintendent H G Heath at Burton on Trent Police Station. My PC number is 282. I live in Scalpcliffe Road, Burton, just within walking distance of the police station, with my wife, Constance, known as Olive, and my two daughters, Connie, who's now 16 and Barbara, who's just six years old. To describe me, well I'm 6ft and I suppose you would say, well built, sturdy, with fair hair.

The funny think about police stations is that we're all given nicknames. I'm obviously known as Mac, but the boss, Supt. Heath, is known as 'Snowball'. It was a good name, at the time, as basically it referred to a snowball getting bigger and bigger as it rolled, which was symbolic of the way he ran his team – as his exemplary conduct and connection with others on the team increased, this in turn amplified each individual's behaviour and encouraged a high-

4

performance workplace culture. So, yes, we thought a great deal of him.

However, some of us has another nickname for him – 'Ted', although we were careful though not to let him know this, as that would not be proper. Some of you may be wondering, why 'Ted'. Well, of course, because of the popular Ted Heath Band, who were prominent at the time – a large, jazz-orientated band featuring five saxophones, four trombones, four trumpets, piano, guitar, double bass and drums. Ted Heath and his music was officially formed on D-Day, 1944, 6th June this year, as a British 'All Star Band' playing only radio dates, although they had been to the Middle East to play to the Allied Forces based there. 'The Very Thought of You' had been recently released and the rest of the lads would have a laugh behind his back, singing the words, especially after the Super had called one of us out for not being up to date with their reports. You could hear, the words mumbled as Heath had returned to his office,

'The very thought of you,
  and I forget to do,
  the little ordinary things
  that everyone ought to do…'

…followed by muffled sniggering giggles. Of course, then would come a shout from his office, "Get on with your work!" and we'd have to buckle down.

………

I was out most days on my rounds, and sometimes nights, depending on what was going on in the area – thefts, mishaps, whatever. In September I had to deal with penalties against a Rolleston butcher – alleged contraventions of the food regulations act against 34-year-old Harold Joseph Dewey of 'Brooklyn', Chapel Road, Rolleston. He was up in court on 12 charges of failing to produce a record of the movement of animals on May 26th; numerous examples of giving excess rations; allowing a pig to be slaughtered without licence; and unlawfully possessing pork not purchased by an authorised person.

I felt a bit sorry for him as people were hungry and he must have had a kind heart. 'Ted' had asked me to get involved and I had gone along, asking the butcher to produce his book. Mr Dewey said he couldn't find it but produced it the next day. However, enquiries had already started with the Ministry Inspector, Mr Blower, checking the contents of Mr Dewey's delivery van. I had gone round to his house with the Inspector, but he was out.

While waiting for him to return, we found the slaughter house had been recently used and two live pigs were in the sty, plus there were intestines in the fowl house. Expecting pork, ham and bacon to be in the locked fridge, we waited for Mr Dewey to return and were astonished to find the fridge empty. Mr Dewey eventually said he had 'bushed' the meat, meaning he had hidden it.

At court, Mr O D Somerville-Jones of the Treasury Solicitor's Office, London, was the prosecutor for the Ministry of Food and Mr T H Bishop was for the defence.

Addressing the Bench, Mr Bishop pointed out that the defendant had a country round. The bare meat ration was little enough in all conscience, and people who lived near the shops had the opportunity of getting their share of offal.

There was no suggestion of selling the meat on the 'black market'. Mr Dewey expressed regret for the trouble he had caused and gave assurance that, in future, he would confine himself to the regulations.

For the records, Mr Dewey was fined a total of £351 5s, which was paid immediately.

Speaking to Joe Cooper, a son of Mary Cooper, he said "A lot of people did a lot of things just to live, didn't they. There was a lot of black market going on. Everyone was involved in a small way."

Another case that got into the South Derbyshire Weekly Mail in June 1944, was about an Anslow Farmer, who allowed 10 cows to stray on the Anslow-Bushton Road on 23rd May. '

I had been on cycle patrol when I saw the animals grazing on the grass verge, moving slowly towards Bushton Farm. Nine of them had forced their way into a corn field belonging to another farm. For allowing 10 cows to stray on the Anslow-Bushton Road on 23rd May, George Alfred Collins (48) of Mill Hill Farm, Anslow, was fined £1.

In his defence, the defendant said he had taken the cows for a bit of grazing, and left them for a short time to get a cup of tea.

One thing that caused us a problem was that we did not have enough PCs to man the station. A lot of our PCs had enlisted so that left us very short on the ground. However, in May 1944, 'Ted' announced that we would be getting three police women. A few whistles went up at this news. "Hush everyone. Yes, you might know not that there have actually been police women on the force since the First World War, even though, at the time, women had not been given the vote. Anyway, that's your bit of history, so no need to get your knickers in a twist. Yes, as soon as they are trained up, three women PCs will be joining us here. I expect you all to be courteous but I also expect them to do their jobs. I don't want to hear of any hanky-panky. I'll have no slacking here. We are greatly understaffed, as you know, so this extra help will be gratefully appreciated."

Well, there was a lot of chitchat after that little announcement and, as you can imagine, a bit of flirting started up when they arrived, but the girls were having none of it, so the playfulness eventually died down.

…..

Sometimes, on my rounds I would meet up with my PC colleague, Ron Thompson. He lived in Tutbury but it was only a 20 minute cycle ride to get to Burton. We'd arrange to have a drink in my local, or his local in Tutbury, if either of us weren't on nights, and, of course, if there weren't any air-raid sirens, warning of overhead German bombers. Of course, in those cases, Ron and I would be out and about, making sure people were ushered indoors or a safe place and that the black-out blinds were drawn.

This one time, we were in the Royal Oak at the top of Wyggeston Street. It was an old Victorian pub but had a great atmosphere and we'd get to play a game of darts. Fred Harrison, who worked for the Prudential Insurance came in and we started chatting. Fred just lived in Wyggeston Road so it was his local and we'd often meet up with him.

"How're you doing old chum?" I said

"Not so much of the old, but my feet feel like they're a lot older than me at present. I've been tramping these streets all day."

"Ne'r mind, come and have a sit down and rest your plates and I'll get you a pint."

"You know, they still haven't cleared up the rubble from those bombed houses. Bombed on 30 August 1940. Of course, all survivors have been moved on a long time ago, or gone to live with relatives. The insurance has paid out though."

"Yes, that was a night," I said. "I remember, there were no warning sirens. The bombing happened just after 10.30 at night. People had no chance to get to cover.

"From what I can recall," Ron added, the bombs were thought to be just from one single aircraft. Eleven bombs were dropped on the Uxbridge area – just casting out the bombs as it returned to Germany. As the bomber was on his own, the local radar stations wouldn't have picked him up."

"Yes, absolutely terrifying." Fred carried on. Two bombs hit separate home in Wood Street, completely destroying those houses and killing Mr Bull, who lived at No. 95 with his wife and their daughter, Betty, just 11-years-old. Then then was Bill Tew of No 22 Wood Street and his wife Emma, and their daughter Mary, The terraced houses opposite were badly damaged. They'll probably have to be pulled down eventually. A total of 31 other houses in Wood Street suffered minor damage, but repairs have been carried out on those.

Some of the bombs also fell near to Fleet Street and Abbey Street. Nos. 2 and 6 are boarded up. There was an old lady, Mrs Annie Brooks, living at No. 94. She was severely injured and taken to Burton Infirmary in New Street. Unfortunately, she never recovered and died three weeks later.

Of course, just last year bombs were dropped on Wellington Street, Carlton Street, the Dairy on Calais Road, and Wyggeston Street, where I live, at No. 8. Too close for comfort that was!"

"Right, that's enough of that," Ron chimed in, "Anyone up for darts?"

The Day the Sun Disappeared, 27 Nov 1944

While we were playing we heard a bit of a ruckus starting. Normally this was a pub with no trouble, but heard a young man shouting out, "You're a liar, that never happened, take that back or I'll punch the living daylights out of you."

Then a scuffle broke out. Ron, ran and got between them. Ron was a big lad, about 6ft 3inches and I myself was not that far behind. I joined in too. We both towered over the two lads. Ron was saying, "Now lads, we'll have none of that here. Now you just pack it in. If you want to fight, go outside." By this time, Ron and I had each in an arm lock and the lads were squealing. We escorted them to the door and threw them out. We could both look after ourselves whenever there was any mischief brewing. Ron shouted out after them, "Now get off both of you, otherwise we'll have you down the nick as quick as you like." - showing them his badge.

So, that was Ron – both of us really, ready to muck in and never back off.

So, that was the life of a country PC. That was until 27th November, 1944.

CHAPTER 3

THE MACKAY HOME

"Yes, hope you have a good day. Oh, and don't forget your gas masks."

"No mum," 6-year-old Barbara replied, but it's so cumber..., cumber."

"You mean to say, cumbersome," I interrupted.

"Yes, that word. I hate it. It bashes against my back as I walk. I'm sure I've got bruises. I hate wearing it too. I feel I'm being suffocated."

Gas masks were chunky, tin covered in perforated metal that stuck out just below the chin. They had a revolting smell of rubber too. Adjustable straps fastened over the back of the head. The eyepieces steamed up and soap was rubbed over the inside of the eyepieces, to try to stop this happening, but this just meant you couldn't see properly.

"Well, I don't think you'll have to put up with it for that much longer. I hear they may put a stop to people having to wear them soon, as the war is going in our favour and the Germans are on the run. But, in the meantime, you'll have to put up with it, like everyone else, lady, they're for your own good to keep you safe – don't want you coming home gassed!"

"Oh, you're a laugh mum, the things you say!"

The Day the Sun Disappeared, 27 Nov 1944

"None of your cheek, you know there are checks from the roaming vans that come round the schools to check there are no leaks and you don't want to be caught out. Now be off with you. And that applies to you too Connie. Even though you've left school, you've got to earn your keep now."

"OK, mum," Connie replied

Popping my head out of the door I remarked, "It looks bright and sunny, so that's good, although a bit chilly, as to be expected."

Anyway, while I was clearing up after breakfast, I started thinking what the day held for me. Various things were running through my mind. I had to start doing the washing – it was Monday, so wash day. That was a task ahead, collecting all the dirty washing, then boiling up water for the boiler, to wash the shirts and sheets.

However, Tom had got me a new gas oven – it was on the never-never, mind, so we were paying for it bit by bit. I was really pleased with it, though. Cake tins were stored in a drawer integrated into the cooker, under the oven. It had gas burners on top, over the oven. It was finished in white enamel with black fittings in contrast to the more normal grey enamel of the cast iron grey of kitchen ranges. What's more was it had a pilot light for the burners. Most of the gas burners in other houses had to be lit with matches or a flint gadget. There was a white enamelled lid that could close down, presumably for tidiness. However, I never did close it down as the kettle was always left standing on top of the rings.

I wondered what to cook for tonight. There was a grill under the burners and above the oven. So, in the grill pan would go your rashers of bacon, if we could get hold of any, that is, as bacon was scarce as a new-born's teeth. The rashers would be cooked and they would have a taste all of their own – delicious. Yes, it would be so nice to taste a piece of bacon. My taste buds were just relishing the memory of the salty texture. Hmm. "Oh, stop thinking of bacon, Olive," I said to myself, "What you can't have, you can't have, so there!" But I'd be glad when the war was over, just to taste a piece of bacon again.

Washing was hard work, but it had to be done – sorting the clothes into piles of woollens and cottons and colours and whites. Tom's white shirts had been standing overnight in cold water containing a 'blue' whitener, which I had stirred regularly using a Dolly peg. Then the electric copper was turned on, and I would transfer the clothes that had been soaking to the copper, adding soap flakes for boiling. Handwashing was next on the list, in the big white sink, using the bar of Lifeboy green soap which was great for getting the stains off Tom's collars, then rubbing them clean up and down on the serrated glass washboard. Of course, the sheets needed changing too. Then the handwashing had to be squeezed roughly by hand before being put through the mangle, which stood on the floor, followed by the clothes in the boiler. I would feed the folded clothes through its two eight-inch diameter rollers, whilst turning the big iron handle with my other hand.

I then had to hang the clothes out on the line to dry. It was chilly this November day, but there was a good breeze and not wet. I was so glad that we had electricity installed and I had a nice new electric iron, such a boon from the old cast-iron irons. Yes, the ironing would have to be done tomorrow, if the clothes were dry enough.

Washday Monday's were always such a busy day. A woman's work was never done!

My thoughts played out while I was busying myself.

The Day the Sun Disappeared, 27 Nov 1944

The family had had a hard few years, since the 2nd World War started. It was now 1944. Farmers didn't have to enlist as the spare fields they had previously used for pasture for the dairy cows, had to be ploughed to grow crops as food production had to be increased.

Looking out of the window I was surprised to see Joseph Cooper. I didn't really know him, just through my husband Tom, but I'd seen him around as I did my shopping. He had been working as a loco driver in the gypsum mine at Fauld for the past three years but he would help farmers at sheep-shearing time. He was well known in the area for his skill at sheep-shearing. Maybe he was in Burton to do a bit of shopping.

Farmers would have had to take on more help to deal with the harvest and, as our men and lads were at war or helping with the war effort, help was hard to come by. Luckily a few families had taken in evacuees escaping the bombing in London.

There were other Italians stationed at the RAF Fauld ammunitions store – known locally as the 'Dump'. These were prisoners of war originally, from the Hilton camp. However, ever since the Italians had changed sides in the war, they were being used now to help out at the Dump, They were basically treated as civilians, earning a little bit to send home. The 'Dump' was supposed to be a secret to the rest of the world, except us of course. Imagine if the Germans knew about it! Then again, they probably did as we were constantly being told on the wireless broadcasts to beware what you say, as you don't know who could be listening in.

Workers would go off daily to the site, and I knew truckloads of used bombs were going there to be defused, put back into working order, and then sent out on their single-track railway, to awaiting planes at the nearby RAF aerodromes. It all came to be part of life.

The Day the Sun Disappeared, 27 Nov 1944

The Dump had been there since 1939. The thought of thousands of tons of bombs underneath the Stonepit hills had sort of lost its edge. People had put up with the comings and goings of RAF traffic since the site was opened.

In 1937 the Air Ministry had purchased the disused gypsum workings next to Peter Ford's plaster works for weapons storage, about 450,000 square feet. In fact we were grateful as it provided so much work for those people who could not join the war effort, through age, needing glasses or even having flat feet. That was weird – I never thought of people having flat feet, apart from the local police, but that was just a joke – the plodders we called them! My Tom was a police constable, but I can assure you he didn't have flat feet! But then again, he wasn't out walking, he had his trusty bike – but he did enough miles on that, going from town to village to little hamlet. He'd come home fare wacked after a long shift, ready for his tea and a long soak in the tin bath. Getting back to flat feet, I suppose it was no fun for the soldiers, marching with heavy back packs straining every joint and muscle, then having their feet ache with the weight and not able to keep up. That's probably why the army wouldn't have them.

So, we were just getting on with our everyday life as best we could. The main thing that worried us was the enemy aircraft dropping bombs on neighbouring cities, like Derby, Coventry and Birmingham. Any one of those aircraft could be shot down in our vicinity, so we did feel vulnerable.

The Italians at RAF Fauld were a good lot, a bit rough and tumble, but they were hard workers. Tom said he could see them through the wire fence. They liked a laugh and, although most of them couldn't speak English, they liked our young ladies of the village, flirting with them through the fence, calling out, "bambino" and such like, and blowing kisses. I mean, if the girls didn't like it, why go all the way out there? It was all harmless fun. I think most of the Italians at the Dump were glad to be away from the front, and safe, although they were desperate to hear of news of their families back home, and this bit of innocent banter gave a bit of light relief from worrying about what was happening in Italy.

Farms in the area had land girls, who had come from the big cities. Most of them had never seen a farm, let alone worked on one, turning up with their coiffured hair, city shoes and manicured nails, but they soon caught on, and mucked in, wearing Wellington boots, overalls and scarves keeping their hair in place. Some of them were a bit flighty though, and any time they had free, you would see them chatting to the Italians or the RAF or checking on when the next dance was to be held.

News got around that the Goodwins at Upper Castle Hayes farm had a 16-year old evacuee from Wallasey, Cheshire, but they were really a bit away from us in Burton, on the southern side of the Dump, nearer Tutbury.

They had cows and I imagine they would harness the horses to their cart and load it up with the churns of milk from the dairy cows the same as most farms around the area. The milk would be dropped at the bottom of their lanes for the Milk Marketing Board to pick up, although some was taken to the Nestlé factory at Tutbury. Milk would arrive from the neighbouring farms in metal churns on the back of wagons and leave in tin cans via the dedicated railway siding. None of the families around here had these new-fangled refrigerators, we'd seen advertised in the newspapers. We just made do with our cool cupboard, which most houses had. These were the coldest place in the house, so the milk wouldn't go off, especially in hot weather. So, these tins were just the thing. The Tutbury factory was opened in 1901. Dairies frequently delivered milk straight from the cow, warm, unpasteurized and not always free from contaminants. Tinned milk was the only option for consumers that wanted the nutritional benefits of cow's milk without the health risks. The factory at Tutbury had also set up production, packing of powdered eggs and Red Cross food parcels to those in need, and to the war front.

If anyone had pigs any sour milk would have been saved to feed them.

I then started thinking of Christmas. It wasn't that far away. I was hoping we would be given a bit more on our rations, otherwise Christmas just would be a dull affair, but I knew we would make the best of it, making paper chains, and it would be lovely going to church and singing carols. But, my mind went to thinking of the poor soldiers, out there in the cold, building trenches, dealing with bomb disposal, fighting for their lives, fighting for our country, waiting desperately for parcels coming to them containing the long-awaited letters from home, plus newly knitted socks or, if they were extremely lucky, a bar of chocolate, which no-one could get hold of. Oh how I'd love just a teeny square of chocolate – the memory of that succulent taste just melting in my mouth. "No, Olive, get that out of your mind" I said to myself - It just didn't bear thinking about.

As I occupied myself, wiping the sweat off my forehead as, with the fire lit and the hot water in the boiler, and the hard work, it was like being in a Chinese washroom, I found myself thinking of our daughters, Constance or Connie for short, named after me, and Barbara. They were great kids. Barbara was now just six years old and Connie was now 16 – quite an age gap but that's how things worked out. We had to be wary what Connie was up to as

The Day the Sun Disappeared, 27 Nov 1944

any young lads were after a nice looking girl like our Connie and she also had an eye for the RAF we saw down the local. Connie had got herself a job at the local pub, The Elms in Stapenhill Road, of an evening, just picking up glasses, washing up and bits as she was under age to serve drinks. The RAF, mainly Americans, would come in in their smart uniforms and shiny teeth, and chat her up. But Connie had a head on her shoulders, plus she was also working on a farm, digging up cabbages and carrots, so I suppose she was too busy for any romancing – well, I hoped, anyway!

Elms Inn, Stapenhill Road

My dad, John Pittaway was living with us too. He was getting on a bit now – 79 years old and not keeping all that well, so he'd come to live with us. He used to be a tube fitter. He'd help me where he could, hanging out the washing, getting shopping for me from the local shops and so on, but as he couldn't walk very far now, he spent most of his time reading the papers in front of the fire or down the local.

The rest of the family were in Wolverhampton, not all that far away but, with the war being on, we didn't get to visit that often.

The Day the Sun Disappeared, 27 Nov 1944

Maybe we'd get to see them at Christmas. Tom's parents Edward and Agnes were there and his sister Florence Ellen, who we called Nell. Tom himself was born in Wolverhampton but we met, at a dance, married and came to live here –a Victorian end of terrace at No. 12 Scalpfliffe Road, Burton-on-Trent, having a side path and gate leading to the garden. Tom was born in 1904, so that made him 40. He'd just had his birthday last month, on 4th October. I am two years older than him, coming into this world on 8th May 1902.

At night you could see searchlights from the searchlight station at RAF Tatenhill, just west of Burton, sweeping the skies for enemy planes. A brewery sports ground in Burton also had search lights, a listening post, two small barrage balloons, and an Ack Ack Gun for anti-aircraft, all spread around the edges of the field.

If the unnerving wail of the siren went off at night, that would mean it was time to take cover, normally under the big oak table, which we had moved to the far corner of the room and put mattresses around the sides and cushions on top. All windows had black-out blinds which would help stop the panes of glass careering through the room if they got shattered. To begin with, when the sirens sounded, our hearts felt as if they had ceased to beat. We'd all jump up then hurry to our safe place. I'd put blankets and pillows under the table and we would try to get as comfortable as possible. It was impossible to get to sleep though with all the worry if a bomb was going to land on us. So, I made up stories for the girls, trying to keep their minds off the racket and whoosh of the bombing. If Connie was at the pub I knew she could shelter in their cellar. Tom would normally be out, getting people off the streets and I lived in dread that he would be hit. We

The Day the Sun Disappeared, 27 Nov 1944

waited there until the "All Clear "sounded. Tom would come home and we'd all hug him, glad that he was safe for another day but then he'd be out, checking if any bombs had actually landed and, if so, helping with the rescue teams.

Although a few bombs descended on the area most of the raids were intended for the Rolls Royce factory in Derby, but as we were en-route we had many disturbed nights, with the feeling that, until we heard the 'All Clear' we were still at risk - a Jerry pilot might decide to off-load any bombs before heading back.

If the sirens went off at night and the all clear was after 1am, children didn't have to go to school until 10am so they could get a bit of sleep.

There were obviously other places of safety, underground. Some people had cellars and neighbours would be invited down there in air raids. Tom said that over by the gypsum mines, people would flock there and take shelter in those mines.

We sort of lived on cups of tea, what with the rationing – just to give our stomachs a feeling of being full.

CHAPTER 4

OCTOBER 1944

John Pittaway, my father, was sitting by the fire reading the Burton Observer.

"Ay, it says 'ere that the coal board are gonna restrict the amount of coal we use from now until January."

"Ay, give over, they can't cut our coal use, not with winter almost on top of us. That's just not on." I went over to dad to read that section of the newspaper.

"Ah, but they're saying 'controlled premises'. I think that means places where people are working."

I read on, out loud. "No controlled premises may be supplied, except by licence from the Local Fuel Overseer, with more than one ton of house and kitchen coal (including coalite). Stocks at any premises, including any delivery made, may not be raised above 25cwts….. then it goes on. 'These are maximum quantities, not rations. Merchants will not have enough coal to give everybody the maximum quantity and only very limited supplies of coke and anthracite are available.

These are maximum quantities, not rations, dad. Merchants will not have enough coal to give everybody the maximum quantity, and only very limited supplies of coke and anthracite are available." I read on, "'The supply position remains exceedingly

The Day the Sun Disappeared, 27 Nov 1944

difficult and it is essential that the strictest economy in the use of all forms of fuel be exercised this winter if serious hardship is to be avoided during the colder weather. Consumers who have been able to build up reserve stocks should draw on these as sparingly as possible, since they will be urgently needed later on.

The exemption of hospitals, schools and other educations institutions from the restrictions will cease as from 31 October, and the only premises exempt will be those which receive a special certificate of exemption from the Regional Coal Officer.'

Migh, dad, so the schools and work places will be freezing and we'll have to cut down on the amount we use here. We'll be walking around in our coats, hats and gloves, indoors. It's fine when I'm doing the washing but we'll have to get a couple of electric fires, then the electricity bill will go sky high!"

"You've got that wrong, Olive. Electricity is produced by firing coal. So we won't have electricity either."

"Oh, I can't be 'aving that, not with Christmas in the middle of it all."

"Oh, well, we'll have to grin and bear it, Olive. We'll have to find something else to put on the fire – chop some wood up maybe."

"Are you offering?"

"Well, I'll do my best. That will keep me warm anyway, and it's probably no good going down the pub as they'll be cold there too."

"Little Barbara will be at school with no heating. She'll be coming home with a cold if she doesn't wrap up well. I'll better get some Veno's cough cure in store, just in case…. Oh, here's an advert for Eezit for headaches. 'When a raging headache just spoils your evening, take Eezit. It is quickly assimilated into the stomach and does not upset the digestive organs. It calms the nerves and is good for colds and flu.' So, I'll get some of that too."

"Oh, talking about Christmas, have you seen this advert."

"Ok, 'Food Facts, how to get your Christmas extras.' Read it out to me dad."

"Well, it says, 'The extra food rations for Christmas have already been announced. These are extra sugar, margarine, and meat. There will also be extra sweets for the younger generation and extra cheese in place of meat for vegetarians. For holders of adult buff ration books, child's green ration book and junior blue ration book.

Sugar: 8 oz obtainable once only between 10th December and 6th January. Preserves may not be taken instead. Coupon K for week 22 will be used.

Margarine: 8oz for the same dates. Fats coupon for week 22 will be used.

Meat: value of each coupon increased from 7d to 11d. The value of each meat ration authorised on form RG48 will also be 1s10d (child's 11d). Obtainable between 17th and 23 December.

Cheese for vegetarians who are authorised to get cheese instead of meat 6oz. Obtainable only between 10th December and 6th January. Cheese coupon for week 22 will be used.

Chocolate and sweets: 8oz (for young people only). Obtainable between 10th December and 6th January.

Tea for over 70's: As announced in last week's Food Facts, tea for the over 70's can now be obtained from the local Food Office.'"

The Day the Sun Disappeared, 27 Nov 1944

"Oh well, at least that answers my question about extra rations for Christmas….Oh, and I know it's only October, but I've just noticed an advert for children's books for Christmas. I may keep that in mind for Barbara."

DARLEYS

CHRISTMAS BOOKS FOR CHILDREN

A CHRISTMAS CAROL	8/6
JOLLY LITTLE JUMBO, by Enid Blyton	2/6
AT APPLETREE FARM, by Enid Blyton	2/6
COME TO THE CIRCUS, by Enid Blyton	2/6
THE TOYS COME TO LIFE, by Enid Blyton	3/6
THE DOG THAT WENT TO FAIRYLAND, by Enid Blyton	3/6

BURTON

CHAPTER 5

THE COCK INN, HANBURY

It was Friday, 24 November, 1944. Many of the farmers and townsfolk had gathered as usual at the end of a hard week, to whet their whistles at the local pub.

The Cock Inn wasn't much of a pub in those day, a bit spit and sawdust sort of a job, but it was their pub and they loved coming there to relax and have a laugh. It wasn't a family pub, so to speak as the wives would stay a home with the children. It wasn't really seen in those days for respectable women to go 'down the pub'. Anyway, it was good for the women to not have their men under their feet. They'd give them their tea, then wave them goodbye.

Maurice Goodwin was there (from Upper Castle Hayes Farm) with Stephen and John West. He wasn't much of a drinker but he wanted to treat Stephen and John for their hard work. John Hardwick, Fred Ford and Horace and Dick Utting were there when they arrived. Dick lived at Fauld House. Horace was the older brother to Dick and worked in the Dump. John Hardwick and Fred Ford lived close by Top Farm.

Jim Heathcote, from Fauld Manor Farm, was on a nearby table. Jim was now out of his usual overalls but still had on his peaked flat cap. He had a young son, David, who was only about two, and would be at home with his mother. He was a very nice, easy-

The Day the Sun Disappeared, 27 Nov 1944

going sort of a chap though a bit on the slow side (according to Joe Cooper)

John Hardwick was talking to Dick Utting of Fauld House, saying that he'd heard about the RAF conducting air-raids over Europe with bombs supplied from Fauld. Then went on to talk about Hitler employing pilotless V bombers that had started a few months earlier.

"Those blasted unmanned doodlebugs are causing havoc in London. According to the papers up to 100 were being fired, daily, at London and the South East." I feel really sorry for the people who have been bombed out of their homes."

"Yes, luckily most of the children were evacuated to safe areas, like Wales."

"Still, I've heard that our allies have managed to blast the last firing site in France to smithereens. The Nazis had set up there as the doodlebugs are just short-range."

"So, pleased they can't reach us."

"Ay, I've heard the Bosch are now firing them at Antwerp now and other industrial sites in Belgium and Holland. The worst thing about them is there is no real warning apart from the buzzing sound they make first of all. These bombs are like little planes with plywood wings and they're dropped from a German plane well out of range of our guns. The Germans can control them to some extent by radio transmitters. They are put into a power dive as soon as they are over the target, which stops the engine, then there is just an ominous moment or two of silence, in which to scarper for safety, until the bomb explodes on hitting the ground. They can leave a crater 20-30 yards wide."

"Still, our troops and allies have rid Paris of the Germans. They're on the back foot now, what with the First Allied Airborne Army strike on Holland on 17 September – us Brits, the Americans, Poles and Dutch Commandos, giving them what for, dive-bombing them, and holding the Arnhem bridges until the Second Army had advanced through Holland to join up with them."

"Yes, there've been some heroic acts of bravery, they deserve all the awards that can be handed out."

"I think we've got Hitler beat. By next year, the war will be over. The War Office reckons we won't be having to use our blackouts for much longer."

"Fingers crossed old pal."

Nearby were William Ford and Harry Hill, who had made their way over from the Purse cottages, at the edge of the Peter Ford's works. They both worked at Peter Ford's, Harry being in the office. They lived next door to each other with their respective wives, Nellie and Sarah. They must have both been in their mid-50s. To look at, Harry had thinning grey hair with grey eyebrows Sarah was the seamstress in the area. She was quite fashionable with waved dark hair, as was the style at the time.

They overheard a bit of the conversation between Dick Utting and Jim Heathcote.

Harry Hill butted in, "My two sons, Bill and Jim are in the armed forces – Bill's in the RAF in the Middle East and Jim is in the Navy – on submarines - and up in Northumberland at present. My

The Day the Sun Disappeared, 27 Nov 1944

youngest are twins, Kathleen and Ronald and they are doing their National Service away from home. Kathleen's in Coventry working for the Hospital Co-operation. So they're all doing their bit."

"Good for you old timer." Jim answered. "Yes, hopefully this war will be over soon and they'll be home again."

"I hope so," Harry Hill replied.

Just coming from the bar, Maurice was saying, "Oh, I'm so pleased the last of the carrots and cabbages have been taken up and we've got them to market. You've all done a grand job lads, so here's a pint on me." and brought the pints he had ordered for Stephen and John West, to the table, which were taken up greedily.

"Ay, it's that time of year we can relax a little now. Just tending to the cows and sheep – a never-ending job." Joseph replied.

"Ay, it's time now to do those repairing jobs I couldn't do before." Maurice added. "I've got a hole in one of the stone walls needs repairing and there's a bit of fence wiring that's coming away. One of my sheep got herself caught up in it. She'd got herself wrapped up that tight, it was a job to get her free." He continued, sipping from his pint. "I've got a mind to go to Burton market on Monday, we could do with a new heifer." Maurice then lit up his pipe and most of the others joined him – cigarettes or pipes as was their choice. The smoke began to billow in circles above their heads, mingling with the smoke from the coal fire they were sitting by.

"Oh, that's a lovely roaring fire, that, Mr Goodwin." Joseph chimed in.

The Day the Sun Disappeared, 27 Nov 1944

"Ay, sure warms the cockles as the nights draw in, as long as they can still get supplies of coal. There's a definite chill in the air now. Like as we'll soon see a spot of snow ont' hills."

"What're you gorping at, Fred?" Horace Utting asked, following Fred's line of sight across the room.

"Nowt much, just those girls there, making fools of themselves with those RAF lads over in the corner."

There was a small group of men in American RAF uniforms at the other side of the pub. They were obviously stationed at one of the RAF camps close by and two or three land girls were nestling up close to them, one was even sitting on the knee of one of the men. They were all giggling.

"Yer, bet she wouldn't do that if her parents were here." Horace replied.

"These girls all swoon over men in uniform." This was John Hardwick, getting in on the conversation.

"Ah, yer only jealous, mate." Fred replied, "Then again, he does have those film star looks – all these Americans seem to – white teeth and wide grins. Donna see her going google-eyed over you, John, with your buck teeth and ingrained dirt in your hands."

"That's good muck, I'll be telling you, from hard graft and I haven't got buck teeth! In any case, have you looked at your own hands lately?"

John looked down at his hands. "S'pose you're right there."

"If that one doesn't behave herself, she's likely to get more than she bargained for." Fred added, giving a raised fist and elbow.

"Ay, she'll get something else raised, not just an elbow."

The Day the Sun Disappeared, 27 Nov 1944

At that, the girl and the American got up and left the pub, waving to the others in the group.

"That's it," Fred said, "They'll be round the back of the pub, doing what comes naturally."

"And three months down the line, she'll be up the duff and he'll be nowhere to be found." John added.

Just then, the door opened again, letting in a gust of cold air. In came a man in an old, well-worn tweed jacket and flat cap, carrying a splice of rabbits.

"Been poaching again, Jack, I see." The barman piped up.

"Not poaching, but yes, these two just walked into some traps I found, so I had to put them out of their misery and what could I do about it but bring 'em here to see if anyone wants."

"Give 'em here, Jack. They'll go into a good stew." Mr Melvin Zucca, the pub owner barman took them. I believe money was paid but didn't see how much. "So, everyone, there'll be rabbit stew tomorrow. First come, first served, thanks to our Jack here."

Voices were raised, "I'm up for that. Put me down for a serving."

Yes, what with rationing, any bit of meat was more than welcome to supplement their meagre meals.

Robert Wagstaffe, talking to Maurice Goodwin, said, "The Zuccas with their two children, have really settled in here, by the looks of it, especially as they only took over the Cock last June."

There was talk about a social event coming up on Monday 27th November. Bernard Harrison (husband of Clara, and father of a large brood including Ida, was standing at the bar. He lived 200 yards past the village hall in Hanbury and worked at Staton's mine.

"Strange day for a social event on a Monday," Bernard replied, "but anything for a bit of light entertainment during this war to raise the spirits. Our Ida is looking forward to it and is even getting a dress altered for the event. It's her birthday the day after, so a sort of celebration for her. She'll be 17.

John Hardwick was listening in and said to Bill, "Sweet 17 and never been kissed. I've seen her around, she's not too bad. Might try my hand there," and winked.

"Oh, you're too old for her. She'll be wanting someone her own age." Bill replied.

"No harm in trying though."

So, the group stayed for a few more, with Jim and Dick going to play darts, then they wended their weary ways back home.

The Day the Sun Disappeared, 27 Nov 1944

CHAPTER 6

BURTON NOVEMBER (Olive Mackay)

I was just thinking to myself and the situation we were in. Everything was rationed. The Co-op used to come round with horse and cart with limited supplies of bread and milk. Saturday was the day you queued for your rations at every grocers you were registered with. I was registered with Hubbards in the indoor market in the town centre. If you had a garden you were expected to grow what you could to help your basic rations along.

After one bombing raid, on a Saturday, while going to get the rations, I was surprised to see a Heinkel Bomber, positioned on its side, with the wing on that side broken off – it had been shot down. It had been so close to our house, just a few blocks away. Tom came back to say it was going to be left there as it was thought it would boost morale to see that our little bit of Burton had actually brought down an enemy aircraft. Well, I must admit, it did give me somewhat of a feeling of elation. Yes, we did that!

Our iron railings outside of the house had been taken, along with everyone else's. They were to be melted down and used for armaments. Even vehicles were confiscated for war use. Tom used his bicycle so that was alright.

We'd had a few bombing raids in Burton, 11 bombs were dropped in the Uxbridge area, two of which hit separate homes in Wood

The Day the Sun Disappeared, 27 Nov 1944

Street. No 23 was repaired, but there is a gap where 21 and 22 once stood. The terraced houses that once stood on the opposite side of the road were badly damaged and demolished. The Gladstone Inn, in Wood Street, suffered minor damage. The licensee's wife escaped with shock after having been thrown across the bar. A total of 31 other houses in Wood Street, had to be repaired. At other times, bombs had also been dropped on Wellington Street, Wyggeston Street, Charlton Street and the Dairy on Calais Road. Those streets were just 40 minutes' walk away. Then a Spitfire crashed in Stafford Street, killing two people.

The factories had all been re-modelled to help in the war effort, working flat out, producing ammunition, army uniforms – anything and everything to produce what was needed. Branston Factory, the original home of Branston Pickles was turned into an ordnance depot for the war effort. What used to be a virtual man-only staffed factory was now staffed by women and even crèches were set up for those women who had young children. Women were even being used to construct roads. The concrete road from Newborough top towards Manbury was made, by women, to close the road from the New Inn to Newborough leading to the Tatenhill Airfield, which was a bomber base.

Burton had prisoners of war, Germans but also Italians. The Italians were allowed to go out now, and wore brown with yellow patches on their backs.

Just then Connie came home and rushed to the fire to warm herself. The fire was burning wood logs now. "Move over grandad, let dog see t'rabbit please, let me warm myself. Oh, it's piddling down out there. There's sleet in the air." Turning to look at the back page of the paper John was reading, she noticed what was on at the cinema. "Oh, The Song of Bernadette is on next week at the Gaumont. I must see that. Jennifer Jones plays a French peasant girl who has visions of the Virgin Mary. I believe people gradually start to believe her and masses of folk come on pilgrimages to be healed. Eventually Bernadette is deemed a saint. I've heard so much about it. Oh," and looking further down the page, "Deanna Durbin is in 'Christmas Holiday' with Gene Kelly, at the Gaumont Electric from 14th December. It's her first really serious part. I've heard she acts in a grave, proud way, and sings, 'Spring will be little later this year' and 'Always'. I must see that too."

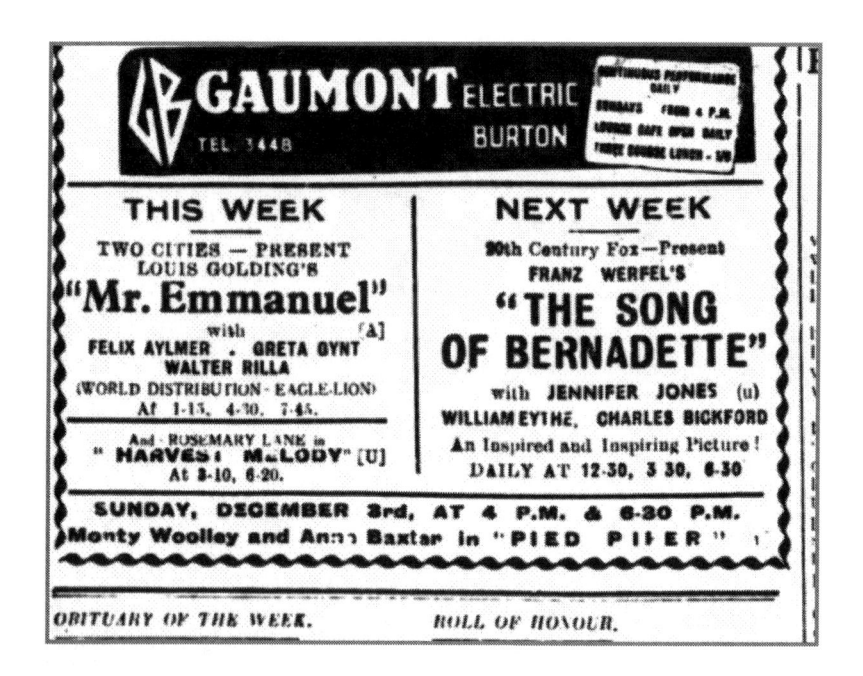

CHAPTER 7

UPPER CASTLE HAYES FARM

Maurice Goodwin and his wife Mary, lived on and worked Upper Castle Hayes Farm, on the southern edge of the alabaster mines. Maurice's first name was actually William, but with so many Williams and Bills around, he decided to use his second given name. The Goodwins had two children, Marie, and Gordon, who had just started to attend the Grammar School in Uttoxeter. Mary's sister, Lizzie, was also staying with them.

It was Monday, 27th November, 1944. "Come on you two, you'll have to get a move on to get the bus to Uttoxeter, Gordon. The bus leaves at ten past eight, as you know, so hurry up.

(Joe Cooper said the Hellaby children would have made their own way to the respective schools. It was a hell of a walk for their children. They would walk on a track across the field, up Hanbury Hill.)

Gordon and Marie appeared, satchels and gas masks over their shoulders. Gordon looked smart in his new uniform.

I waved goodbye. Maurice was already out of the farm, in his work overalls.

He returned a little bit later, I've seen John Hardwick (John was 21 years old) and Fred Ford going off from John's father's farm. We had a bit of a chat. They were supposed to be feeding the cattle at the farm but, because the weather was a bit frosty this morning, they have set off to cut roots elsewhere. By the way, I need to go to the cattle market in Burton-on-Trent. I want to see if there is anything worth purchasing."

"I'll go with you. I want to look at the stock too and make sure you choose a good cow. You have to be so aware at these markets, they can shove you off with an old has-been that's well past her prime. I've even heard of tricksters who fill a cow's udder up with milk, to let you think the cow's a good milker. Then, when you get it home, after producing the milk she has, doesn't produce any more."

"Ok, Mary. I know you've got a good eye for that sort of thing, but if we are both going, we'll have to hold back as I'm expecting a delivery of grain."

"Good, that will give me time to do my chores."

"Yes, I'll just finish off planting the broad beans and putting in supports for them to grow up. Give me a call when they arrive. Oh, by the way; I've arranged with Robert Wagstaffe for him to come over this morning to cut some of the hedges."

"Oh, he lives in Draycott-in-the-Clay, doesn't he?"

"That's right, in New Road. He does a lot of thatching and hedge-cutting for farmers in the area. I suppose he's getting on a bit, but still manages well. He must be about 68 now but that's not saying much as there are miners of his age and older, still digging out the alabaster, as most of the young men having enlisted. Robert likes to get out as much as he can as, unfortunately, his wife, Ann, died so, rather than sitting at home on his own, he gets out and about, going what he can. His wife is buried in All Saints churchyard in Denstone, Staffordshire."

The Day the Sun Disappeared, 27 Nov 1944

So, Maurice picked up his bucket of seed, put on his wellington boots again, slung the bucket around his neck, and trudged out.

My sister, Lizzie, who was staying with us, was busy upstairs, changing the sheets, sweeping, dusting and polishing. I could hear the floorboards creaking as she went from room to room. She was also humming a song that was around at the time. It sounded like, 'Don't Fence Me In' by the Andrew Sisters.

I decided to put the wireless on, not that Lizzie had a bad singing voice, but then again she wasn't all that great. I just hoped she'd get the message with the wireless going on.

The wireless doctor, Doctor Charles Hill, (later became Lord Hill), had just finished his daily broadcast to remind the nation to "Keep your bowels open and be exuberant with health by taking a daily intake of the trusted dandelion leaf."

"Oh, I'm glad he's off," I said to myself, "Of all things, talking about keeping your bowels open", I thought to myself. It's alright if you're in the doctor's surgery, but that talk should be private, kept between you and the doctor."

I stared for a while just looking out of the window, while washing the breakfast dishes, then washing out a few bits of hand-washing. It was so peaceful. You could see for miles. Past our land you could make out the water tower and the tower of the church, standing out at the highest point of the Stonepit Hills. The farm looked out on the flood plain of the River Dove, the boundary between Staffordshire and Derbyshire. Before that were the Stonepit Hills and the Queen's Purse Wood. If I were to go outside, I could see the Derbyshire hills to the north and, in the distance, the Peak District and the Weaver hills and North Staffordshire moorlands. The hamlet of Fauld was directly north.

The Day the Sun Disappeared, 27 Nov 1944

The area was mainly farming, although there were two Gypsum mines, worked by The Peter Ford's & Sons and Staton's. The Peter Ford's Works were based in the lower part of a hidden valley – a long strip of woodland leading off Fauld Lane. The alabaster obtained from the Gypsum mines had been mined at Fauld since Roman times. We all knew that the gypsum mine workings extended, in a labyrinth of tunnels under the Stone pit Hills for a number of miles west, south and east of Hanbury. Part of the works were covered by Queen's Purse Wood, which the locals called 'Little Wood', with Heathcote's field directly to the north. There was also a lovely little coppice of wood before you get to Peter Ford's Alabaster work – this was Brown's Coppice, but known to us as 'The Old Wood'. This was lovely to walk around, especially in spring, when the bluebells were out in force.

Children would often wander over there and Gordon would climb the trees, pretending to be Tarzan. Yes, quite often he would drag himself home, bearing the wounds of his escapades - grazed knees and hands – feeling very sorry for himself for a couple of days, but then raring to go again. Marie was quite quiet and disciplined, no tomboy was she.

Tutbury Castle sat about 2½ miles to the east on an escarpment. This was just a ruin – just the north tower remaining - a bleak tower rising up. It had formerly been one of the main seats of the Norman Lord Henry de Ferrers, ancestor of the earls of Derby. That thought reminded me of Gordon telling me about a history lesson he had had at school. He seemed really excited to find out that Mary Queen of Scots had been a prisoner there, on and off in 1569. Gordon had quoted from his history book, "On the 4th February 1569, Mary Queen of Scots and sixty attendants, including her gaoler Knollys, rode into Tutbury Castle. She had been many hours in the saddle and for the first time since her arrival in England, she realised that she was now in prison." Gordon went on to say she had been a prisoner for 18 years and was finally beheaded on 8th February 1587 at Fotheringhay Castle. Gordon had emphasised the word 'beheaded' and had brought his arms down in a swiping motion, as if he actually held the axe to behead Queen Mary, then he ran off outside shouting and hollering "Queen Mary of Scots is dead." Well, I've got myself a typical lad, I thought to myself. Lads seem to revel in killing and murder stories.

Tutbury Castle

I laughed as he pranced off. So, anyway, we had our bit of history.

Just to the north west of us, near the entrance to the mines, there was a thirty-foot-deep reservoir. It had been built for the use of Peter Ford's alabaster mine and mill. Maurice had told me that the wall of the dam held back six million gallons of water – what did he say – that's it, the dam was thirty feet high and thirty-five feet thick at its base. It didn't bear thinking about if all that came down. I'd heard about dams breaking and the subsequent disaster.

Our RAF Lancaster bombers, managed to breach three dams in May last year. The squadron was nicknamed 'The Dambusters'. Our Dambusters were trying to obliterate the Ruhr valley industry – power plants and turbines, using what they called 'bouncing bombs' to skim across the reservoir into the dam wall. No-one thought these bombs would actually work! I know it was war but huge holes were blown into three dams, the Möhne, the Edersee and Sorpe dams, resulting in at least one and a half thousand people being drowned plus two hydroelectric power stations were destroyed and several more damaged. However, the Germans weren't going to be put off by this as I'd heard that, with a Herculaneum effort from German manpower and Hitler youth, the dams had been repaired. So much for that! We had lost eight aircraft and over 50 men.

I hoped the Germans wouldn't retaliate and find our dam, but then again there were a lot bigger dams that could do a lot more damage if their walls were breached. Anyway, there was nothing much here apart from the Gypsum works. Oh, dear, what am I talking about, of course, the huge bomb store in the disused mines! .....Then again, those bombs are deep underground, they'd be flooded out, but that's all. Oh, I was getting myself into a bit of a state now, all this thinking of war and floods.

Thankfully Maurice returned to get me out of the doldrums – it must have been about an hour later. "We'll have to go or we'll miss the beginning of the sale at Burton and might miss the opportunity of getting a good heifer. Robert Wagstaffe is here so he can help unload the grains." So, we got in the car and started to drive down the hill. Just then we saw the grain lorry coming up. "Oh, blast 'em. I knew this would happen. I can't get by, so I'll have to back up and turn around."

So we returned to the farm. "Well, I suppose I've got to get changed yet again."

"Yes, dear."

Then Maurice helped Robert to unload.

The Day the Sun Disappeared, 27 Nov 1944

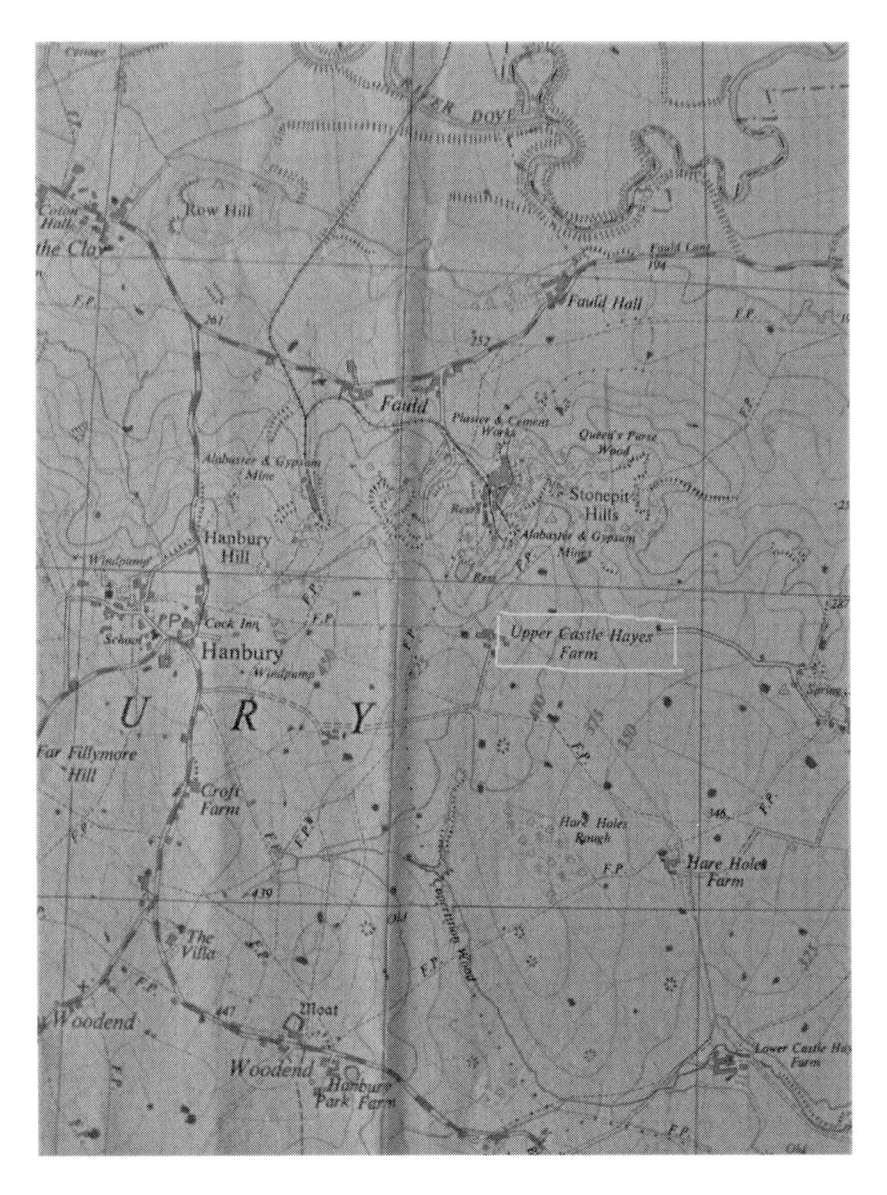

The Day the Sun Disappeared, 27 Nov 1944

So, after we let the grain lorry get on its way, we finally set off again for Burton market, giving a wave goodbye to the farm workers, Stephen and John West, a young evacuee boy, aged just 16, from Liverpool, called Russel Miles; Robert Wagstaffe and, of course, Lizzie. The farm dogs, chased after us as we went down the drive. Lizzie went back into the house to make some breakfast.

No-one was to know that this was the last time any of them would see each other.

Just further along the road, past the reservoir, the grain lorry was almost forced off the road with the force of the blast. He did an emergency stop, feet pounding the clutch and brake, down to the floor. The ground beneath him was rocking violently. He jumped out of the cabin, clasping his hands to his ears to try to drown out the uproar of the tumultuous eruption that defied all known memories. Looking south west he saw the mushroom cloud and heard above it all, a cracking sound and saw the whole wall of the dam disintegrating, spewing forth the total contents therein. Through the smoke, fire and water, he could just about make out the ground crumbling where he had just been, and the farm at Upper Castle Hayes descending in broken fragments of brick, plaster, steel and wood, deep into the massive pit that had formed.

He crossed himself and got on his knees to thank God that he was still alive.

CHAPTER 8

RAF FAULD

War had broken out on 3rd September 1939. Nazi tanks were driving into Poland. However, RAF Fauld had readied itself for war a couple of years before. In 1937 the Air Ministry acquired the disused Gypsum mines that belonged to Peter Ford's Works.

It seemed an ideal site as, during the mining process, natural pillars of rock had been left to support the roof, every 20ft or so. The Air Ministry chose such places as Fauld because they kept dry and seldom suffered from rock falls. The mine shafts were 90ft below ground with enough capacity to store 10,000 tons of bombs. The RAF took on converting the mines into a usable site by adding a concrete roof lining, and the building of two walls – an internal 10ft thick wall sub-dividing the High Explosive store, and the other, a much more substantial barrier, 50ft thick, separating the HE store from the area where incendiaries were to be held. A light railway was built branching off into the mine areas and, at the other end, leading off to the main railway line, over the River Dove, at Scopton, about a mile away to the north. These bombs needed to be transported there. From there, they would be transported to airfields across the country, via the North Staffordshire Burton to Uttoxeter main railway.

There was a lift shaft, where bombs were loaded and descended 100ft, then hauled from the lift with chains onto trolleys then wheeled through the long tunnels to wherever they were to be stored.

This storage area was known as Maintenance Unit no. 21 (or 21 MU for short).

The underground rail tracks at RAF Fauld.

The first RAF men arrived on 8th September, manning machine gun posts. Three days later, 14 airmen arrived on anti-aircraft duty, with tents to live in. The storage and sending on of explosives was beginning to grow, although the men were camping out with no basics like canteens, or dormitories. There were practice runs, shipping empty bomb cases out, then armed bombs were being shipped to places like Iraq and Singapore. In April 1940 502 tons were sent out, mainly to neutral Turkey. That was not much more than a day's average by 1944.

Fauld was always casting around for labour, if RAF men and local civilians ran short. Between November 27 and 30, 1943, Fauld could not find extra RAF men so the local US Army depot very kindly lent 100 other ranks. This saved the situation in the meantime. In February 1944 20 USA personnel were employed daily due to the incoming of heavy American bombs.

Even though the USA had not joined the war until 1941, they supplied bullets. At this time, Britain was losing the war. America joining in was a God-send. Britain was aiding the Soviet Union after Germany invaded in June 1941.

They still needed more space to accommodate a further 10,000 tons of bombs and in 1941-2 they enlarged the storage into unused parts of the mine, thus doubling the storage capacity. However, this new storage area ran precariously close to Peter Ford's working gypsum mines, but it was agreed that the wall of rock separating this new storage area from Peter Ford's mines, which varied between 15 and 50ft in thickness, would be enough to provide a sufficient barrier should there be a blast.

Britain did have stocks of chemical weapons and the RAF officers on the maintenance unit side were trained to handle them, like any other weapon of war, undergoing training at RAF Tatenhill, near Newchurch. Officer students there did 'practical light demolition and the breaking down of ammunition' at RAF Fauld and visited other maintenance units to see how chemical weapons were stored. So, they could handle chemical weapons but what kept the front line ticking were bombs and bullets. In February 1942 alone, Fauld overhauled 37,934 hand grenades; in April 1942, 23,954. Another site was opened at Linley (between Aldridge and Walsall) on 15th October 1942. This was staffed with one squadron leader, a non-commissioned officer and 38 airmen. No matter how many sites Fauld opened, even keeping bombs loaded in the open at Scropton railway sidings, the unit needed enough workers to keep the stocks moving.

In April 1944 Fauld sent out an average 383 tons a day. RAF Fauld took off after the fall of France with outgoings and incomings monthly rarely falling below 3,000 tons. RAF Fauld couldn't cope with this amount and had to take on ever more men to cope with the surge in demand and supply. Airmen were posted from Blackpool and Morecambe. They were being billeted into spare buildings, halls and church buildings. Finally buildings went up for billets

Duke of Gloucester's Visit – photo from Graham Shaw

The Day the Sun Disappeared, 27 Nov 1944

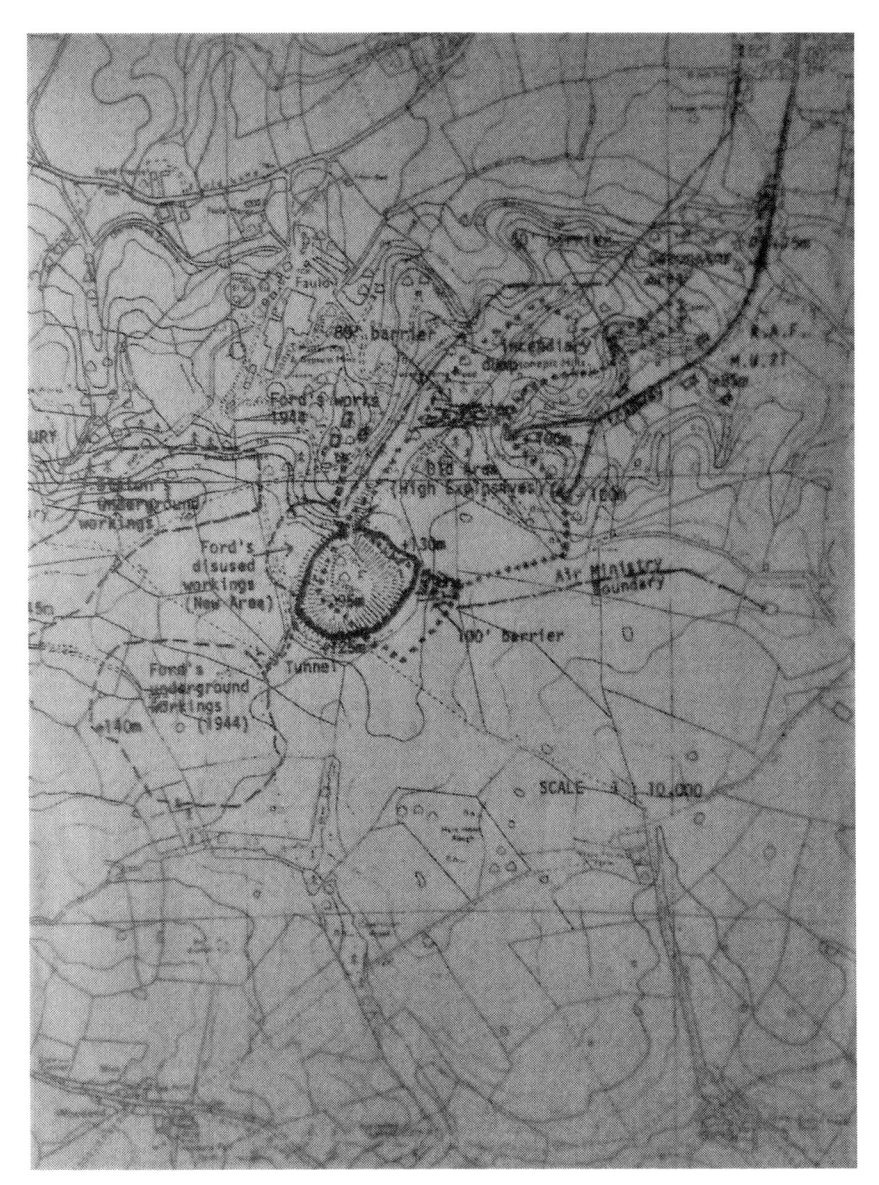

Map of the site (provided by Graham Shaw)

The Day the Sun Disappeared, 27 Nov 1944

Fauld was not just an area for storing bombs, repair of jettisoned bombs was also carried out. Strangely enough, the RAF was not responsible for this task, but it was put onto a team of civilians trained in bomb disposal and employed by the Armaments Inspectorate Department (AID), formed in May 1943. They were responsible for the overseeing and inspection of all new and repaired armoury storage units. Their members were not there to supervise the RAF armourers employed in removing the heads from these bombs that contained the fuses and detonators, but to check over the finished article. Some of the useless bombs were being prepared for return to factories where they would be broken down. Once the exploder pocket had been chipped away it would then be safe to steam out the high explosive and the casing could be melted down and the steel used again. But, if the exploder pocket was jammed, it would sometimes be necessary to chip out the composite explosive with a copper chisel. It was imperative that this was made of copper as copper did not create a spark, which could possibly set off an explosion. This chipping out of the exploder box was done in a remote area known as the 'exploder bay'. Once a bomb had been checked over by the A.I.D. it was marked ready to go.

The requirement for 4,000ln HC type bombs crystallised into a regular requirement for 100 bombs per day. More labour was required. In May, Fauld took its first 46 Italian prisons of war from a camp at Hednesford. Another 50 came on 6 July 1944 and 100 more in September. They were referred to as Prisoners of War but, in actual fact, as Italy had already signed an armistice, they were no longer so, and were now known as co-operators and usually paid a wage for their work. The number of men and women crept up and by October 1944 21MU was manned by 18

The Day the Sun Disappeared, 27 Nov 1944

officers, four WAAF officers, 475 other ranks, 445 civilians and 195 Italians (1 officer and 194 men)

Field Marshall Sir Graham Donald was in charge of RAF Fauld.

Bombs in the Dump - Donated by Graham Shaw

CHAPTER 9

SQUADRON LEADER ANNESS

I had only been at RAF Fauld since September that year, so was still fairly new to the workings of RAF Fauld. I was the Squadron Leader, Squadron Leader Anness, and acting chief equipment officer at the time. I knew what went on there but, in those two months had seen quite a bit that I thought was unsavoury in the management of the site. I had been posted to 21 MU as I wasn't allowed to fly anymore. After a stupid car accident in Iraq, while off duty, I had lost the sight of my right eye. A half-blind pilot is useless up in the sky dog-fighting the German Messerschmitts.

Wing Commander Kings was in charge of the camp, but then again, he was in charge of every munitions camp in the area and, basically hardly ever there. He was, though, a qualified X officer, meaning that he had undertaken the RAF explosives course. Field Marshall Sir Graham Donald had overall charge of all the bomb storage sites and so, again, we never saw much of him.

People were working on disarming 1000lb bombs when they arrived. This involved removing the nose and tail plugs, along with the exploder pockets, which contained a primary charge of explosive. If, as in some cases, this proved impossible to do, then the men would have to chisel out the composite explosive from the pocket and collect it in an ammunition box.

On first arriving there I did an inspection to get a feel for the place and the work carried out. Going into the caverns, or galleries as they called them, was eerie. They looked like Aladdin's caves, cave after cave, through passages ablaze with electric light that lit up the main thoroughfare but left the corners in darkness. I could still faintly make out the tiers and tiers of enormous high explosive bombs though. In other sections there were piles of incendiaries.

"These must all run into millions of pounds" I said to myself, "enough to make hundreds of raids on Germany."

My first thought was what would happen if an explosion took place in any one cavern, and whether the resultant fall of earth would damp down, before he blast reached other parts. That didn't bear thinking about. At least there was 90ft of earth above the tunnels, which would act as protection should there be an air raid.

Then, on investigating further, it occurred to me that there were just not enough people supervising the civilians and the Italians. Yes, Mr Salt was there, the foreman. (He was 37 and lived in Goodman, Burton-on-Trent). It was his job to give out work to 30 of the civilian labourers. He had an underground office in the mine. This included loading and unloading bombs onto trucks. All of these bombs coming in from Scropton would be inspected for the presence of detonators. However, I was wondering who was supervising all the others? There were just not enough RAF men on site. I knew the civilians and Italians had had rudimentary training in what was required, and they were getting on with their jobs. The problem was that the RAF would obey orders and do everything to the book, whereas the civilians and Italians didn't have this discipline instilled into them and, with not enough people supervising, in such a dangerous environment, I was beginning to wonder when there would be an incident.

Looking at the records, written up by James Pollard, the chief inspection officer for the Aeronautical Inspection Directorate

The Day the Sun Disappeared, 27 Nov 1944

(AID), there had only been one bomb found at Scropton, since July 1943 that had a detonator, so it seemed the work appeared to be going according to plan, and that eased my fears a bit.

The station engineer, John Bell, had two men in the mine each day, checking lamps. The lamps had to be checked because of the poor quality of wartime electric bulbs, which often failed. Also, there weren't enough lamps for use by the people going into the mines and these were mostly shared or even, because the lamps were not working, just one for use by a group. My thinking was, if only there were enough lamps, these could act as a number count as to how many were down the mine at one time – or even something simple like a number tag, to be picked up and removed on their return.

What came to my attention was a constable standing guard at the mine entrance, a Constable Skellet. I questioned him, "Do you keep a record of who is down the mine at any particular time?" He was a bit hesitant, "Come on constable, I would appreciate a straight answer."

"Well, sir, it is my job, along with Air Ministry Constabulary Sergeant, Howard Langley, to check everyone who enters the mine to see if they have cigarettes or other combustibles on their persons."

Giving the appearance of having gone on elsewhere, I re-tracked and watched from a distance. What I noticed was that only about one in ten people were actually checked. This meant that someone could easily take a lighter with him and light up, undetected and not be prevented from doing so. I didn't think anyone would do such a foolish thing, if they valued their lives, but that's not to say a chain-smoker wouldn't think he could get away with it. Maybe that person had done so before and hadn't set off a bomb. He may

The Day the Sun Disappeared, 27 Nov 1944

even think that, as the detonators were in one place and the bombs in another, there would be no harm. I reported this to Kings but, again got the excuse that there just weren't enough men to supervise but he would arrange extra training sessions.

I didn't see how extra training sessions would help, I mean, if a man was bent on lighting up, who was going to stop him?

I did manage to ask him, trying to make light of it, with a smile on my face and a bit of a chuckle, to try to cover up my anguish. "What do you think would actually happen if a bomb were to go off in one of the galleries, sir?"

"Oh, with 90ft of earth above them, I reckon the resultant fall of earth would damp down, before the blast reached other parts. That 90ft of ceiling also acts as a protection should the Germans find out where we are."

Another job being carried out at the site was replacing pistols, where necessary, and painting lugs of the bombs to prevent corrosion. This was being done by Edgar Higgs, an AID viewer.

Ken McLeod in his uniform

LAC (Leading Aircraftman) Ken McLeod's job was in the mine itself, putting steel bands around .5 ammunition boxes with two other airmen armourers. He was just 21 years old, working with Corporal Lionel Poynton, LAC Patrick Sheridan and two groups of Italians. McLeod had collected paint boxes and brushes and had set one group of Italians to painting and stencilling boxes. In the underground office, I was talking to Foreman Rhodes when

The Day the Sun Disappeared, 27 Nov 1944

Sheridan came along, "Well, I've got one group of the Italians working on stencilling but don't know what to give the other group to do, any ideas?"

It all appeared quite dreary to me and the Italians were there, just twiddling their thumbs, waiting for orders. One of them, who I found out was Soldato Salvatore Ruggeri, started singing, an operatic aria or such like, in Italian. Another of the Italians produced a mouth organ to accompany him – he was Soldato Salvatore Trovato. In the cavern his voice echoed and sounded really quite wonderful. I went back to him and asked him what he was singing, "Vergin Tutto Amor" he replied.

It was wonderful and I applauded him. He then produced from his breast pocket some photographs. I asked for the torch to be passed over. "Mie bambini, my children and my Maria." Looking at the photo I saw a dark-haired lady, presumably his wife, and two little girls. "Very nice, " I said.

"They are just outside ofa Roma, near Tivoli." Salvatore continued, "Everything is white there, on the ground. My familee, worka with the stone, 'ow you say, ornimenti, orniments, and grave stones. I donna not know eef they are safe. Mie povera bambini and my Maria. I getta no letters."

I felt sorry for poor Salvatore, "Hitler is on the run, Salvatore. Your family may be with relatives or friends." And urged him to write to the Consulate to try to find out if his family were safe.

....

I left the Italians and came across LAC James Kenny, an armourer, in a small cavern, near a triangle in the old HE area. This was the first place I saw where the work could actually be dangerous. He was preparing useless bombs for return to factories to be broken

The Day the Sun Disappeared, 27 Nov 1944

down. He was working with LAC Fairbanks. Their job was taking the exploders from 500lb bombs in the AID compound. As far as I could see, the men were just working unsupervised and the bombs would be inspected at the end. I got speaking to Kenny about what was involved, "This is a skilled job, requiring strength. Some of the bugger exploders just won't come off. They can be a right phaff. I've known it take two days to remove the exploder container. One particular explosive was a right pain in the neck – it just wouldn't budge. I had to call on Mr Nicklin, an AID viewer, (Aeronautical Inspection Directorate) he's down 'ere quite regular, but he couldn't budge the thing either. What we had to do in the end was use a special steel spanner and white spirit to ease the RP cement."

"But isn't white spirit inflammable." I added, astonished at the thought.

"Yer right there, but what else could we do?"

Looking around I added, "What if there was an explosion or fire – do you have fire-fighting equipment down here?

"Oh, there are buckets, but they're hardly ever filled up."

I was astonished. That had to be looked into too. I would have a word with the senior fireman, William Jefferies.

"Tell you what though, Sir, flying against the Germans, even though I could lose my life, that's really what I want to do. That's what I joined the RAF for, not blooming dismantling bombs. I'd rather lose my life up in the air, fighting for my country, than lose my life down here in a dungeon, Plus I've got pals in the RAF, and they've stormed through the ranks while I'm stuck here kept on the same rank, Leading Aircraftsman – that's a joke – Aircraftsman, when I don't ever see an aircraft! It's not fair."

The Day the Sun Disappeared, 27 Nov 1944

I agreed, especially as I was in the same boat. I had heard the same from so many of the RAF people I had talked to on site. That's probably why there was such a large turnover of staff, plus pilots were needed to fight the war, and why so many civilians had to be brought in to do the work.

I went back to the entrance to see bombs being loaded into the mine by four men, supervised by LAC Frank Rule.

I went to speak to senior fireman, William Jefferies about the lack of water in buckets. "Sir, I am following orders and I believe the equipment is adequate." I was astonished to hear him say this, but Jefferies continued, "However, I know the unit has asked for three more static water pools (man-made ponds, common in RAF stations) but nothing is forthcoming."

Wing Commander Kings happened to be in the master provision office one day. He should have been inspecting the mine but it didn't look like this was going to happen as he was inundated with paperwork and people waiting to see him.

I finally got in to see him about provision of lamps for the mine and static water pools.

I saluted on entering the room.

"Yes, Squadron Leader Anness."

"Sorry to interrupt you, Sir, but I was wondering when we might get a delivery of lamps for people entering the mine, sir, and the order for static water pools."

"All you need to know, Anness, is that they have been ordered. I will chase them, but there seems to be a problem getting the filaments to make the lamps and, as for the water pools, well...."

The Day the Sun Disappeared, 27 Nov 1944

We will just have to make do with what we have, for the time being."

"Thank you, sir." And I about turned and walked out of the office.

An officer passed me as I walked out of the master provision office. I saluted.

I hadn't seen this officer before, although there always seemed to be a big turnover of staff, but I was curious.

I crept back and listened at the door.

"Ah, Group Captain Storrar."

"Yes, sir, reporting for duty."

"Sit down. I do not know how much you know about 21MU but I have heard good reviews about you and I want you to be commander of RAF Fauld. My time is stretched to the utmost and I cannot spent as much time as I should supervising the running of the place. I need a second in command."

Kings went on to describe the type of work that was carried out at the site. "I'll introduce you to the main chain of command here, when I show you the site. Flying Officer Joseph Solomon has actually started a week of leave. His deputy, Pilot Officer Norman Rollo is new here – he only joined us on 13th. He has one day a week off, a Monday. James Pollard is the chief inspection officer for the Aeronautical Inspection Directorate. You'll get to know all of these officers by and by.

"Sir, as you know, I do not have much knowledge of bomb disposal. I have only been on a one week's X-course at 31 MU, RAF Llanberis, which I have just completed.

The Day the Sun Disappeared, 27 Nov 1944

"Yes, I understand your concern, but we have the civilian AID viewers, that know the science of it all, such as brass striking steel could make a spark that could set off a bomb. All the RAF is concerned with here is discipline and getting the bombs moving. You have 17 X-qualified officers under you. We just have to trust the men to do their jobs competently."

"Yes, sir."

I ran for the exit before Storrar left Kings' office. I was a bit bemused. Where did these 17 X-qualified men come from when officers were being transferred constantly and the site was always crying out for more men to take their places? Also, how qualified were these men – had some of them just done initial training, with no actual experience?

What I managed to find out, just listening into conversations, was even more alarming. An Examiner was talking to the Chief Examiner, "All these changes to regulations and working methods, I can't keep abreast of them. It's difficult enough not having enough men and an influx of new recruits who don't really understand the job, but this new lot of technical instructions, just following on from the changes we had last month, well it's well nigh impossible."

"Well, we have to do the best with the new instructions. I'll go through them with you. I know we are working at full stretch, doing a hard, unglamorous job, but it has got to be done to the best of our ability. And, keep this strictly under your hat, top secret and all that, but I myself have had to condone practices that would, in peace time, have merited instant dismissal. So, keep up the good work, as we're apparently doing it well."

……

The Day the Sun Disappeared, 27 Nov 1944

In the mess one day, I saw Corporal Lionel Poynton sitting on his own. He looked quite down. He was sitting in front of a heap of what had been nicknamed 'wooden egg'. It was powdered egg, rather greyish in colour. The cook on duty would serve up mounds of the concoction with plenty of hot tea, bread and margarine.

"Do you mind if I join you, Corporal?" I said as I took a seat opposite him at the table.

"Sir, you should be with the officers, not sitting with the likes of me."

"I sit with whom I wish to, Corporal. Now, why are you looking so glum, surely it can't just be the wooden egg, or maybe it is? Good for plastering walls, if you ask me." I said, trying a half-hearted attempt to bring a smile to his face.

"No, it's not that, Sir, that's something we just have to put up with. No… if you don't mind me saying…. I'm worried. I'm an armourer, been here since July."

I urged him on to speak."

"Well, I was just doing an inspection of the HE mine (High Explosives) and there I saw two of the LACs (leading aircraftmen) trying to remove the nose and tail blocks and the exploder container from a 1,000lb bomb. I believe they were unit returns having been jettisoned. While I was there I saw a bomb with the transit plug in the tail removed and set up horizontally on some form of batten, about a foot from the floor. LAC Fairbanks was with LAC Bailey, who was chiselling out the CE (composition explosive) from the exploder pocket, using a brass chisel and a hammer. Well, the thing is, that work should be carried out in the exploder bay, not the HE mine. Before coming here in July, I had spent three years as an armament instructor at RAF Kirkham so I recognise that the proper precautions should be taken. It looked precarious to me and I warned him to take care. Luckily, Mr Saunders, an AID examiner then joined us. But, Sir, what are they doing dismantling bombs out of the exploder bay? It's dangerous."

"I am sure, corporal, I will give them a right talking to, and put them on a caution. They won't do the same again, but thank you for pointing this out."

Although I was aware that AID inspections were going on, I had no detailed knowledge of these inspections. The Aeronautical Inspection Directorate (AID) were civilians and not governed by the RAF. The RAF men were trained in discipline and following orders from their superiors in rank in the RAF, but would they necessarily obey what the AID inspectors said?

I let Corporal Poynton get on with his meal and I ate mine. There was a lot of chat in the mess, people joking and so on, so it was quite noisy, but, behind me, I heard someone say, "Malcolm, I'm going to get some Stillsons (a large wrench) to take the noses off those crash bombs, then we can send them out again."

"But they're meant to be dumped in the sea, sir."

I turned round to see a young airman talking to one of the civilian viewers. "Hey Kidd, you need to grow up a bit, son. We're in a war here, can't be dumping what can be salvaged." The civilian got up and went, so I joined who I now found out was Malcolm Kidd, not what I first thought was the civilian just calling him a 'kid'. The young airman looked timid and stood to attention when I joined him at the table. "At ease, airman."

"Yes, sir." and he sat down

The Day the Sun Disappeared, 27 Nov 1944

I asked about Malcolm Kidd's job in the munitions dump then asked what had upset him so about the civilian. "Well, sir, I'm working with 1000lb bombs recovered from crashed RAF bombers. My sergeant has ordered me to stencil them as 'For dumping in deep water'. The man I was talking to thinks the bombs can be salvaged. He wants to unscrew the nose-pistols off to save the RAF money. I can't say anything, sir, as he thinks I'm just a junior and have a lot to learn. My father is in the Guards and I have been taught to carry out orders and not to question anything."

"Just carry on obeying your sergeant's orders, Kidd, and don't say anything to the civilian. I will see if I can speak to your sergeant and get someone to have a word with the civilian."

Malcolm Kidd finished his meal and went back to work.

I never did get to find the sergeant. What I had heard worried me and I would have to speak to the new guy, Group Captain Storrar about it.

As it happens I never did get to speak to Storrar, I was just too busy in the never-ending stock-keeping process and so was Storrar.

There were all sorts of problems to sort out with people coming to me about things going wrong. Thomas Mylotte, the storeman, who had been at 21 MU since 1939, was complaining that mistakes were going on all the time. He'd just ordered trucks for loading of 4,000lb bombs. Instead four trucks arrived but only one could take 4,000-pounders. In the end he got one suitable truck and loaded two 4,000 lb bombs on that. He said, "That would normally have been a laugh if I'd ordered something from a shop and got

The Day the Sun Disappeared, 27 Nov 1944

the wrong thing, but this has put my day right back. Stupid so-and-so's – can't even follow a simple order." He was miffed.

It was just too much and I got bogged down with it all and I was getting in a muddle. Nothing added up. I was also, by now, responsible for checking Bagots Wood (12 miles from RAF Fauld), the sub-unit of Linley (30 miles south of Fauld) and explosives at Loughborough, which meant I could only visit Fauld once every week or two. It was humanly impossible to manage. I wanted out. I wanted to be up in the air, but, being half-blind, I was grounded.

I knew Mr Saunders (an AID inspector) kept records underground, so hopefully his records were accurate. I couldn't just let this go unrecorded though as it was part of my remit, so managed, finally, to approach Group Captain Storrar with my apprehensions that I was finding it virtually impossible to keep accurate records because of lack of staff and other commitments on my time.

Storrar said he would take this to Wing Commander Kings, and the situation was related to Air Marshal Donald who wrote to the Air Ministry advising that records above ground had been suspended. That was indeed a relief!

The Day the Sun Disappeared, 27 Nov 1944

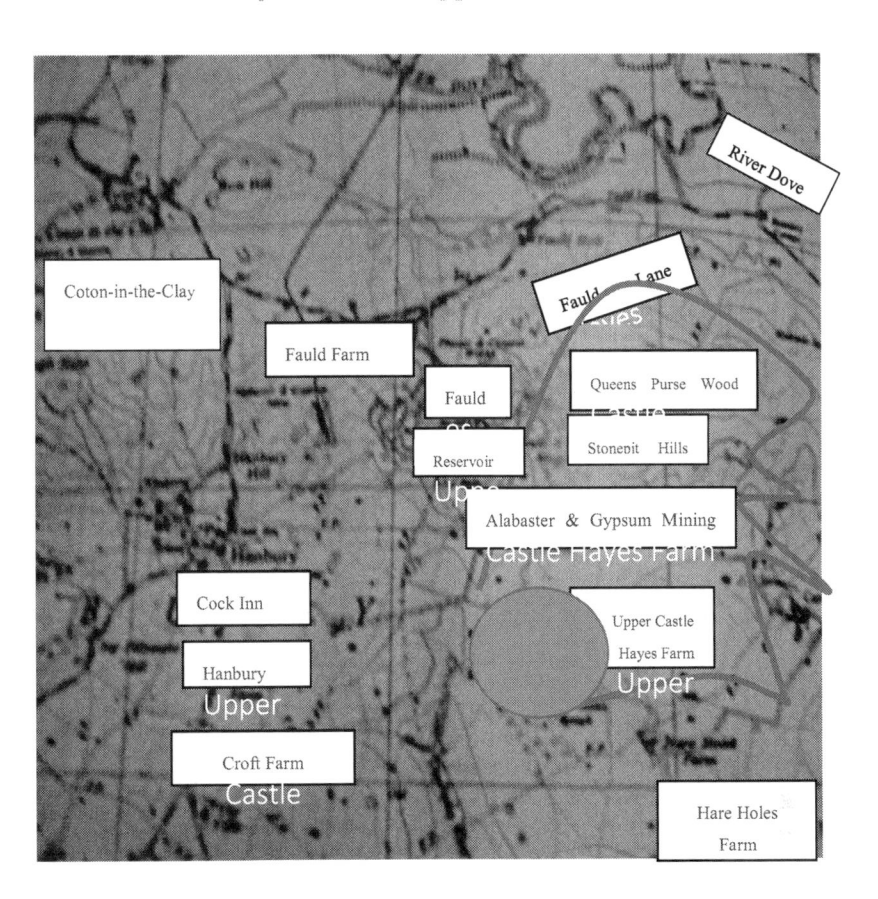

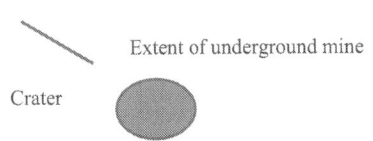

Coton-in-the-Clay

River Dove

Fauld Lane

Fauld Farm

Queens Purse Wood

Fauld

Reservoir

Stonepit Hills

Alabaster & Gypsum Mining

Cock Inn

Upper Castle Hayes Farm

Hanbury

Croft Farm

Hare Holes Farm

— Extent of underground mine

Crater

CHAPTER 10

HARDING FAMILY, TUTBURY

I was 9-years-old, living in Tutbury – Rose Harding.

I went to school that day – Cornmill Lane, Tutbury. The windows of the school were covered in paper criss-crossing the panes of glass, to try to prevent flying glass should the school his bombed. We came to Tutbury in 1938. My dad, John Harding (names changed at the request of the family) had moved up from South London to work for the MOD, at Hilton, just north of Burton upon Trent, in Derbyshire. He'd got a job as a maintenance-fitter, working on the engines. He finally was ready for us to come north to join him. So, we got the train north – my mum, Jane, me - I was just four-years-old at the time and my little sister, Lillian, who was only one.

"What do you think of it, Jane? It's a bit rough-and-ready, so I suppose it's not much, but the MOD has given us these quarters while I'm working for them."

"Well, we'll make do, John, we can't all be so choosy, but it's not much more than a makeshift barrack hut."

"Yes…. well, if anything better comes along, I'll put my name down for it but you can't expect much better. We're in the middle of a world war and troops need to be stationed somewhere. It's right by the railway at Egginton Junction, which is handy for the movement of troops and equipment."

The Day the Sun Disappeared, 27 Nov 1944

"Yes, but they don't seem to be our troops. Are they American? There seem to be a lot of well, 'black' faces."

"Don't be getting on your high horse, Jane. Those 'black' faces are fighting for us. Yes, it's an American barracks for US Army Engineers. There's about 3000 of them here. And anyway, I managed to get a job as the site is totally manned by civilians – the likes of me." John lit up a cigarette to calm himself down a bit. He didn't like arguing with his wife and had been trying to do the best that he could for his family.

As it happened, a house became available in Ironwalls Lane, Tutbury, with the view of the castle and the River Dove to the north. Dad had got a job at RAF Fauld. The house was much more to mum's liking and, when they had settled in, they started to get to know their neighbours, Mrs Rich, the Pattisons and the Cottons. I became best friends with Kate Cotton who lived on Green Lane. These houses had been built for the employees of RAF Fauld.

I had two older brothers. They joined us later, along with the rest of the family, coming to the area to live too – Jane's brothers, along with nieces and nephews. They all had to escape the bombing in London, when it was at its worst.

Mum's brothers would help out on farms, 'Digging for Victory', tilling what had once had been fields, to grow crops. Dad kept chickens for eggs, and when they stopped laying, the chickens were cooked for a nice Sunday dinner. The RAF and the alabaster mines were taking anyone who was fit enough, no matter how old, as so many of our young men were overseas fighting the war.

"Now what shall we have for dinner today, Rose, Lilly?" This was mum, who was very creative in stretching meals, eating the

The Day the Sun Disappeared, 27 Nov 1944

leaves of cauliflowers, even though they were supposed to be poisonous. It was a case of having to be creative.

"I know, how about Spam fritters followed by Dustman's Wedding Cake. I know that's your favourite." There was a cry of glee from me and my sister. We knew no better as we had never tasted real cake. It was basically a bread pudding, as you just couldn't get the ingredients for a proper cake.

Mum had to be inventive. Basic foodstuffs such as sugar, meat, fats, bacon and cheese were rationed. Everyone, including children had been issued with ration cards, and these had to registered with particular shop-keepers, so you could only go to those shops, whether they had a supply of what you wanted or not. Normally you would find yourself queuing outside a shop, sometimes in the pouring rain, queue at the butchers, queue at the baker's queue at the greengrocers. Pregnant women and children were given first options on milk and egg allowances and those others most in need. If you managed to get what you wanted, the shopkeeper would cross that item off the ration book.

As shortages increased, the longer the queues became, then when you'd queued for ages, and finally got to the counter, it was to be told that the shop had run out of what you wanted.

Fruit and vegetables were never rationed but were often in short supply, especially tomatoes, onions and fruit shipped from overseas. We had never seen a banana and it wasn't until the late 50s they started to be imported again. I remember mum's eyes lighting up when she saw them in the shop after so long.

Other things like petrol, was rationed in 1939 and mum received clothing coupons in 1941, then there was a lack of soap in 1942.

The Day the Sun Disappeared, 27 Nov 1944

Of course, people could get what they wanted, if you knew who to ask and where to go and if you had the money – the Black Market, or if you were in with a shopkeeper, he might keep something special by for you 'behind the counter'.

Dad joined the 'Home Guard' along with many of his friends. He often said, many years later, that Dad's Army was a documentary not a comedy, as many of the stories were similar to real life. Yes, and I agreed with him, all doing their drill training, with wooden sticks for rifles – they didn't have the equipment see, so what they would do if they saw a German was anyone's guess. It was only later on that they even got uniforms. They were mostly old codgers, ineligible for military service, either because of age, or otherwise infirm in body or even a bit simple. Most had served in the First World War, but some though had even served in Kitchener's campaign in the Sudan in 1896-98 or even the Boer War. Yes, Jones the butcher comes to mind, when thinking back to the rationing – putting behind the counter a bit of black pudding for his regulars, and Private Walker, a black-market spiv, supplying anything anyone wanted, if they had the money. Still, they were there, trekking through the countryside, on 'manoeuvres' but would be the first to raise the alarm if they saw something suspicious, or get in there and sort it out as best they could.

A typical ration for one adult per week was:

Butter: 2oz (50g)　　　　　　　　Bacon and ham: 4oz (100g) – (1940)
Sugar: 8oz (225g)　　　　　　　　Meat: to the value of 1s.2d per week.
　　　　　　　　　　　　　　　　(was then equal to 6p)
Cheese: 50g (2oz) (May 1941)　　Eggs: 1 fresh egg a week (June 1941)
Jam: 1lb (450g) every two months　Dried eggs – 1 packet every four weeks
1941

The Day the Sun Disappeared, 27 Nov 1944

Other items were added during the war

Fish	Rice – (Jan 1942)
Tea (Jul 1940)	Canned fruit
Peas (Feb 1942)	Biscuits (Aug 1942)
Breakfast cereals	Milk
Dried fruit (Jan 19420	Cooking fat (July 1940)

As a 'sweetener', everyone was allowed 16 points per month to use on whatever food items they wished.

We were lucky dad had chickens – you can't do much with one egg a week, definitely can't make a cake and so much for bacon and egg for breakfast!

Mum told me we couldn't get the food from abroad any more as the German submarines were attacking British supply ships. Rationing was introduced to ensure that people got an equal amount of food every week. The Government didn't want a hike in prices that would mean that poorer people might not be able to afford to eat. There was also a danger that some people might hoard food, leaving none for others.

We were all sat down for dinner one day, except little Lillian, who was in her cot. I had a high chair. It wasn't much, dry bread and some nondescript form of minced meat, and not much of that - mum had mixed onions in with the meat and a can of tomatoes, and peas, to eke it out, with a pot of tea in the centre of the table.

"Well, we won't get fat on this, John." mum said.

"You're right there but, then again, look on the bright side, we've never been healthier. We're getting all we need, even though it's not that tasty.

The Day the Sun Disappeared, 27 Nov 1944

"There's a can of pears for afters, although you'll only get a quarter each, still, better than nothing."

"Never mind, love. Let's just imagine we are having a sumptuous meal. Let's pretend that this mishmash is a juicy steak. Come on, can't you taste that yummy meat just enthralling your taste buds?"

"Ok, I'll go along with you." And pouring out a cup of tea for everyone, resumed with, "I am imagining this is a superb glass of port, can't you taste the fruit of the alcohol just swilling around your tongue, heightening your senses." They chinked cups and all said, "Cheers."

....

The 'Dig for Victory' campaign started in October 1939 and called for every man and woman to keep an allotment. Lawns and flower-beds were turned into vegetable gardens. Chickens, rabbits, goats and pigs were reared in town parks and gardens.

 At the time, mum's brothers were refugees too, along with nieces and nephews whilst the bombing was at its worst in London.

The Day the Sun Disappeared, 27 Nov 1944

CHAPTER 11

FROM VERA POYNTON

George Page and his wife, Alice, were living in Hanbury Road, Newborough. They'd had three daughters, Dolly, Nellie and Marjorie. Marjorie, the youngest was still living with mum and dad. Dolly had married Ernie Horton and they now had a four-month old little girl, Vera.

Just three months earlier, in September, Nellie had got married to John West who was working in the gypsum mine, as was her father George.

It wasn't a grand marriage as Nellie was a war bride and there just wasn't the money to splash out.

Nellie and John were married in Newborough Church.

"Oh, can't I get married in white, mum." Nellie was complaining. "I mean, ever since I could remember, I have dreamt of walking down the aisle, with dad on my arm, and a flowing lace train sweeping out behind me."

"You know your dad and I would get you a dress if we could, but the coupons won't stretch to a wedding dress as well as a going-away suit. It's either one or the other."

"Oh this dratted war. Everything's spoilt - all my dreams."

"Now, donna be like that girl. You love your young man, don't you?"

"Yes, of course I do."

The Day the Sun Disappeared, 27 Nov 1944

"So there, he's your dream, so you'll have to make do with a suit."

"I suppose so."

"Anyway, the neighbours are doing you proud. They've had fair warning and have been saving up their ration coupons, going without themselves, and put them together to make you a wedding cake and sandwiches.

"Yes, that's awfully nice of them.

"You make sure you thank each and every one of them, my dear. Anyway, it's not every day we have a wedding and it's sure to be a grand affair in everyone's eyes, the best we can make it."

So, the day of the wedding came and Dolly did Nellie's hair. As nylon stockings were not to be had for love nor money. Dolly then, painstakingly, drew a thin line with gravy mix up the back of Nellie's legs, to represent the stockings line.

"Oh, if only John was in the American Army, he could have got me real stockings. I've seen American soldiers giving them to their girlfriends.... and chocolate." Nellie moaned.

"Yes, what I'd do for a bar of chocolate," Dolly replied, "Yummy. But, come on now, there's no moaning allowed on your wedding day. Everything's going to be fine and you look beautiful."

The wedding went off well, all the relatives and neighbours were there and the happy couple went off for a little break not too far away. Alice was quite tearful, seeing her second daughter married, but then again, so were Dolly and Marjorie.

"Never mind" Dolly said, to try to cheer her up, "After this dratted war, maybe you can do it all again, and wear white this time."

The Day the Sun Disappeared, 27 Nov 1944

"Oh, it's not just that, but it's just that we can't afford a place of our own just yet. I know we'll be staying with you and Ernie and I suppose that's better than staying with mum and dad, but it's not the same."

"It'll be fine, Nellie. We'll have a laugh while the men are at work. It will be like old times at home. Anyway, you'll soon have that money saved up, you only need a bit more, and a couple of months of saving then you'll have that place you want. There's no rush anyway, you'll have your whole life together, you and John."

So, after the honeymoon, Nellie and John returned to live with Dolly and Ernie and their little daughter, Vera, in Dolefoot Lane, Newborough, which is south of Draycott in the Clay and about 5 miles south west of Fauld.

Ernie left for work, as usual, on that Monday morning, waving goodbye to his wife Dolly.

Dolly was holding four-month old little Vera in her arms, on the door step and working Vera's arm in a wave-like action to wave off daddy.

"Oh, do I have to go, Dolly? She's so sweet.

"I'm afraid you have to John, but you'll soon be back again and can give little Vera one of your famous hugs. Now run along, otherwise you'll be late."

John followed immediately behind, off for the gypsum mine. Nellie gave him a kiss on the doorstep and waved him off as he got on his bicycle to cycle to the gypsum mine. He would probably meet up with his father-in-law, George on the road there.

The Day the Sun Disappeared, 27 Nov 1944

No-one knew, from those tender goodbyes at the doorstep, that this would be the last they would see of John, or their father.

Vera, who was only four months old at the time, writes:

My grandma was still alive when grandad died and lived until the early sixties. My uncle and aunt had only been married three months. Grandad and my uncle John Page are buried in Newborough Church yard (no headstone – I don't think they could afford one as money would have been tight).

In the early fifties Aunt Nellie remarried William (Bill) Dicken. Bill was a little older than aunty. He owned a mobile shop. They first lived in Shobnall Road, Burton on Trent. They later brought Rose Cottage, Hanbury Road, Newborough- just down the road from grandma. They delivered groceries in the mobile shop to Burton and all the surrounding villages. Aunty Nellie went on the rounds with him. They never had any children. Ill health forced uncle to give the mobile shop up in the mid 60s.

The Day the Sun Disappeared, 27 Nov 1944

Now the earth has erupted
In a furnace of flame and mushroom cloud
A searing blast and gas brings death
Consumed in mud-filled coffins, buildings sloughed
Now the earth has erupted

CHAPTER 12

THE MACKAYS – AFTER THE EXPLOSION

On the day of the explosion, Barbara was at school. All of a sudden the windows were breaking, the doors banging, plus the floor rippled (like corrugated tin sheeting). I dived under the table as the shock waves continued, praying that Tom, Barbara and Connie would be safe. I didn't know what to think. We'd had no air-raid warning siren. All I could think was an enemy plane had got under the radar and had bombed us. My mind went back to the awful bombing we had in Burton on 30 August 1940. That happened at half past ten at night. Eleven bombs were dropped on the Uxbridge area of Burton, just south west of us, around Wood Street. Those houses had been completely destroyed, killing five people. In the following days and weeks after the bombing, I scoured the papers for anything about it, but there was nothing. Tom had said that was because of the Official Secrets Act.

As it happens Connie and Barbara came home safely. Connie had been working in a field. She saw and felt the explosion, as the ground wavered and quivered under her feet. She ran home to make sure I was alright. Connie had been at school and related that glass had smashed and chimney pots had fallen.

The Day the Sun Disappeared, 27 Nov 1944

"It wasn't a plane, mum." Connie said, "It was in the direction of Fauld – I think the bomb dump has gone up."

Anyway, they were both safe.

A little while later I saw the milkman going down the road in his milk float. He was a bit later than normal. I ran out and stopped him. I wanted to know if he had any news of what had happened. He looked as white as his milk and was shaking.

"Are you alright." I asked.

"I'm sorry missus," he managed to get out, "just a bit shaken. I was delivering to the Acorn Inn in just south of Anslow when the explosion went off. I was knocked off my float with the force of it. Luckily people in the pub came out and got me, took me in and gave me a stiff brandy. It fair shook me up I can tell you. But I'm alright now, thank you. Yes, the Dumps gone up."

I knew Tom would be investigating what had happened but he didn't appear until the early hours, covered in mud and totally exhausted. I ran a hot bath for him and made him something to eat and drink. In the meantime I was trying desperately to brush the mud off his uniform and shoes. He slumped into bed into a troubled sleep, tossing and turning.

In the morning, before going to the police station, Tom gave me a potted version of what had happened. "Bombs at the RAF dump have exploded underground. Peter Ford's alabaster mill is a wreck and people are trapped in the mines. People are stuck in the RAF bomb storage underground and the retaining wall of the reservoir for the use by Peter Ford's mill has broken and tons of water has flooded the mill, drowning the workers. There were two explosions. As far as people know, only one person was killed in the first explosion and a number injured, but the second, some

The Day the Sun Disappeared, 27 Nov 1944

distance from the first, caused the most deaths. Workmen have been buried and crushed as the roof and sides of the workings caved in or have been shattered by the blast in the administrative buildings nearby.

The first of the dead were brought out from the workings about an hour after the explosion, but others are believed to have been blown to atoms."

I gave a gasp at this and put my hands to my face. Just the thought of it, made my stomach churn.

Tom carried on, "Immediately after the explosion, I could see two distinct columns of smoke rising like gigantic mushrooms, into the sky. The whole area is packed with ambulances, fire brigades from all over and Civil Defence personnel. Diggers and tractors were there trying to clear a path as quickly as possible so that the recovery vehicles could get in. There are no roads – they've all been mangled. It's just mud and rocks. They even have colliery rescue brigades, with nurses quickly taking the injured to hospital. Two farms and a pub have been wrecked by the blast. One of the farms has disappeared into the crater. Police from all stations are there diverting traffic. Nearly every house has been damaged in some way or other. After about an hour and a half the fire brigade had put out the fires, just a bit of smoke from the crater.

Tom then left for the police station.

It was the next day and I was listening to the radio to try to get any more news. Lord Haw Haw came on speaking in his posh English accent, "Germany calling, Germany calling" saying that the explosion was due to the Germans, who had bombed Burton and beer was running through the streets. "Oh, that man. Can't they get him off the radio?" That was being broadcast worldwide. To think that any people from Burton in the forces abroad would hear

The Day the Sun Disappeared, 27 Nov 1944

this and think that Burton had been bombed to smithereens, and their families had been killed. It was unforgiveable!

The Day the Sun Disappeared, 27 Nov 1944

CHAPTER 13

PC MACKAY AT THE DISASTER

From P C Mackay's written report

It was a lovely winter morning, with a clear blue sky and warm sunshine.

Overhead an aeroplane was flying leisurely and the war seemed very far away from this peaceful part of England. I was on patrol at Anslow - about two miles away from Fauld.

Just at that moment, at 11.10am to be precise, I felt the earth shudder violently. My first thought was an earthquake, they were known to happen, not regular, but not unknown. There was a dull 'thud' which echoed across the countryside. Then the houses around me started to rock and glass splintered and masonry started falling. I had to get myself to relative safety and jumped over a wall into a field. Then I saw a huge column of smoke shoot up from the direction of Fauld, the site of the RAF Maintenance Station.

It was a terrifying sight and I couldn't believe my own eyes. Huge billows of what appeared to be black smoke rose into the air for must have been a mile and a half. I could see, mingled with this smoke, patches of red, green and yellow and a white haze spread slowly over the countryside, for some miles. More dull thuds followed the explosion.

The Day the Sun Disappeared, 27 Nov 1944

I didn't know what to do. People were coming out of their houses, wondering what was going on. They saw me and began shouting out, "Mackay, what's happening?" Big cracks had appeared in their houses. Some people started screaming.

Then there were more dull thuds, followed by the first heavy explosion. I counted six explosions.

Then it dawned on me, the underground military dump of bombs had exploded. I knew that, if it went up, this would be followed by catastrophic death and widespread destruction. I thought this was the end and we would all be killed any moment. I got down on my knees and prayed – expecting this prayer to be my final one.

Time seemed to stand still for the next few seconds, and then there was an ominous quiet over the land.

I realised that, by a miracle the predicted death and destruction had passed me by, and the people around me.

It was time for action and I got on my bike and raced to the scene. I didn't know what to expect but little realised that the next twelve weeks I would be continuously on duty there, searching for the dead.

When I arrived at the RAF station, at 11.20am, there seemed to be an unexpected eeriness of calm. Work-people were calmly walking down the roadways to the office for roll call, even though flames were shooting thirty feet high, from the burning incendiary store, and the "pop pop" of these bombs could be heard as still more of them burst into flames from the heat of the others. It all seemed somehow pseudo-realistic. All I can think of to explain this was that my heart was beating ten to the dozen, expecting to leap into action at the first command, not knowing what I would face, whilst, somehow, in comparison, everyone appeared as somehow moving in slow motion to me – a weird feeling. In reality, people were indeed running around in action mode.

Then, time seemed to catch up with everyone around me, as if a button had been pushed, and from all parts of the compass, fire appliances, ARP vehicles and personnel started pouring into the stricken area in a continuous stream. It made me proud to be British! Police Sergeant Kelly of Tutbury must have realised what had happened and must have telephoned his headquarters for back-up. The news had got round quickly to all rescue teams.

From a nearby American Camp, vehicles emerged, laden with GIs armed with spades, shovels, ropes, stretchers, blankets and so on. I saw other parties marching into the area, all desperately anxious to help and all oblivious or uncaring of the peril in which they stood.

Dust was coming down heavily, depositing itself thickly upon everything. The main loss of life was caused by the terrible destructive effect of the descending debris, which engulfed everything upon which it fell.

I decided my job was to take written statements from all the people recovered alive.

After that, I went to assist the coroner, J L Auden and the school hall, then continued as many hours as I could possibly do, just going around with the rescue parties, searching for bodies.

The Day the Sun Disappeared, 27 Nov 1944

As soon as I saw the explosion, at 11.10am, I cycled over, from Anslow Village, arriving at about 11.20. I could see flames visible in two places and could heard the 'pop', 'pop' of incendiaries going off. The flames from the incendiary store were 30ft high. Roll calls were being made in the road for the workers, military and civilians. All the phones were out in the unit, but Police Sergeant Kelly of Tutbury had used his station phone to contact the civil defence report centre and the National Fire Service district officer at Burton, requesting immediate assistance from fire brigade crews and ambulances.

I met up with Superintendent Vodrey, Sergeant Chamberlain and Sergeant Massey of Uttoxeter. "The rescue team all seem to be going to the dump, sirs, but I don't know if they are aware of the Peter Ford's works in the valley, just to the north. I believe they are in dire straits there."

So we all went towards the works and discovered they had been virtually destroyed, along with the Purse cottages and the reservoir. When we got there it was to see an American officer and others carrying off Mrs Ford, who lived in one of the cottages, on a stretcher. I assisted them in getting her to hospital then came back to carry on the search. The news spread to the Air Raid Precaution (A.R.P) station, and a nearby American RAF camp. I started walking around the area to see what I could possibly do to help the recovery teams that were now starting to arrive. The body of the blacksmith, George Cockayne, was found a little bit later and I helped get him onto an ambulance. I then went onto the RAF Fauld site, continuing to get people onto stretchers, then into the ambulances that had started to queue up there. Someone gave me a spade and I started digging, listening out acutely for any sounds of life.

The Day the Sun Disappeared, 27 Nov 1944

The response was immediate, and made one proud to be British. From all parts of the compass, fire appliances and ARP vehicles and personnel poured into the stricken area in a continuous stream.

It was an hour before the telephones were re-opened in the Unit.

Exhausted, after a long day and night, I finally made my way back home.

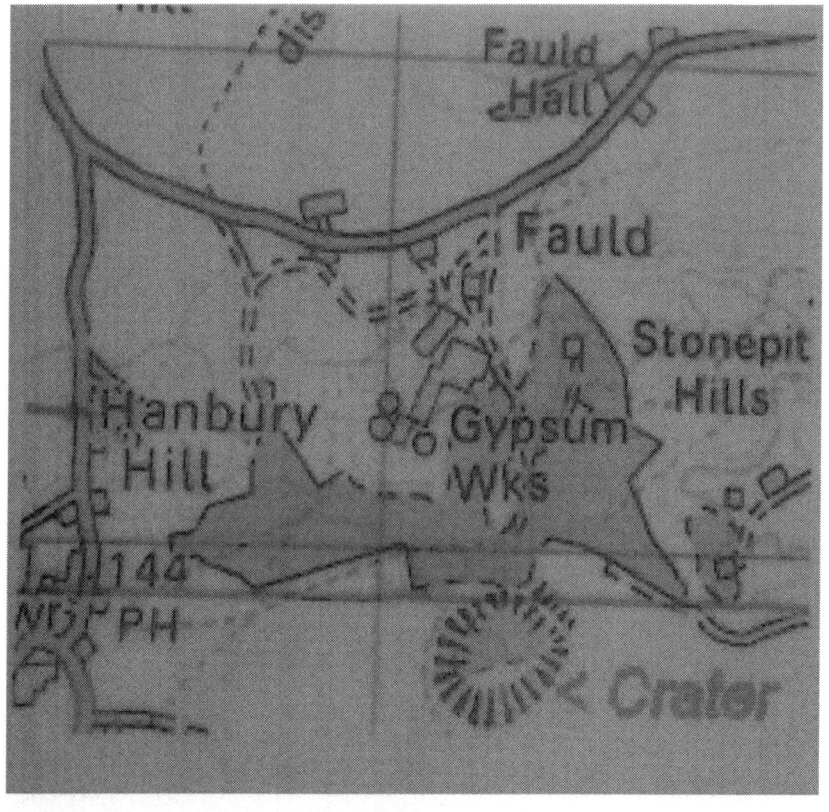

I went out early the next day, firstly to report to the Police Station. The whole police station had obviously been out doing their best with rescue attempts. 'Ted' Heath was manning the phones with

The Day the Sun Disappeared, 27 Nov 1944

the WPCs when Tom arrived, "This is a total disaster, Tom. All the rescue services are there but there's a cat in nine chance of getting most out alive. From what I hear gas is creeping along the mine tunnels. Sergeant Kelly reported in about 12.30pm yesterday that the works of Peter Ford have been destroyed."

"Yes, sir, I've been out there rescuing miners trapped in the alabaster mine." I gave him my report of the people rescued.

However, one good thing, I suppose, is that I have not received any notifications of casualties here in Burton and only minor damage has been caused, chiefly to old residences, with chimney

*Burton Observer, November 30th 1944 – Rescue square working among a tangle of ironwork and timber on part of the site of the plaster worker*s.

pots down and ceilings fallen in – not like Hanbury and Tutbury and the surrounding villages. We've had calls stating doors have been blown open and windows rattled. In parts of Burton people have been quite unaware of the occurrence. Parts of some buildings shook, while other parts of the same premises did not. At a Burton store the entrance swing doors opened to their full extent with the blast and closed again, but no damage was done. However, I've received reports that the explosion was heard and felt at Coventry. Daventry, 19 miles south of Coventry, also felt the explosion. People rushed into the streets thinking a bomb had fallen. Northampton heard the blast too, it shook houses in Leicester and the surrounding area and was heard in most parts of Leicestershire. Public services here have been unaffected with the exception of a suspect slight disturbance of a gas main. Christ Church steeple has been deemed unstable, so I've got some of the men out diverting traffic and cordoning off the areas around the gas mains. The Services Hostel, in the old vicarage, is still open but a notice has been put up warning members of the Forces requiring bed and breakfast that they stay there at their own risk.

So, Burton, on the whole, has been very lucky.

Bomb disposal units are at the site and there's concern about a suspected unexploded bomb opposite Hanbury School. They have detector apparatus and are there with the Civil Defence workers.

From the reports that are coming through, the section where the explosion occurred is widely separated from the remainder. This section is very seriously damaged, but the main part of the depot, and the administrative buildings, received no significant damage. The total number of bombs is estimated to be no more than 4000 tons."

The Day the Sun Disappeared, 27 Nov 1944

"So, that's no more than has been dropped in a single raid on Germany."

"Quite so, and so lucky that the explosion was under mainly farmland."

"Yes, sir. God help the damage and number of lives lost if it had been nearer a city."

"What I want you to do Tom, is to take reports from all the people who have survived the blast. We need this for our records and to stop the newspapers and their reporters making up their own stories."

So, over the next few days I tried my best to help the recovery teams, to assist at the temporary morgue, set up by Mary Cooper, and to interview people recovered from the mines, together with many witness statements. *(These reports can be found at the Tutbury Museum, kindly donated by his son, Donald).*

The Staffordshire police assumed overall control of rescue operations, setting up their headquarters in Fauld. The Air Ministry was, of course, involved and Civil Defence had sent in the 'Mutual Assistance Group No. 7', based in Lichfield.

Shortly after the blast, the Civil Defence controller at Tutbury cabled, 'Hanbury village very badly damaged. Escaping gases have formed huge craters and thrown clay about in all directions. Nearly all houses in the village effected (sic). Civilian casualties estimated between 20 and 30. Military casualties not known. Further information will be available tomorrow."

Major Dobson organised for dead cattle to be removed. He also reported on the condition of Hanbury village. 'Eighty four houses in Tutbury rural have received damage and it is possible that four houses are damaged beyond repair and two very badly damaged.

The Day the Sun Disappeared, 27 Nov 1944

I would like to pay tribute to the management of the Cock Inn (Hanbury) who, in spite of great difficulty are still able to serve their customers.'

MAG7 was initially made up of 170 troops, working in three shifts but were hampered by gas in the underground passages.

I started walking the devastated area, which was up to a thousand acres in all, doing so every day until the following May.

A few days later there was a report in the local paper from the Prime Minister, Mr Churchill. The report stated, "I do not know that we should assume that anyone was responsible. These dangerous explosives have sometimes spontaneous action."

I found out soon after that the school roof had been damaged, with heavy coping stones dislodged. The deluge of debris had made a hole in the roof, coming down with such force that it shattered a corner of the teacher's solid oak desk, which she had been sitting at a few seconds earlier.

I don't know if horses have a sixth sense of imminent disaster, but I also discovered that a young lad, who had been working with a horse and card with the farmer on a local farm, would have been killed if it had not been for the horse - well, suddenly the horse stood in its tracks and would not move. Seconds later a great boulder of alabaster came crashing down out of the sky, directly where they would have been, if the horse had not stopped.

The Day the Sun Disappeared, 27 Nov 1944

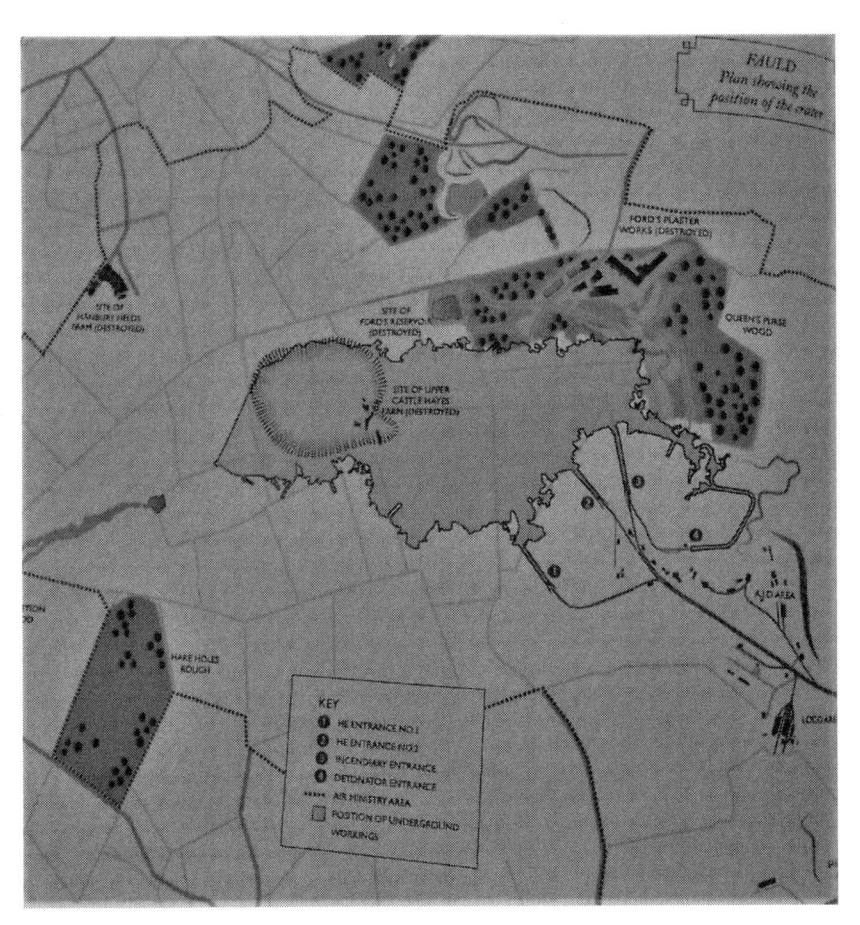

Eight-year-old Peter Harrison, brother to Ida Harrison, came home to find his home totally wrecked. The Harrison family lived quite close to the village hall and Featherbed Lane, which led to Hanbury Fields Farm. Luckily his mother, who had just come out of hospital, was safe and his father worked in Staton's mine, which had not been affected.

The Day the Sun Disappeared, 27 Nov 1944

Remains of Village Hall - picture by John Pye

It was not just the volcano of rock and earth that caused the loss of life but the 30ft dam, 200 yards from the centre of the explosion. The dam crumbled, sending a 15-ft torrent of water, mud, boulders and trees to pour down into the Ford's plasterworks, destroying the buildings and burying the workers there.

The resulting crater from the Fauld Explosion is about ¾ mile long and half a mile wide. Some say it is 90ft deep as the mine was 90ft deep and the explosion blew the top of it off. Deep down there are gigantic pieces of natural gypsum pillars, what is left of the pillars that once supported the roof of the mine workings. People round here call them 'hard arse' 'Hard arse' is the bright white gypsum that cannot be mined. The whole area is surrounded by massive boulders of gypsum that were blown skywards and landed making huge indentations in the torn up landscape. The whole area was covered in 3ft of debris, the fields were unfit for anything and 200 sheep and cattle died or had to be killed. There are still unexploded bombs down there so the whole area is restricted.

The Day the Sun Disappeared, 27 Nov 1944

Prisoners from Sudbury Open Prison were brought in to move the material, a very slow procedure. Bodies were still being dug out some time afterwards. Two years later I heard that a prisoner clearing the earth and debris hit something metal. He immediately put up a red flag to attract his supervisor's attention. What they found was a buried tractor, and beneath it was the body of a farmworker had had been driving it on the day the dump went up.

The Fauld crater following the explosion in 1944 (Image: Donated by John Cooper)

CHAPTER 14

GOODWIN FARM

(Extracts from Burton Observer and South Derbyshire Weekly Mail 30 Nov 1944.)

Sometime later I trudged through the mud to the other side of the crater, where once stood the Upper Castle Hayes Farm, owned by the Goodwins. I knew a house had been there but it had disappeared so completely that it was impossible to say where exactly it had stood. The area where the farm had been had continued to smoke for two days.

There were loads of people digging – quite a few from Tutbury, who I managed to speak to. There were also mechanical diggers down in the depths of the crater.

What I found out was the farmer, Maurice Goodwin (aged 42), his wife, Mary, (aged about 40) had just left the farm on the way to the market at the time of the explosion. No-one had heard of them since and it was presumed they had been drowned. Elizabeth Smith (about 38), who was Mary's sister was left behind. There's no trace of her. They were still looking for Stephen and John West, brothers employed as farm hands and a man named Runcorn, a Liverpool evacuee.

Luckily, the Goodwin's two young children, Gordon and Marie, escaped as they had been at school, in Hanbury, at the time of the explosion. Friends of the family would have the harrowing task of collecting them from school and telling them that their parents had not survived.

At another farm, one of two workers on the land had been found dead, but there was no trace of the other, or his wagon and horses. Speaking to people there from Tutbury, it seems that Tutbury had lost so many well-known members of the community in the explosion and the whole town was grief-stricken.

Jack Gorton was amongst the diggers though he was really too ill still to be digging and breathing heavily. He stopped for a while to rest, "Harry Shepherd was one of them. He'd lived in Tutbury all his life and worked as a plaster miner for over 40 years. He was a great guy. The whole family had been devastated, especially his wife Eliza, as they had a son, William Henry Shepherd – also killed."

Someone else shouted out, that was Bert Hardwick from Top Farm, "Yes, William had been a member of the Tutbury Bowling Club – the same one I go to. He was popular with everyone and I don't say it just for myself but for everyone that knew him, that he'll be gravely missed."

Somebody else got my attention. "Well, I dosna know if thou knows but it wasn't just the two of them in the family who lost their lives. Joseph Bell was a nephew. He was a Tutbury lad too, living wi' his father, Eli. That's three in one family. I never want to see the likes of this, ever again."

One of the men chimed in, "George Priestly died too. You all know George don't you." And there was a shout out of "Yes" from everyone. "A well-liked guy was George. A real family man. He has five sons serving abroad and luckily, so we've heard, another of his sons was working at the pit but managed to get out safely."

The Day the Sun Disappeared, 27 Nov 1944

Someone else said, "Yes, he has a sister. She's lost her husband, Ellnan, too. He was only 39. He was born and bred in Tutbury and worked in the pit as an engine driver for nigh on 43 years. He loved his football and we all remember going to see him play for Tutbury Town Football Club. He was a half-back on the team. His wife and son will be sorely grieving for him.

We've lost so many from Tutbury." One of the lads shouted out, "Don't forget George Cockayne, the blacksmith at Peter Ford's mill" This was Vic Price from Tutbury. "He has a son serving abroad, and not forgetting his brother-in-law, George Smith, who also worked in the alabaster mine."

"Well, we're all hoping to goodness they're going to find George. He's still missing. For your records, Mr Mackay, he's about 60 and has three sons serving abroad. We're also hoping that young Samuel Pickering will be found too. His father's also a plaster miner but we believe he got out."

"The bodies of Robert Wagstaffe and Russell Miles should be hereabouts. They were working on the Goodwin farm at the time."

The Day the Sun Disappeared, 27 Nov 1944

FATALITIES OF PEOPLE LIVING IN TUTBURY

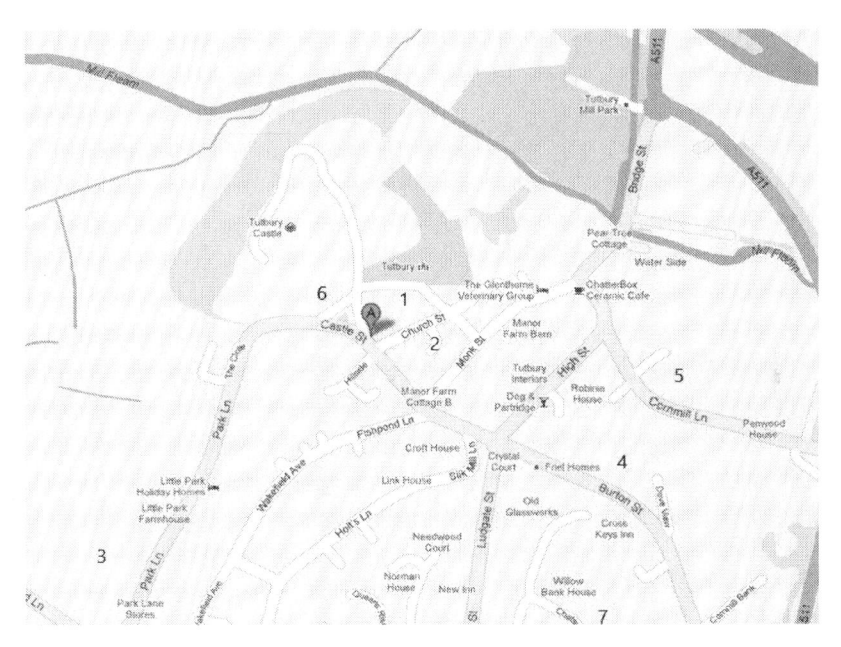

No. 1, Church Street –	George Powell – 7 Church Street, TUTBURY
	George L Cockayne – 9 Church Street
No. 2, Monk Street -	James Brassington, 55 Monk Street
	William Gent, 8 Monk Street
	Samuel Pickering, 44 Monk Street
	Frederick Nicklin, 16 Monk Street
No 3, Park Lane	George Priestley, 13 Park Lane
	George Smith, 16 Park Lane
No 4, Burton Street	Henry Shepherd, 15 Burton Street
	Eli Bell, 24 Burton Street
	Joseph Bell, 32 Burton Street
No 5, Cornmill Lane	William Shepherd, 15 Cornmill Lane
	Edman Woolley, 3 Cornmill Lane
No. 6 Castle Street	Lewis Frow, 24 Castle Street
No 7, Green Lane	Ambrose Patterson, 96 Green Lane

The Day the Sun Disappeared, 27 Nov 1944

Just then I heard 'Mac' being called. This turned out to be a policeman from Tutbury, Police Sergeant Kelly – doing his bit, digging.

I'd known Sergeant John Kelly as I was serving under him when I had been at Rolleston. He had been stationed at Tutbury since 1939 and didn't have all that long before he retired, which would be in 1947.

He had served with the Royal Field Artillery in the 1914-18 war and served in Mesopotamia and Salonika. On his demobilisation in 1919, he joined the Staffordshire Constabulary and his earlier duties took him to Biddulph, Wolstanton and Madeley. He had been stationed at Kidsgrove for 15 years before coming to Tutbury, on his promotion to the rank of sergeant.

I was in line to be his successor upon his retirement.

"Hello, Eyes" I called out. "Hard graft this. Have you and the other lads found anything?"

"Well, we've found red and blue bricks scattered all over the place, from the rim of the crater. Theer the same type of bricks as the farm. Pieces of dead animals, as are everywhere. The mechanical diggers have found a 9x9" oak beam about 60 yards from the crater. It had been broken in two. This was also part of the Dutch Barn on the farm for storing the hay and straw. Theer were pieces of iron, mixed in with the straw, all twisted out of shape like, and pieces of roof asbestos. I stuck a red flag 30 yards inside the crater, as I believe this is the spot where the farm had been. We also found an iron bedstead inside the crater, some bedclothes about 50 yards from the rim, but so far, no sign of any bodies. It is possible that some of the farm has been swilled down the valley towards the Ford's factory, with the water from the reservoir and is covered with earth and mud, and very possibly the blast wave has actually sucked some into the bottom of the crater."

"Yes, everything's gone. An awful state of affairs."

"That's an understatement if I ever heard anything, Mac"

"Yes, sorry, there are really no words for it....I knew the Goodwin family, and the sister, Elizabeth. I used to visit quite regularly, even coming to help them for a week with their harvest....I'm really sad.

I've been walking around the area, must be about 200 acres, I suppose, and only one head of cattle had escaped unhurt and one slightly injured, the rest have had to be destroyed.

Changing the subject Eyes, well, I never found out why you were called Eyes?"

"Well, I wanted to be No.1, as in the bingo call – 'Kelly's eye - Number 1,' but none of the other lads would agree to that – and I dosna blame them, having to call me No. 1 - above me station and all that! So, I'm 'Eyes' after the song, 'When Irish Eyes are smiling'."

I left them to it and carried on my weary trudge. I became aware of notices that had gone up around the edge of the crater, 'Government property. Most dangerous. Keep to the road.'

....

I met up, on my walks with Ron Thompson, a police pal from Tutbury. He was a big guy but he looked stressed and worn out. I suppose I did too, but we knew we had to carry on. He had been busy directing rescue workers and civil defence workers. He was also assisting in with the search and rescue of casualties,

The Day the Sun Disappeared, 27 Nov 1944

administering first air, where necessary. He also took a part in cordoning off and guarding bomb-damaged buildings, and keeping members of the public away from the dump. Obviously there were anxious people waiting for any news of their loved ones but he had to move them on. He also was going to the damaged houses to offer reassurance and ensure that the occupiers were being helped out either by neighbours and make sure they were directed to where they could get proper meals.

PC Balance was doing his bit too. He had been living at 17 Burton Street, Tutbury since 1923, a police house. It still had the old cells there, with a barred window. He was an old guy and actually retired in 1939, but had come out to help, where possible. Most of the younger policemen had joined up, so the force was left with a lot of older men.

His original beat had covered the villages from Stretton and Rolleston right across to Newborough, as well as Tutbury.

The police station was at No 15 Fishpond and the adjacent Nos. 16 and 17 were police residential property.

CHAPTER 15

JIM HEATHCOTE

In the meantime, Jim Heathcote, living at Alabaster House, Fauld, had been at Fauld Manor Farm, the north side of Fauld Lane –. there was a bit of a track in front of his house that led to the pit and the mine. Jim's farm belonged to Gypsum – William Newton's as it was then.

He farmed there. Jim was a youngish man - he was dressed, as normal, for working on the farm, in his overalls, wellington boots, jackets and flat peaked cap. The deafening roar of the explosion drew him outside to see an enormous black cloud erupting upwards above the Stonepit Hills and across Fauld Lane. The cloud had taken on the form of a gigantic mushroom shape that appeared to be about fifty yards wide and reached upwards almost out of sight. The top of the 'mushroom' began to spread and there were large white objects appearing beneath the smoke, falling to the ground. He realised that these must be huge pieces of alabaster, some the size of railway engines, falling, along with trees and great mounds of earth, having been blasted up into the heavens. He knew then that the Dump had gone up. He watched in anguish as one of his fields, close to the Dump, where his sheep and cows were, was being blasted up into the sky. He dove to the ground as objects were flying through the air, landing on the roof of the house and he could see the force of the wind blowing the doors off. His first thought was to his wife. He ran back to

The Day the Sun Disappeared, 27 Nov 1944

Alabaster House. Luckily she was alright, but shaken as the blast had shattered all of the windows. "Oh, I was so lucky, Jim. I was just in the hallway, by the cellar door, sorting out things I needed in the hallway cupboard. Then I heard the explosion and all the window panes just smashed and there was all this banging and crashing I thought the roof was coming in on top of me. There was splintered glass just flying around. I ducked down and hid my face in my hands. I didn't know what else to do. I'm so glad you're safe, Jim. What's happened?"

"I believe the Dump's exploded, love." Mrs Heathcote gasped, "Oh no, all those people working down there. They'll have been killed! Have you seen George?" (George was their four-year-old son).

"No, I thought he was with you."

"No, he was interested in what Dorothy Harrison was doing on the farm, so she took him with her."

"Oh God (almost screaming). They could be lying injured in the field. I sent Dorothy down to move the sheep and the cows to the lower field. That fields now a wreck!"

Luckily, at that moment, they saw 19-year-old Dorothy Harrison, who had been working on Jim's farm as a Land Army girl, rushing along the lane, holding onto little George's hand. Jim and his wife were so relieved.

"It's OK, Mr and Mrs Heathcote, George is safe." Jim picked up little George and cuddled and kissed him. She continued, "I know I should have been moving your sheep and cows up into another field, but I had something in my eye and took little George back home with me, so that I could see to it." (Dorothy lived at Fauld

Cottage with her parents and her brother, Tom. They were not related to the Harrisons in Hanbury).

So relieved, Jim responded, "And good job you did go home, Dorothy, as..." going outside, "just look, that field no longer exists. I'm so glad you're safe. You would be dead, duckie, as are my cows, mostly dead, from what I can see, or on their last legs. My sheep are dead too. We won't be able to go on, that's the last of me as a farmer. I've lost everything."

(Joe Cooper confirmed that Dorothy Harrison was working on Jim Heathcote's farm. Dorothy was a different family from the ones who got their house blown up, opposite the village hall. She was with little David Heathcote (3 years old). She wouldn't have been in the field, not at that time of day. She could have been moving the cows. Dorothy is still alive. A very nice girl. Dorothy Harrison lived in Fauld Cottages.)

Looking around outside, they could see part of the roof of Jim's house and buildings had gone and the doors had been ripped off their hinges. There was also a great block of alabaster lying in front of the house.

So relieved, Jim hurried down the drive to find Dick Utting, who lived at Fauld House. Debris had crashed through the cowshed roof, where he had been doing the milking, and he was driving the cows out. "I think they'll be safer outside, what with the roof shattered, although there's all this earth and stuff plummeting down." Dick said.

"Yes, I think we've been lucky, even though we're only 700 yards from the blast, but the lay of the land has meant the blast has gone over us, over the ridge between the farm and the mines. I dread to think what the destruction is down there.

The Day the Sun Disappeared, 27 Nov 1944

On getting to the top of that incline he could see the huge crater, the size of six football fields. All of the land had been shredded, leaving this gigantic hole where once there were fields with cattle and sheep grazing, the Peter Ford's works, the bomb store.

Purveying the now completely unrecognisable landscape, Jim took a sharp intake of breath and uttered, "Oh my God." The Goodwin's farm has gone – it's no longer there. It's disappeared into the hole."

The farm belonged to their friends, the Goodwins. Jim found a tear forming, but shook himself, this was no time for sentiment.

www.helenlee.co.uk/tutbury/imges/fauld/aerial2.jpg

Dick was looking totally shaken too and in a quavering voice managed to say. "My brother, Horace is down there somewhere….

Don't know how he could have survived that….. He was working on the bombs in the mine."

Jim, managing to control the tremor in his voice, just about succeeded in getting out, "I heard they were going to Burton cattle market this morning, the Goodwins. I'm hoping they got away in time and that they're safe."

Dick didn't answer, he was still thinking of his brother.

The Day the Sun Disappeared, 27 Nov 1944

The Crater – Donated by Graham Shaw

The Day the Sun Disappeared, 27 Nov 1944

"We'd better see what help we can be." Jim said. Dick replied, "Wait on, I may have some stuff in the shed that might be useful for rescue equipment." So, armed with spades and rope and strips of material Jim's wife said might come in handy for bandaging, they started walking, through the rubble and upturned land, towards RAF Fauld. Their little track leading to the mine and Peter Ford's had disappeared.

Soon after they met up with what looked like a whole squadron of American RAF, probably from the US army camp at Sudbury, just to the North West. They'd come in jeeps, but had to get out after the turning off Fauld Lane to the gypsum works, basically as the road had come to an abrupt end, it just didn't exist anymore.

The sergeant got out of one jeep and Jim stepped forward. "We've come to help with a rescue attempt, sir. Do you know the site? We need directions on where we should start."

"Yes, I am the farmer at Fauld Manor Farm," Jim said, pointing behind him. "I believe the best place to start would be in what remains of the Peter Ford Works. As you can see there is no path left, not much is left in fact. The whole area has been torn up and what used to be regular walks for me and my family, and fields of sheep and cattle…, and farms…"

At this point Jim lowered his head, thinking of the Goodwins, at Upper Castle Hayes Farm, (he gulped and took a deep breath to recover himself, before continuing), "…are no longer recognisable or have disappeared into the crater….. The works are in this direction. Follow me."

Together they made their way through to Peter Ford's works, looking for survivors. That's when they realised that the dam had burst too. The flood water mixed with fifty thousand tons of blast debris, had destroyed Peter Ford's works and the Purse Cottages.

The Day the Sun Disappeared, 27 Nov 1944

Dorothy had been joined by her brother, Tom, and they walked off ahead, looking for anyone they could rescue.

Tom stopped and bent down, investigating something he'd seen, "Oh... don't look Dorothy," he called over to her.

Tom had picked up half a body.

Dorothy turned around, away from the body, she didn't want to see the gruesome sight, - and the thought of it sent shivers down her spine. What she saw though was more and more people joining them on the track. After the Americans came the A.R.P Big diggers and trucks, making their way down what was left of the path.

"You can use Alabaster House, where I live, as a consultation point, if you wish. We still have the telephone in operation." So, RAF were picking up bodies and transporting them back to Jim Heathcote's garage for the time being.

....

In the meantime, Joseph Foster, manager at Peter Ford's works came across mill workers in the plasterboard room and had then gone onto Purse Cottages. Nothing remained of the Purse Cottages, just rubble.

"Help." He heard a feeble whimper, Help me."

Going towards the cry Joseph Foster found 51-year-old Mrs Ford on top of a heap of earth, almost unconscious. She had been blown out of her cottage and landed 20 yards away from where her cottage used to be, her body slumped and supported against the broken ruins of a wall. Trying to scramble over the piles of mud he found it impossible to get to her. He kept slipping down and getting bogged down up to his waist in the mud. It was like trying to wade through quicksand. Luckily, at that moment, he saw American soldiers and an officer.

"Hello, help. Mrs Ford is just here." He called out to them. They were on the other side, nearer to Mrs Ford and were able to find some planks of wood from the wreckage, to get over the mud to get to her. She was seriously injured and was unconscious by the time an unknown American officer gallantly struggled through the glutinous mud to get to her and carry her back to the trucks to get her to Derbyshire Royal Infirmary. It looked like she had been blown through the air a distance of what must have been about 20 yards. She'd suffered broken ribs, a broken arm and lacerations to the scalp. Every stitch of her clothing had actually been ripped off through the immense force of the blast.

It wasn't until near Christmas that rescue workers were able to burrow down through the mud around what had formerly been the Purse Cottages. They were digging just with spades, having to heave up the great slabs of earth manually. The body of Mrs Sarah Hill, neighbour to Mrs Ford, was found on Boxing Day. The body of Mrs Hill's husband, Harry, was not found until 3rd January 1945.

Just eight days after the funeral of his wife, Mr Harry John Hill was laid to rest in the same churchyard on Friday, 5th. Mr Hill had been employed as a clerk at the plaster mine for 25 years. The service was attended by his children and family as well as friends, George Ede Jnr and Miss Nora Ede. The councillor for Burton-on-Trent and members from various lodges were there too along with Mr and Mrs J Foster, Charles Gibbs, Mrs and Mrs William

The Day the Sun Disappeared, 27 Nov 1944

Watson, Mr Harry Wetherill, Mrs J Jones, Mrs F Ford, Mrs H Downing, Mrs J Key, Mrs William Bowring and Mr Thorley. The bearers were his friends Mr G Ede, Mr Jeff Hellaby, Mr Jim Heathcote and Mr L J Shotton.

....

Mr Frederick Harrison, a Prudential Assurance Company agent, had arranged to visit both Mrs Ford and Mrs Hill. He had been with the firm for 32 years in Burton and about three weeks prior had transferred to this area.

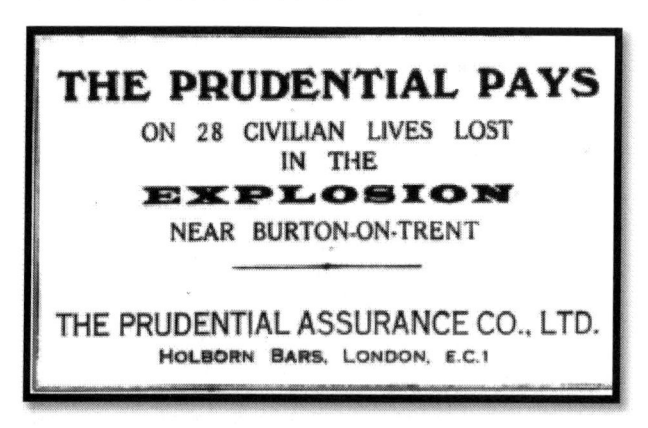

THE PRUDENTIAL PAYS
ON 28 CIVILIAN LIVES LOST
IN THE
EXPLOSION
NEAR BURTON-ON-TRENT

THE PRUDENTIAL ASSURANCE CO., LTD.
HOLBORN BARS, LONDON, E.C.1

He had been to visit Mrs Pegg at about 11 o'clock, then gone onto the cottages of Mrs Ford and Mrs Hill, close to the plaster mine. He knocked at Mrs Hill's door. Mrs Ford heard them chatting and came out, "Oh, I thought it might be you, Mr Harrison. You stay there and I'll just go in to get my insurance book. I'll be out directly." No truer a word said, as that's when the bomb exploded. At that moment the walls of her room just ripped apart and fell outwards. Mrs Ford was sucked up and out.

PC Mackay stated, on looking at the remains "Why she was not buried by the descending debris was beyond understanding."

The Day the Sun Disappeared, 27 Nov 1944

The Hill family had been at Purse Cottage for 11 years. Mr Harrison's body was found the day after Boxing Day. We heard many months later that Mrs Hill had eventually died. She'd lost her husband and her house, everything. Her death was stated as shock due to her traumatic experience. On the memorial erected later, her name appears as one of the victims of the explosion.

The Day the Sun Disappeared, 27 Nov 1944

CHAPTER 16

PETER FORD'S GYPSUM AND ALABASTER WORKS

Peter Ford's works before the explosion - donated by Graham Shaw

Peter Ford's works were in a hidden, narrow wooded valley heading off Fauld Lane. There are a labyrinth of tunnels under the Stonepit Hills, which extend for a number of miles west, south and east of Hanbury. Gypsum is mined for alabaster for buildings. The entrance to the mine followed paths into the Stonepit Hills, the lower slopes of which were covered by Queen's Purse Wood.

The mines became air-raid shelters for people living nearby, when the air raid sirens were sounded.

At the head of the valley, to the south, was a 30ft deep reservoir overlooking Peter Ford's that supplied water for the site. The reservoir held six million gallons of water, was thirty feet high and thirty-five feet thick at its base, tapering to 14ft at the top.

At the entrance to Peter Ford's, on the right stood the two Purse cottages. Mr Harry Hill and Mrs Sarah Hill lived in one. Mrs Hill was a dressmaker. Harry worked in the offices at Peter Ford's. In the other cottage lived Mrs Nellie Ford and her husband William. William also worked at Peter Ford's.

Further on, on the right, heading north, were the mill with the plaster house, sheds and store. There were open-fronted tin sheds, at the far end of the mill where the plaster was crushed and rolled into powder, then put into barrels. Immediately crossing over the railway track was the blacksmith's shop. George Lawrence Cockayne was the blacksmith. He was 49 (born 1895) and lived at 11 Church Street, Tutbury.

Coming back, southwards, on that side to the main entrance, you came to the joiner's shop, the store, then the offices. An unfenced track led south from there passed Brown's Coppice (also known as Bluebell Woods), then you got to the reservoir. Following that track, through a gate, led directly to the gate for Upper Castle Hayes Farm.

The Day the Sun Disappeared, 27 Nov 1944

Fred Lindsay was working in the plasterboard room with his brother, Arthur, who was busy spreading plasterboard at a large table in an adjacent room. It wasn't a very sound structure, just a corrugated iron shed but it served its purpose.

Arthur was calling out to his pal, who was up in the rafters. They were talking football.

"Did you hear the match on Saturday, on the wireless? Port Vale versus Stoke City."

"Yes, it was 3:0 to Port Vale. Shame there's nowt much on closer by but, as we all know, everything's been cancelled because of the war, unless you want to watch the locals having a knock around on Sundays."

"Yes, most of the players are out doing their bit in the war although I hear Derby County might be starting up again next year if the war continues to go our way. Still, it was a good match. McDowell, Bellis and P Griffiths scored the three goals. Yer, before you say anything, I know these matches are just in the war league and they don't really count, but it's all we 'ave. Just a few teams in the north and a few teams in the south but I'm for Port Vale to go through."

"Yes, you've got a good team there."

That was the last Arthur heard from his pal.

Also working on the surface were William Lovatt from Uttoxeter, working with John Redfern, William Gent and William Moseley from Tutbury.

William was calling out, "Has anyone seen Doddy?" Doddy was the nickname for Jack Key.

The Day the Sun Disappeared, 27 Nov 1944

John Redfern replied, "It's Monday, you know where he'll be, curled up under his blankets trying to sleep off last night's pints of Marsden from the Crown Inn."

"That's true, you can rely on him never being here on a Monday." William replied, "Don't know how he's still kept his job - just that we're so short-handed, I suppose."

Sandy Harrison was busy working in the yard shovelling crates of plasterboard into the drier. He was whistling a tune he had heard on the wireless before he left for work that morning. It was "You always hurt the one you love," by the Mills Brothers, then Sandy broke into song, "The one you shouldn't hurt at all…."

Norman Worthington was the youngest one there, only 17. He was working in the powder house.

Joseph Foster, the Works Manager from Hanbury, had walked across the Botham's and Goodwin's farmlands to get to Ford's Works that morning, the same route as many of the workers at Ford's.

He had worked at Peter Ford's all his life and knew most of his men as good friends.

He passed the air shaft from the mine, nearly a hundred feet below, passed the reservoir and Purse Cottages. That morning he was helping Harry Wetherill to put up plaster board in the mess room. Frank Cartwright, a clerk appeared, "Mr Foster, sir, I've got a message that you are wanted in the office."

"Thank you Frank." Joseph Foster returned to the office, then went back to join Harry Wetherill in the mess room. That's when he heard a sound that he thought were loud detonations. He thought the Nazis had let go their cargo of bombs over the area. The explosions were deafening, followed by a resounding crack.

The Day the Sun Disappeared, 27 Nov 1944

Everything went black. When he began to see a glimmer of light, he went outside to inspect what had happened.

"Harry, there's a rush of water coming this way." But before he could get an answer the water had cascaded into the mess room and they were up to their knees in water and floating debris. Luckily the heavier debris was being held back by the strong walls of the mill, thus saving us from being crushed in the mess room, but we didn't know how long the mill would stand up to that weight. We couldn't do much but wait, wait for the water to subside and pray the mill would hold up.

Looking outside Joseph saw Alf Hurstfield, a worker there, lying on the tramway, trapped under timber. He was trying to keep his head above the water that was swirling around him.

"Harry, come we've got to get him free." They waded through the water and with the aid of another worker, James Radcliffe, who went to support Hurstfield's back to keep him above water, they managed to get him out and all four of them splashed through to the comparative safety of the mess room, closing the doors, just in time to see the full force of the water swirling like an eddy at body height, past the door. It was coming in under the door, so they grabbed what they could to block up the door to try to stop the water coming in. The water was still knee-deep.

Harry shouted above the noise of the flooding water, "Did you manage to see what's happened....parts of the work shops have been totally destroyed and also the offices?"

Hurstfield was collapsed on a chair, obviously in pain.

"Yes," Joseph replied, "If I'd been any longer on that call in the office, I would have been a gonner."

The Day the Sun Disappeared, 27 Nov 1944

"Too right," Harry replied, "And we would have both had it, if it weren't for this mess room. It's amazing it's stood up to the flood. A pile of debris has been lodged against the wall. It's six foot high. The wall has saved us - it didn't collapse!"

"God help anyone out there." James said rather breathlessly, "It's a nightmare."

Clods of earth were now raining down into the swirling water. "What's happened, Mr Foster?" James asked.

"Well, all I can think, what with the huge explosion we heard, is that the Dump has exploded – it's finally happened - and the explosion has cracked the dam open."

"God in heaven." Was the almost unanimous reply.

"We'll wait until the water has subsided a bit then see what the damage is and if we can help anyone." Joseph replied.

So, as soon as they could, they made their way through the soaking mud looking for people. The sky was still raining earth, big slabs of alabaster, bushes, and trees, anything that had once been in the fields covering the Dump. They managed to find broken off pieces of hardboard or corrugated iron to act as protection over their heads as they squelched through the mud.

....

The Day the Sun Disappeared, 27 Nov 1944

Remains of Peter Ford's Works - Donated by Graham Shaw

Twenty six bodies were recovered from the Peter Ford's & Sons yard, adding to the five found in the mine.

CHAPTER 17

CONTINUING THE SEARCH

Jim Heathcote and Dick Utting met up with Jeff Hellaby, their neighbour from Fauld House Farm at Peter Ford's mill. They found the blacksmith, George Lawrence Cockayne. It was an horrific sight. George had the anvil protruding out of his spine.

Of course, there was nothing they could do for George, so they carried on, then found Tom Bowring. Tom lived at Brickyard Cottage, Hanbury Woodsend. Tom didn't have a stitch of clothing on him, covered in mud and shivering. Jeff Hellaby, seeing the situation, immediately removed his great coat and put in on Tom. (Confirmed by Joe Cooper. Joe Cooper stated, "I knew Tom Bowring as I used to work at Peter Ford's when I came out of the forces, when I was 20, about eight years after the explosion).

Tom was covered in cuts and bruises but no permanent damage.

He was shell-shocked and trembling. "You're alright lad," Jim Heathcote said soothingly, "You're safe now." He sat Tom down on a rock. He didn't really know what had happened. He spluttered out, through chattering teeth. "I, I was working outside. I…I make….made plaster and cement in the mill. I saw this plane buzzing around then heard an explosion. I…I thought it had dropped a bomb. I just ran and threw myself down. Then the hill sort of exploded. I saw this huge ball of flame going end over end into the sky and then bricks, earth and stones came crashing down

The Day the Sun Disappeared, 27 Nov 1944

half burying me. My...my brother, Fred... he was working in the mine. He'll, he'll be dead." Then he started crying. Dick Utting put a comforting arm around him. Dick needed the comfort himself as he didn't know whether his brother was still alive or not.

The RAF and A.R.P. carried on their search while Dick stayed with Tom.

Tom carried on, "I saw William Gent about an hour after I started work this morning – in the cement place in the Mill. Have you found him?"

"Unfortunately, the mill's totally wrecked. There were bodies inside. You've been very lucky. If you'd returned to the mill, you wouldn't have survived."

"Well, Percy Cooper, who lives in Hanbury – you might know him - well we had a bit of a chat. I suppose it must have been about 11am when he went up to the Mill and I went outside." Dick shook his head as Tom mentioned Percy Cooper. So Tom knew that he was dead too.

Tom carried on, telling his story. "I saw little bits of something falling on the ground all round me and I looked up to see what was happening.

Well, you've seen it yourself, the sky was full of huge lumps of dirt and debris of all kinds and it seemed right over the Works. It looked like it was coming down from a great height. I dashed across the yard to the bag room where there were some corrugated tins reared up and I got under them just as the stuff came down and knocked these tins down onto me. A blackness descended over everything and I heard terrific noises, the noise was deafening, sounded like walls being blown down, crashing and banging. I gradually saw a bit of light, it seemed a long time, and I crawled out from under the tins. It was then I heard the noise of water rushing down the yard and I ran to the top of the tip, where the old gypsum rubble and waste was piled up, and over the top into what had been Jim Heathcote's plough field, but found myself in a bog. I landed waist-deep in mud. I managed to crawl out and back up the slag heap. That's when I saw the works had been destroyed and were under thousands of tons of soil, rock and water.

Millions of gallons of water was flooding the site and I guessed then that the reservoir had broken. It hadn't actually burst, but just disappeared. I felt nauseous. My stomach was churning up into my throat. I didn't know what to do." Tom looked up at Dick, like a poor lost pup with sad eyes.

"We're all in the same boat, Tom. We're just doing what we can."

"I don't know when I lost my clothes, must have been in the mud. I was covered in it. I don't remember ripping them off.

Dick, seeing that I was alright, went on to search for others. Tom then went back to the bag room, which was still standing." His bare feet were sloshing through the mud, which was oozing up between his toes. There he found Mr Foster.

"So glad to see you lad, "Foster said, then led him into the board room, which was badly damaged but still just about standing. He sat Tom down on a sack of cement. Tom noticed there were just a few other workmen there for the mill, William Lovatt, Bill Phillips Alf Hurstfield, James Radcliffe and Mr Walker, all looking totally done-in and some injured. None of them spoke, it seemed like too much of an effort, just absorbed in their own violent recollections of what had just happened.

The Day the Sun Disappeared, 27 Nov 1944

"These you see here are what looks like the only survivors, Tom. I think all the others must have perished."

Mr Foster sat himself down, with his head bowed in his hands. "Try as I might, there was nothing I could do for the others. I couldn't find them. They had just disappeared under the mud and rubble.

You'll see the total picture of the disaster for yourself if you go up onto the hillside. I've already been to the two Purse cottages, where Mr and Mrs Hill and Mr and Mrs Ford had lived. The RAF managed to get Mrs Ford to hospital. I couldn't get to her, and came back. The RAF have been brilliant."

My legs just wouldn't carry me – I was too dazed and in shock, but with Mr Foster's help I went out and had a look around. Most of the buildings had gone, including the Purse cottages. They just weren't there anymore, just rubble. I could see what remained of the reservoir. There was a huge gap at the top of the Works yard and our mine entrance was not visible.

"We've had a good look around here, Tom, looking for any survivors." Foster said. "From my count we have lost 26 men who had been working on the surface here. I don't know about the alabaster mine.

Doddy has been lucky too. From what I can gather, he had that 'Monday morning feeling' and didn't come to work. He would have been working up top too.

As you can see, the boiler house has been ruined. Only the chimney stack is left standing."

I looked and saw this mass of piled up shearing and twisting steel girders, as one would twist copper wire.

The Day the Sun Disappeared, 27 Nov 1944

"Underneath this horrible mess, are the dead, mutilated bodies of the people we knew and loved." Here Mr Foster groaned putting a hand up to his eyes, in an effort to wipe away some tears. "There was just no warning, Tom." He gasped. "They couldn't escape. The water just poured down, mixed with soil, clay, trees and other debris, turning it into a quagmire, moving slowly, taking everything in its path, down upon the crushed chimney stack. We here are the only survivors."

Tom found out later that his brother, Fred, had not survived.

....

Some did escape from the Peter Ford works. William Lovatt, aged 37, from Uttoxeter, worked with John Redfern and William Gent, who both died. "I was at work that morning. I saw John Redfern at work but didn't talk to him. John wasn't one of those talkative types. He was a specialist alabaster carver and needed to concentrate on his work. His job was to prepare alabaster for a range of decorative uses. We all knew that, so kept our distance. I saw William Gent, in the Mill, and we exchanged a few words. I was still there when the explosion went off. The whole mill started to shake and a huge beam broke off and came down on my foot. Then the lights went out. I don't remember much after that."

Others had miraculous escapes from death. William Philips, from Marchington, was working as an electrician at Peter Ford's and was a colleague of William Rhodes (see chapter 22).

One of the rescuers shouted out, "Hey lads, I've seen something here. I need some help. Others came over, answering his call, and saw what they could only make out as a hand, rising above the mud – just a hand. They immediately set to work, grabbing hold of the hand, then the arm came out, then the head that had been

The Day the Sun Disappeared, 27 Nov 1944

buried in the swamp of mud created by the flood water from the reservoir.

Finally they heaved him out, just seconds before the flood water oozed in and covered where that hand had been, never to be seen again. They started pumping at his chest to try to resuscitate him. Finally, the rescuer shouted, "I've got signs of life, lads, he's breathing. My God, he's breathing!" They hauled him onto a stretcher and sent him on his way to hospital.

I (PC Mackay) went to see William Philips at the hospital. He had suffered serious injuries, but heard later that he made a full recovery.

I reported his story. "I was standing about two hundred and fifty yards from the mine entrance, when I heard a sort of distant cracking sound. I looked up and, in that split second, saw the whole hill erupt Everything on that hill had gone skywards, whole trees, complete with roots, huge rocks, pieces of fencing, railway tracks, machinery from the mill – all muddled up together, flying up into the sky. Then this great blast of wind tore into me. I tried to grab onto the nearest thing, which was a telephone pole but I couldn't hold on, the wind was so strong and I was just wrenched away and thrown up into the air. I landed in Jim Heathcote's field, about 90 yards away. I suppose I must have passed out then as I don't remember anything after that. The next thing I vaguely remember was being hauled by my arm out of what I can only describe as a mud coffin. I was told afterwards that the torrent from the reservoir, now mixed with over 50,000 tons of debris had swamped the field and I was being sucked into a mud mire. I don't know who rescued me. I never found out, but it seems someone saw a hand raised above the mud and slime and pulled me out. I thank you, whoever you are."

The Day the Sun Disappeared, 27 Nov 1944

Lynn Noreen McNamara, a niece of Bill Philips stated that Bill Philips was doing some electrical work there when the dump went up. "He always had an oxygen tank in his bedroom after that. It was not really spoken about. I imagine this was down to the injuries he sustained."

…………………..

Joseph Foster, the works manager at Peter Ford's, had the grim task of identifying bodies. He had worked with most of the men all his working life. It was distressing for him to have to identify the pitiful remains of people he considered to be his life-long friends.

A body was found on 2nd January 1945, but no-one could identify it, not even Joseph Foster. "We thought it could be that of John Redfern, just owing to the clothing." William Moseley from Tutbury, who had worked with John Redfern also failed to identify the body; 'Doddy Keys' could not confirm it was him. Doddy hadn't turned up for work that day because he'd been on the razz the night before, and was still hung over. Others such as Ken of Hanbury and Ernest Gibbs of Draycott failed to recognise the body. Even John Redfern's sister, Daisy Kirk, from Draycott-in-the-Clay was convinced this was not the body of her brother. However, (and this is taken from PC Mackey's records), there was one vital fact and that was his clothing. The body was wearing a brown serge jacket, grey pin-striped worsted waistcoat, white shirt with a thin black stripe, grey socks, size eight studded black boots with iron tips at toes and heels - but the vital piece of the puzzle was that the body was wearing a piece of sacking taken from a cement bag, being worn like an apron. This would suggest a skilled man who worked as a stone-dresser, carving alabaster, for ornamental purposes. The body was laid to rest as 'unknown man' in Hanbury Churchyard on 5 January 1945.

Mr G J Walker of Hanbury, found himself wedged in against a machine that had been imbedded in concrete. He could not get out, no matter how he tried, and the worst thing was the water from the dam was swirling around in great waves, with the incumbent wreckage piling up against the machine, getting higher and higher. He was crying out, "Help, help, somebody help me. I'm here."

"I've 'ad it" he said to himself, his voice trembling, as the water swirled around his neck, "That's the last of me. I'm gonna drown." Just then, he heard voices, American voices, "You alright, Jack. It's OK, we're coming fer yer." He'd never heard anything so welcoming. They were big lads. They chucked the debris out of the way, while the water was swirling up to their chests, and with a couple of good heaves, Mr Walker was freed. The Americans saw him to safety. I don't know how many times, Mr Walker repeated to them with a sob of sincerity in his voice, "Thank you all, I thought I'd 'ad it there, thank you, thank you."

He told a reporter for the Burton Observer, "Six or seven men were trapped and killed when the place collapsed. They were still under the wreckage. It was the water that was the worst. When the reservoir was blown up, the water came down on us like a sea. It came up to my knees and we could not get out because of the water and wreckage but after we had been struggling for about 18 minutes, some Americans rushed us and yanked us out."

....

Joseph Foster, the foreman at Peter Ford's works, spent his days advising the Staffordshire County Surveyor, Robert S Murt, O.B.E (who had taken on the task of managing the recovery of victims) and also in the agonising task, along with all the survivors, of identifying the bodies of those with whom they had spent all of their working lives and often childhoods. Bulldozers, mechanical diggers of every type (many loaned from the Americans) were employed in the following months, often in bitter weather, to recover the bodies of their former work mates. Around 10,000 tons of debris had to be removed.

Frank Cartwright had lived in Uttoxeter and had been the Transport Manager. His grieving wife was told his body could not be found. They had three daughters and she had to explain to them that their father wouldn't be coming back.

Reginald Cartwright, Frank's brother, was the head clerk there. He died. He was 46 and left a widow and three daughters.

Norman Worthington – it was his first job and he was only 17 – the youngest working there. He, with others, got inside some of the big plaster barrels and suffocated. Fred Lindsay worked in the plasterboard room. It wasn't a very sound structure but none were killed there.

The Day the Sun Disappeared, 27 Nov 1944

The aftermath of the explosion at RAF Fauld – Peter Ford's Works (Image donated by Graham Shaw)

RURAL COUNCIL AND NATIONAL APPEAL. . Mr. T. E. Foster, chairman of Tutbury Rural District Council, in a message of sympathy to relatives of the bereaved, states that all possible steps will be issued on behalf of members, taken to alleviate distress caused by the disaster. The Rural Council is considering the question of launching a national appeal fund fur the relatives of the victims.

At a meeting of a Rural District Council on Thursday it was decided to open a national appeal.

The Day the Sun Disappeared, 27 Nov 1944

CHAPTER 18

JOHN COOPER

I was 9 years old in 1944 – at school, the junior school in Hanbury, with my friends, Peter Flint, Peter Harrison and Philip Allen. We had all been given repeated instructions as to what to do in an air raid. We all had to hide under our desks, not that that would have protected us much from lumps of building and flying glass. Our desks were just two by two wooden desks with lids that opened up to reveal your books, a ruler, pencil case containing pens, pencil, rubber, maths instruments, and anything else you wanted to put in there – sweets or even a frog to frighten the girls with. We were just normal boys out for any bit of fun we could get.

Miss Farden was our head-mistress and gave us lessons. She lived in the school house. She wasn't much to look at – some would say she was no oil-painting - and must have been in her late 30s, but most days, after school, while we were out in the playground having a bit of a kick-around, you could guarantee that by 4.30-5pm we would see her, sauntering in the direction of the vicarage with her handbag under her arm. On these days she always seemed to have a smile on her face and we would see her patting her hair down as she walked, trying to neaten it.

"There she goes again," I said to the others, "out for a bit of you know what again, with Rev Crook."

"How can you tell," Peter said, "Maybe she's just going to help him with the vicar's wife – she's been ill you know."

The Day the Sun Disappeared, 27 Nov 1944

"I know – no woman would tidy herself up and have a smile on her face just to look after an ailing old lady. No, I know what's cracking off. Haven't you seen the vicar smiling when he sees her? I've actually seen him put his arm around her. He wouldn't do that to a normal parishioner, now would he?"

Then a chorus started up amongst us, after she had passed by - very quietly so she wouldn't hear, "We know where you're going. We know what you're up to."

Then Peter said, "Well, who can blame him. Old Mrs Crook's not up to much and I hear she's gone a bit doolally – what's it they call it, that's it, she's got dementia."

My mum was working at Hanbury Fields Farm just south east of Hanbury itself. Being a Monday, she was doing the washing at the farm. The farmer and his wife had gone to market, leaving the father's mother at home.

All 50 of us at the school had just come in from the playtime break and I was in my class having an English lesson with Miss Farden, the Headmistress, when we heard the blast – a tremendous bang and the whole school shook and the blackboard fell over. There were tiles flying everywhere.

7-year-old Bill Moore, Brian Cooper (no relation) and Fred Allen – well we looked at each other from under our desks. In that look, we knew we were going to make a break for it. There were six of us in all, who made a run for it. Miss Farden was shouting out after us to come back and stay under the desks but, being lads, we ignored the teacher's warning, and escaped to investigate. We tried getting out by the front door first, but there were slates from the roof and rubble being driven against the door, so we tried the

The Day the Sun Disappeared, 27 Nov 1944

back door (which faced the crater). We were stunned at the damage. Everywhere we looked was covered in dust and clods of earth and plants were still raining down on us.

We were skipping around, trying to dodge the fallout. The air was thick with the dust, so thick that it blocked any glimmer of sun and the whole area was dark. There were huge lumps of rock that had made great indentations in the ground. In front of us was the remains of Rock House (owned by the Shelleys).

Amazingly, none of the six of us were injured although there were huge coping stones flying off the roof of the school. We were all scared stiff. So much for our little jaunt to escape and investigate. One of us was whimpering, "I want to go back". I called back, "Can't you see the massive hole in the school roof – no you'd be in just as much danger there, the whole place could collapse on you. Just make your way home."

Rock House, provided by Graham Shaw

The Day the Sun Disappeared, 27 Nov 1944

A huge boulder had descended through the roof and the kitchen (built on the side of the house) of Rock House. It was a complete ruin. We saw Sarah Shelley running out of the house, but seeing all the debris flying around, ran back in. At that moment the roof collapsed. We went to check on her and found her under the table, she hadn't been harmed. Just above her was a huge hole in the ceiling with the upstairs carpet sagging through it. The carpet had save her life. Going into the village we saw the local pub, The Cock Inn had been ripped apart. There was a bed hanging out of the first floor and great holes in the front yard, which were rapidly filling up with water from a burst water main. Looking across in the direction of where the RAF bomb storage was and Peter Ford's gypsum mine, we could see this huge mushroom-shaped cloud in the sky. It seemed to go up for miles. We'd never seen anything like it. Every building we came across, buildings we passed by daily, had been ruined in some way, chimney pots off, roofs off, walls blown in, doors blown out, smashed glass from windows. We were walking through a bomb site, literally. "I want to get home," I shouted to the other boys over the noise of the descending rocks and foliage, and ran off, actually to Hanbury Fields Farm, as I knew my mother would be there.

The Day the Sun Disappeared, 27 Nov 1944

The Cock Inn. Photo donated by Graham Shaw (Cooper family)

Bill went home, meeting up with his twin brothers George and Ted and Tony Deauville.

The children in my school were collected. One lad, collected by his neighbour, was taken home to Hanbury Woodend. He was just six years old. The sights that met his eyes on his way home will always stay in his memory. Everything was covered in mud and he saw a wellington boot with part of a leg. "Come away, lad," his neighbour urged, but everywhere he looked there were parts of cows strewn in the trees. A truly horrific sight for a child to witness).

Out of 50 children at the school only two were hurt, one by falling debris.

The Day the Sun Disappeared, 27 Nov 1944

I found my mother at Hanbury Fields Farm. She was so pleased to see me, grabbing and hugging me, so pleased to see that I was safe.

"Oh, John dear. What a disaster. I was so scared. The mine's gone up….. the bombs…. The noise was horrific. I just grabbed old Mrs Botham and pulled her under the oak table. It's a miracle we survived."

"What about dad?" I managed to get out.

"I don't know, dear. As you know, he's the locomotive driver inside the mine. I think you will have to prepare yourself that your father isn't coming back. I don't really think he would have stood a chance, but I'm obviously praying that he managed to find shelter."

I then burst into tears. "My dad…. never coming back." I managed to get out through my sobs.

"Oh, we don't know that yet, for certain. I'm just saying, be prepared."

Mum continued, "I got granny into the yard, then next moment we saw John Hunt running over. (He was a neighbouring farmer, living at Ebernezer House). He was out of breath but delighted we were all safe."

John Hunt had said, "I saw a huge column of something black shoot up into the air, then heard the explosion in your direction. I thought I'd better check on you." Looking around, he said, "Have you seen anything of the men, Chawner and Rock?"

"I went out and shouted for them and went into the chop house but there was no sign of them. It was then that I saw across the fields

The Day the Sun Disappeared, 27 Nov 1944

towards the Goodwin's farm and saw the farm had gone and all the fields torn up in all shapes."

Totally shocked I just said, "I guess they had been out in what had been the fields, cabbage-cutting."

"Thank you, Mrs Cooper. There seems to be smoke coming from the hay-barn, I'll go have a look."

Walking further he found Mr Botham's horse, lying dead, and the remains of the cart just yards away. He came back to the farm.

"There's no hope, Mrs Cooper. The field is just holes and hills. No-one out there would have survived. As you know, that field adjoined the Upper Castle Hayes farm fields, belonging to the Goodwins. The farm has gone….. disappeared into the crater."

The farmer and his wife, Mr and Mrs Botham, eventually returned from market, at about 3.30pm, with their daughter, Lucy (who was about 3 or 4 years old). "We've had all sorts of trouble getting back, what with the vast numbers of police, RAF, fire engines and rescue vehicles. The police had even tried to prevent us from getting onto the Hanbury Road." Mrs Botham reported.

They were so pleased to see us all safe, then went out to survey the damage. Mr Botham looked shell-shocked when he returned, "I cannot believe what has happened. It's beyond belief. The farm is ruined. It's amazing you and mum survived. It looks like, as we are on the same level as Upper Castle Hayes Farm, we got the blast too. That's the end of our farm."

Mr Botham then asked mum, "Have you seen any sign of George Rock and Sydney Chawner, Mrs Cooper?

"Sorry, John Hunt went to look and he said they had no chance."

The Day the Sun Disappeared, 27 Nov 1944

"Oh, it's all so utterly dreadful." Mum was saying. "It had been such a nice day. At 11am I had gone across the yard to get a bucket of slack for the copper fire. I saw Sydney Chawner, standing by the chop house – the door was open. He had a pitch fork in his hand and he was smoking a pipe. I remember saying to him how nice the weather was, cold but sunny. Then I heard George Rock shouting out from the chop house 'Hello, Mrs Cooper, how are you?' I said 'All right, George, going to be busy like you.'

I didn't actually see him at all, but I knew his voice well. Then I heard him say to Chawner, 'Is that all Syd' and Chawner said, 'Yes, let's go'.

I then came back to the house to carry on with my chores. I was in the wash room, must have been about ten past eleven, when I heard such an awful roar and what I thought was the chimney pot falling down the roof, then saw dirt and stones going past the window. Granny was with me, and we stood together with my arm around her. I heard more awful noises, then saw the legs of a bed and other bedroom furniture shew through the floor above and I grabbed granny and we got under the table together.

Everything then went very dark for several minutes and I thought we were buried alive. We were so relieved when light gradually came back and I crawled out from under the table and looked out across the yard to see everything in ruins with debris everywhere.

Harry Botham went to the chop house and saw that the knife always used by Rock was missing, but that the gorse-hook, always used by Chawner was still there, making the assumption that they had gone cabbage-cutting with Chawner acting as carter.

The Day the Sun Disappeared, 27 Nov 1944

He returned and Mr Hunt then told Mr Botham, "I saw smoke coming from the barn but the water supply had gone. It caught fire and I couldn't put it out. I'm sorry."

"Thank you for trying, Mr Hunt, but I'm afraid that's the least of our worries." was all Mr Botham could muster to say. Looking around all he could see was his farm was in ruins and his home and farm buildings. His livestock were dead - his livelihood, home and future had been blasted to smithereens, gone. There was nothing left!

(Taken from the Burton Observer and South Derbyshire Weekly Mail 30 Nov 1944)

The Vicar of Hanbury, the Rev Crook, was the next visitor, coming to check if he could be of assistance. He was in a sorry state, covered in muck and dirt and obviously in a state of shock. He had his story to tell, "I'm so pleased to be alive." He began, "I was just leaving the vicarage garden when a terrific pressure of air struck me. I felt the earth shaking all around and a pinnacle fell off the church with a mighty crash. Luckily I was just outside of the grounds otherwise that would have been the end of me. Then there was a violent explosion, like an earthquake. A huge cloud of smoke and dirt shot into the sky to a terrific height. I made my way to the school to see about the children. It took me about four minutes just to get there and you know how close the two buildings are. I was being buffeted around and had to hold on tightly to whatever I could, otherwise I would have been blown across the way. The ground was just heaving up and what appeared to be shells, stone and rock were flying in all directions. Then there was a falling of fine earth, which covered me from head to toe. I had to dodge flying debris.

The Day the Sun Disappeared, 27 Nov 1944

I could hear singing coming of children's voices coming from one of the rooms, 'They'll always be an England'. So, I thought, Miss Farden was trying to comfort the children by getting them to sing and take their minds of the disaster happening around them.

You haven't seen it Mrs Cooper, the whole place is shrouded with dirt - and before I could think about it, holes were being made in the roofs of houses, made with huge stones blasted into the elements, and the recreation room just vanished before my eyes. One moment it was there, then the next it wasn't.

Chimney's started to fall, telephone and electricity wires were swirling around and the whole landscape changed in the space of 50 seconds. Where there had been trees and grass, there is nothing, nothing but bare earth and craters.

I went into the school and found the children wondering what had happened. Miss Fardon had got the children under their desks. As soon as the danger seemed to be over, I had them all sent home as soon as it was safe."

Mum couldn't even mash the vicar a pot of tea as there was no water. It was decided that mum should take granny to a friend's house and a friend, Mrs Cox, helped her. After that, I went with my mum and the Vicar back to the school. Mum knew there would be bodies to be recovered and, mum being mum, offered to set up a mortuary of sorts. She suggested the village school hall. So messages were passed around for bodies to be taken there. Half the school hall was set aside, divided by a partition, to lay the shrouded bodies of the victims.

It wasn't until later that evening, about 10pm that Rev Crook knocked on our door in Martin Lane, and said solemnly, "I'm afraid Joe won't be coming home."

The Day the Sun Disappeared, 27 Nov 1944

Mum was expecting this news, but she set herself, valiantly, to the abysmal job of preparing the school hall to receive all the dead. She had been told that her husband's body had been found but had to wait three more excruciating days for the body to be recovered. Gas had prevented recovery parties from getting into the mine.

I heard a little whimper from her as she unwrapped the sheeting from the first body that arrived. It was indeed that of her own husband, Joseph….. my father. I looked at her, astonished, waiting for her to break down in floods of tears, but my mum was stoic. She must have prepared herself, mentally, for this and, although a tremendous shock to have the blinding reality right in front of her, she just wiped the hair out of her face, wiped a little tear from her eyes and set about the dreadful task before her, that she, never in her wildest nightmares, would ever have thought would have happened. Dad had been found at the bottom of the lift shaft at the plaster works, brought in with Arthur Harris, the mine foreman. The work was indescribably gruesome – bodies, parts of bodies, that used to be living, breathing, working people, having a laugh and a joke with their pals, now mangled wrecks of what once was. Maud Foster was with mum, Joseph Foster's wife (the Works manager at Peter Ford's). Mr J L Auden, the Coroner for East Staffordshire, was there too.

My mum worked in this temporary morgue, of her own free will, for an incredible 72 days! Her daughter, Margaret, was there to help her. She did the undressing and washing of the bodies, washing the clothes removed from the bodies. She lit the pot belly stove daily and kept the makeshift mortuary scrupulously clean – it was winter time and to keep anywhere clean under the existing conditions was in itself a very difficult task but Mrs Cooper did not flinch. She prepared the bodies for viewings and identification by relatives.

The Day the Sun Disappeared, 27 Nov 1944

She also had survived the wrecking of the farm where she was looking after old Mrs Botham, and it was probably due to her action that the old lady's life was saved.

(Interview with Mrs Cooper recorded by PC Mackay in a police statement witnessed by Mary Cooper's eldest daughter, Margaret Nicklin)

(Confirmed by Joe Cooper, "Mum used to go washing there as it was Monday. Mrs Botham was about 80 odd. They heard it going up and they both got under the table. It smashed the house up. There was only the little kitchen that they were in that wasn't damaged. The rest of the house was demolished and the farm buildings. Some of the cattle were still alive but they had to be destroyed. They definitely destroyed the bull. Some idiot was on about letting the bull out, but they shot the bull in the pen. They let the cows out I think, though, a lot of the fencing and gates would be off anyway. As for George Rock and Chawner, who worked on Botham's farm - they never found George. Mum always reckoned that, as George Rock always smoked a pipe and the barn was on fire, he must have dropped his pipe. Of course, he would have been burnt to death and they never found anything of him. There were cows blown to bits, and horses, with cows up in trees. It was horrific really. Everybody, who was in different place, would have a different tale to tell.)

I (PC Mackay) managed to work myself way round to Harry Botham's farm (Moat Farm, also known as Hanbury Fields Farm), through the woods and over the devastated field, where I witnessed the damage and shattered buildings, including this in my report to Supt. Heath.

The Day the Sun Disappeared, 27 Nov 1944

Everyone was in such a distressed state, as you can imagine. The farm was gone, the buildings wrecked, the cattle and sheep all dead. Mrs Botham was trying desperately to sweep up, but it was a hopeless job. I think she just was doing something to keep herself busy and not contemplate what the future held for them.

Mr Botham was just staring helplessly at the fields and over to where the Upper Castle Hayes Farm used to be.

LOOKING BACK... John Cooper sifts through mementos of that terrifying day

CHAPTER 19

THOMAS HUDSON

From Claire Talbot (granddaughter):

Thomas Hudson, was working at the Peter Ford mine as a cement worker. He, and his wife Nelly were living in Newborough. They had six children and times were very hard but, as long as Thomas had a job, they were doing alright.

Before he left for work on 27 November 1944, all the family sang 'happy birthday' to little Raymond, who had just turned seven. His brothers and sisters had made little drawings for him as birthday cards. Mum was saying, "I'll see if we can get something special to eat for your birthday, when you get home from school." She wouldn't be able to make a cake as it was so difficult getting the ingredients, what with rationing, but she was thinking of getting little candles to stick into a bread and butter pudding.

Raymond skipped along to school with his other school-age siblings, Thomas, James and Brenda, holding onto his dad's hand. He'd put all of his cards into his school bag, which he would show his friends and teachers at school. He was scared about getting the bumps and hoped they wouldn't drop him. Every child got the bumps on their birthday. After seeing the kids off at school, Thomas would get the bus to Peter Ford's works and start his day at work, a new day, a new week. Thomas was working above ground, in the cement-making works. The alabaster, dug from the mines would be churned up in the huge machines to be turned into cement, then packed up into sacks. It wasn't that interesting a job, but it provided food and a roof over their heads for his growing brood. In fact Nelly was pregnant again, with their 7th child.

Thomas had been whistling a tune, feeling in a good mood – then, at 11.10am, the explosion happened and everything was coming down around him. The building was shaking and bits flying everywhere. He tried to get out but something heavy had smashed against the door. A heavy beam collapsed onto him. He was trapped in the twisted ruin of the building. Water started seeping in, higher and higher. All he could think of was that the reservoir had smashed, but he couldn't get out.

Thomas died that day.

....

It wasn't just the loss of a good husband and father, but there were far-reaching consequences.

Nelly had to sit them all down as they made their way back from school and tell the distraught children that their father had been killed in the explosion.

For Raymond, that tragedy was to stay with him for the rest of his life as he would never, ever, celebrate his birthday again. He refused to have cards or a party. The memory of that tragic day marred the rest of his life.

With no wage coming in and no immediate help from the RAF or charities, Nelly found herself in desperate straits. She had to resort to begging for bread at the village shop. The children would go at closing time and get any food that was being thrown out. Brenda had to go to work rather than continuing at school.

The Day the Sun Disappeared, 27 Nov 1944

Nelly, luckily got to meet a man, who was willing to take on her and the children. She didn't love him and was still in mourning for Thomas. It was as though she was surrendering her body due to the need to care for her children.

All the kids had to get work as soon as they were old enough to support the family financially.

In Memory Of
Civilian

THOMAS HUDSON

Civilian War Dead who died on 27 November 1944 Age 38

At Peter Ford Works, Fauld, Staffs.

Remembered with Honour
TUTBURY, RURAL DISTRICT

COMMONWEALTH
WAR GRAVES

COMMEMORATED IN PERPETUITY BY THE COMMONWEALTH
WAR GRAVES COMMISSION

The Day the Sun Disappeared, 27 Nov 1944

CHAPTER 20

THE COCK INN, THE NEXT DAY

The Cock Inn - Donated by Graham Shaw

The Cock Inn had virtually been split in half and the roof ripped off those parts remaining standing. All the licensed part of the premises had been destroyed with the exception of the tap-room, which was untouched, not even a window being broken. The bar, however, was a scene of desolation as also was the club-room. In the cellar it was found that an 18 gallon barrel of best beer had been burst open. Most of the glasses and bottles were shattered. However, not to be defeated, even though water was still spouting out from broken pipes at the front and a bed was suspended halfway in and out of an upstairs bedroom, the Zuccas decided to try to open up. The beer pumps were still working and they could get water in a bucket, for washing up, and heat it up on the range. The Zuccas began serving with the remaining supplies and glasses as soon as possible.

The Cock Inn - Donated by Graham Shaw

Leading Aircraftsman J Gair was helping Mrs Zucca salvage her home. He had been cycling through the village when the dump went up and had been thrown from his bicycle. Seeing flames in the bar, he immediately came to the rescue, accompanied by two other men, Herbert Massey and Arthur Clark, to make sure the occupants were alright, then trying their best put out the fire and clear rubble. A picture was taken of him retrieving a headless rocking horse from the rubble. Mrs Zucca and her husband, Melvin, and their two children remarkably escaped unhurt

She was saying to LAC Gair, "We all had a miraculous escape. I had just brought in the washing and made a cup of coffee when everything began to shake. I thought it was a bomb and the best thing was to get into the cellar but there was that huge bang before I could get to the cellar door, so I grabbed the kiddies and dived under the table. We were so lucky with everything coming down around us, the roof coming off, bricks flying everything, coming smashing through the windows, crash, bang, boom. I was scared out of my life, I can tell you, but I just managed to get a cut on my hand, that's all."

They really felt that, as the Cock was a community pub, it should be still a place where people could come and relax, especially at this time when villagers had lost their homes, and others had been out day and night looking for possible survivors. People needed somewhere to commune to tell their stories and have a well-longed for beer or two, or even a brandy, in the circumstances.

So, that evening, with the help of neighbours and borrowed glasses, customers were served by candlelight.

The dart board was still there, in the unharmed tap room, through at a strange angle, with the darts still stuck in from the last customer to use it.

The Day the Sun Disappeared, 27 Nov 1944

A huge boulder had descended through the roof of Rock Farm, opposite the pub, where Sarah and William Shelley lived. The kitchen, built on the side of the house, was a complete ruin.

Margaret Cooper stayed with Mrs Zucca as Mr Zucca went to Wales to take the two children to their grandparents. Margaret was the eldest daughter of Mary Cooper, who started up the mortuary in the school hall. They slept in the pub, under a tarpaulin. All that remained upstairs were two bedrooms, one of which was used as their living room, and the kitchen downstairs.

Margaret helped in the pub when it opened, for a little while, then went back to Fauld where she worked. She was also helping her mother at the makeshift mortuary.

A shout went up from everyone, who had been lined up for the opening of the pub door, "The Blitzed Inn carries on!"

As they all entered, you could see they were all wearing black armbands, made by their wives from any bit of old black cloth they had to hand. Most of the men were in their work clothes, mud-splattered and dirty, after trudging through the mud of the crater, searching desperately for people they might be able to rescue, but this didn't seem to matter.

Sarah Shelley and her husband, William, had taken refuge in the Cock Inn. They were elderly people, grandparents. Rock House, just opposite the pub, where they lived, had been ruined. Mr Harrison (husband of Clara and father of ten, including Ida) had brought Sarah a brandy as she was shaking and crying. She was talking to Mr Harrison. "I'd run outside to see what was happening, but all this mud and debris was coming down, so I ran back inside and hid under our table. There was such an awful crash and the whole place shook. I could see slates and bricks flying around out of the window. I knew something large had hit

The Day the Sun Disappeared, 27 Nov 1944

the roof, Plaster from the ceiling was coming down all around me and on top of the table. I stayed there for a while, not daring to move. A little while later, when the racket had ceased, I peeked out. The ceiling had a huge hole in it, so I knew then that the roof had been badly damaged. I was so lucky as the carpet from the room above was protruding through that gaping hole, obviously full of cement and bricks and tiles."

Rock House - Donated by Graham Shaw.

"My, you had a lucky escape there, Sarah."

"I did. That carpet saved my life. But, the kitchen built on the side of the house has been damaged beyond recognition and the roof damaged beyond repair. We have nowhere to live."

The Day the Sun Disappeared, 27 Nov 1944

"We've got to get that sorted. People are here from various services, taking details. They may be able to put you up somewhere."

Mr Harrison told his own story, "You know we live quite close to the Village hall, opposite, just a bit lower down, on top of the hill. I don't know how my wife got out to be honest. The house has been completely smashed. All the windows are out and the roof off. Clara was on her own because the kids were at school. Our two eldest are away from home, 16-year-old Ida was in Uttoxeter. Our youngest, Colin, was with a neighbour and the rest were at school. Clara told me she was sitting by the fire when everything started moving. She'd never seen anything like it and went outside to see what was happening. Frightened out of her life, she ran for the cowshed and hid in the far corner. She was so lucky she got out of the house, don't know if it was instinct or what but it saved her life as a massive boulder and loads of debris came crashing through our cottage roof. The roof's gone, the cottage is just a ruin now, but at least my Clara is safe."

"Oh, so you're in the same boat as us, plus you've got a big family. What are you going to do?" William interrupted.

"Well, I see there seems to be someone taking names and details, so we'll go there when you've finished your drink. But we definitely need somewhere to stay tonight. Luckily I'd been down Staton's mine, which wasn't affected."

The Day the Sun Disappeared, 27 Nov 1944

Harrison Cottage - Donated by Graham Shaw

After finishing her brandy, Mr Harrison, Sarah and William went to speak to two people who had set up a desk of sorts at the back of what remained of the pub. William told them that he had had a lucky escape too. "I'd been in Hope Field, just close to the Cock Inn. When the dump went up I sheltered under a tree. I'd taken some tools with me from the Stalford Buildings to clean out the spring at The Hope pub. It's lucky I didn't dally at the Stalford Buildings as the farm buildings have been completely wrecked. We were lucky to escape being another statistic of the explosion."

The two people sympathised with them about the loss of their homes and took details to see if they could be relocated.

Sarah and William had nowhere to go except back to the ruined Rock cottage. They stayed there one night but luckily their eldest daughter and son-in-law, Nora and Ted Hidderley, came over, "There's an empty cottage near us, where we stay at Chapel House

The Day the Sun Disappeared, 27 Nov 1944

Farm, Tutbury. It's recently been completed for the farm and is vacant at the moment. Come on, you can't stay here."

So Sarah and William went, rather reluctantly leaving all their possessions and memories.

The Harrisons moved into the Roebuck Inn at Draycott, run by a member of the family, Annie. Ida Harrison went to the vicarage where her sister, Gladys, was working. Another sister, Vera was away from home in the A.T.S.

(Joe Cooper stated, "I don't know how Mrs Harrison got out, to be honest. The house was completely smashed. Their house was on the other side to the village hall, just a bit lower down, on top of the hill. All the windows were out and the roof off. Clara got out. She was on her own because the kids were at school.)

....

Jim Heathcote showed his face for a bit, to get a refreshing drink and a pie, but he wasn't long there as he was, as were most of the others, still out there searching for bodies.

He joined Fred Ford and Dick Utting, who were already there. "I'm sure going to miss Maurice Goodwin. I remember the last time we were all here having a drink around the coal fire. I don't know if they'll ever find their bodies."

"That's a real shame" Dick Utting commented. "Anyway, I've some good news. My brother, Horace managed to escape unscathed. I thought he must have had it, having been in the incendiary area."

"That is good news, Dick.

Tom Bowring then came in. He had been rescued at the Peter Ford's works. Dick bought Tom a drink of Burton's finest.

The Day the Sun Disappeared, 27 Nov 1944

Retrieving it from the bar, he spilt some. "Sorry about that Dick, I'm still a bit shaky – my nerves are shattered"

"That's alright Tom. Only to be expected, but you'll get there. Have you heard anything from the others where you worked?"

"Twenty six of us were killed, Dick. There aren't many others left. I believe William Phillips is in hospital. He was found unconscious, having been tossed nigh on 90 yards through the air. He landed in Heathcote's field, where I was found. He was so lucky with a rescue worker seeing just his hand above the mud and debris.

John Hardwick, from Top Farm, came in and joined them.

Everyone was pleased to see him. "My you had a lucky escape, John," Dick Utting said.

"You never spoke a truer word there, Dick. I should have been feeding the cattle at the other end of my dad's farm, and I wouldn't be here telling my tale if I did. But due to the early frost a neighbour asked me to cut roots at the edge of the wood. It was a super, frosty, cloudless morning then suddenly, as you all know, there was this almighty bang – WOOoom, that was the noise. Everything shook. It must have been what an earthquake is like. As I watched the entire 2 and a half acres went up into the air and out of sight, then I saw the trees returning to earth, which such tremendous force that they ploughed into the land with their roots uppermost. Blast does funny things. They say it rocked houses in Rugby, but I can't remember the earth moving. I ran for cover, crouching behind a small hillock. The stones were coming down. I watched as this huge piece of alabaster that must have weighed about 20 tons landed three-quarters of a mile away."

The Day the Sun Disappeared, 27 Nov 1944

John paused there, seeming to be lost for works, finding it hard to describe what he saw.

"This beautiful morning gave way to rain. Then the sky started to come down. A sky full of soil." John gave a sigh. He looked sad and crestfallen.... Then, after taking a gulp of beer, all of a sudden, he picked himself up and was his usual self, saying:

"Do you know, the 3,670 tons of bombs that exploded was three times greater than the amount dropped on London on the worst night of the blitz – that would be 10 May 1942. Those damn Bosch are trying to claim that it was one of their V2 bombs hit the ammunition dump – I heard it on the wireless in Lord Haw Haw's propaganda programme. It wasn't but someone's got to be to blame."

There was a bit of a laugh at John's expense, just to see him back to his normal self. There was nothing going to keep John down for long.

"There'll be an inquest." Jim commented but, in the meantime, we've got to carry on searching for bodies, clearing up, repairing, and funerals to attend. A body has been found in Peter Ford's but no-one has been able to identify it. We think it may be that of John Redfern the alabaster carver, but not even his sister has been able to say it is definitely him. Anyway, his funeral will be held on Friday and I've told the vicar I will be one of the pall-bearers. I believe Leslie Shotton of Knightsfield Farm and George Ede, from Coton Hall Farm, and Jeff Hellaby from Fauld House Farm will be the others."

Mr G J Walker, a Hanbury man, had walked in and heard their discussion. "I worked with the lad, if that's who you think he is but, even if not, he needs a proper funeral. I'll be there."

The Day the Sun Disappeared, 27 Nov 1944

"Thank you Mr Walker."

Jim brought up a seat for Mr Walker. "How are you old chum?"

"Oh, not so bad now, but that was a hell of a time for me and I'm still a bit shaky. I've been having bad dreams – the nightmare keeps haunting me. I'm lucky to be alive. I was lodged against a machine and just couldn't get myself free. Then the water from the reservoir started coming in. I thought I was going to drown. I was saying my prayers, praying for someone to get me out, and shouting for my life for anyone to rescue me. I've never been so scared. You should have seen the relief on my face when these Americans appeared and pulled me out. I'll never bad mouth any Americans again. They saved my life. They all deserve medals."

Tears began to well up in Mr Walker's eyes. "Give it time old fella, give it time." Jim replied, standing up and putting a hand gently onto Mr Walker's shoulder.

There were no RAF in the bar this time as they were all out, all hours, looking for bodies and doing running repairs to damaged houses. Also they had all been told not to speak to anyone about what had happened, as it was all meant to be hush-hush, so were barred from the pubs in the area.

However, sitting sadly in one corner were two younger people in uniform.

Mr Walker looked at them. He hadn't seen them for some time and didn't immediately recognise them. Then it dawned on him who they were.

He went over and introduced himself. They turned out to be the children of Mr and Mrs Hill of Purse Cottages – Kathleen and Ronald Hill.

The Day the Sun Disappeared, 27 Nov 1944

Mr Walker uttered his condolences. "I heard that Mrs Ford, your parent's neighbour has been found. She was in a dreadful state and she was taken to the Derby Royal Infirmary. Unfortunately, and they looked and looked but the rescuers found was no sign of your mother."

"Thank you for condolences." Ronald said, "There is really nothing to say, so many people have lost their loved ones. We actually heard from Marjorie, Mr and Mrs Ford's daughter and she and her husband, Frank, have been to see their mother in hospital."

Kathleen Hill stated, "We are so devastated though. Our mum and dad…. gone."

"The explosion was so,… well, words just cannot explain it. I am sure it was all over in a second. They would have felt nothing." Mr Walker added with sympathy in his voice.

Kathleen ignored this, she didn't want to envisage the horror of what her parents would have gone though. "I heard the explosion. I am doing my National Service in Coventry. I tried to telephone but couldn't get through until past midnight. It was then that I was informed that our parents were 'missing'. Strange, I think I had some sort of premonition as I had a dream that my dad was on his motorbike and had been in a terrific collision. I remember phoning him at the time as I was worried, just to warn him. I told him, 'Don't go out on your motorcycle.' I knew something was going to happen, but dreams don't tell you the whole story. I don't think he's alive. Kathleen started to cry again and her twin brother, Ronald, put his arm around her.

Ronald said, "Our brother, Bill, is trying to get back, but he's in the Middle East. Our other brother, Jim, is making his way back from Northumberland."

"Where will you be staying? Obviously the cottages have been smashed to smithereens."

"Oh," Kathleen tearfully replied, "We'll stay with our sister Eileen for a couple of days. She lives near Abbot's Bromley. She' can't get her head round it all - none of us can. Then, we've had an offer to stay with the Edes at Coton Hall Farm until the funerals – that is if they ever find their bodies! At this poor Kathleen started to weep again.

"It's just so unimaginatively awful." Ronald added. "Nothing's left, just a pile of mud – not even any family photos. All gone, everything's gone."

"No Roland," Kathleen interrupted, "We've been lucky there, Ronald. Don't you remember, mum had her photo taken two months ago, and gave all of us a copy. You must have your copy. It is the only picture we have of mum now. There's one of dad taken at Peter Ford's in 1937 – he's on the photo with a group of workers. I've got that."

....

Since that time the public had continued to be served in the remaining premises, a portion of the smoke room and a small tap room.

It wasn't until four years later, October 1948, that planning was approved for the Cock Inn to be demolished and replaced. The pub had sustained severe damage - the lounge downstairs, the clubroom and one of the tenant's bedrooms were totally destroyed.

CHAPTER 21

BODY RECOVERY

It wasn't until a month after, shortly before Christmas, that the Goodwin's bodies were found. If they hadn't been delayed that morning, leaving for the cattle market, they would have driven well past the reservoir, and be safe. They were, no doubt, concerned with closing the farm drive gates, to keep the cattle in, delaying them even further. The grain lorry that they were following, got away intact.

The body of John West who, with his brother, Stephen, had waved goodbye to the Goodwins on their fateful trip to market, was found ten days after the explosion, 200 yards from the edge of the main crater. His elder brother, Stephen, wasn't found until after the Inquest on 6 February, 1945, although just a few yards from where his brother's body was found. Stephen had been one of the nineteen deemed "missing, presumed dead" at the Inquest. His body was found by prisoners from Stafford Gaol, who had been attached to land restoration teams. The prisoners were commended for their work and the four prisoners who had assisted in the removal of the remains had their sentences remitted by 21 days.

The bodies of the young evacuee, Russell Miles and 68-year-old Robert Wagstaffe, were never found.

You wouldn't necessarily think it of prisoners, but those involved must have been so moved by the experience that they actually attended Evensong at Hanbury Church - occupying a whole aisle of the church - the grey of their prison uniforms standing out from the rest of the congregation.

The name of Robert Wagstaffe was added, on the Thursday after, to the list of those missing, as it was found that he was working on Mr Goodwin's farm on the Monday.

Where John West's body was found a number of ledgers and office books had been recovered and it was believed that some bodies lay further down.

One of the aspects of the disaster which is perhaps less obvious, apart from the actual loss of livestock, but none the less real, is the damage to highly productive farm land. Field after field is dotted with crater and will need levelling before anything can be done in the way of fresh tillage.

The Day the Sun Disappeared, 27 Nov 1944

CHAPTER 22

WILLIAM RHODES
Information from Keith Wilson and Paul Rhodes.

William Rhodes (known as Bill) was working at RAF Fauld. He was born in 1906 near Bolton, Lancashire but had moved to Uttoxeter during the Depression in the 1930s with his wife and young family.

The reason they chose Uttoxeter was because his wife, Violet Sampson, was born there. She was the eldest of seven children and I suppose she'd just had enough of being in a large family, with her dad trying to scrape a living, in the depression, to feed his ever growing brood. She ran away, in the 1920s, and ended up in Bolton where she got a job as a maid to a doctor.

It was in Bolton that she met Bill and they married. Bill was an overlooker in a cotton mill but things were tough in the depression and he found himself out of work several times.

The move to Uttoxeter was a bid for a better life, away from the smog of the Lancashire mills, which was aggravating Bill's chest complaint. He found it difficult to catch his breath sometimes, coughing and spluttering to try free the phlegm in his lungs. His doctor said tiny particles of fibre from the looms had got into his lungs. Yes, everywhere you went in the mill, you could see tiny specks of fibre wafting about, especially when the sun shone – in

The Day the Sun Disappeared, 27 Nov 1944

the beams of light shining through the windows, tiny bits of dust floating in the air, wafting around with constant movement of the treadles and bobbins.

The doctor couldn't give him anything for it, apart from a cough linctus.

The symptoms were aggravated on wet days, which were often. The mills relied on the damp climate and the rivers as the soft water allowed cotton fibres to be separated more easily and for the washing and bleaching of cotton.

On these damp days the smoke billowing out from the chimneys of the factories was prevented from escaping upwards and formed into a smog that crept menacingly through the narrow streets.

On such days, Bill found himself coughing and spluttering and no medicine that his doctor gave him could relieve the pain that tightened across his chest in a vice-like grip. Of course, it didn't help that he was a heavy smoker too.

"I can't be mithered with all this". Bill said to his wife, through a fit of coughing, while his wife was desperately rubbing liniment on his chest to try to help him. To be honest, she was having trouble breathing too.

"May doctor sees way 'as to lyev, or ah'll dee. Aw'v a hankering te go somwheer else."

"Yes, love, your body can't tek any more. How about we go back to my home town, Uttoxeter. The air's pure there, with green fields and farms and no belching factories, just the smell of cattle muck, and that won't harm you."

"Ok, sorted, sweet. At'll doo. Weer gooint Uttoxeter.

The Day the Sun Disappeared, 27 Nov 1944

So, they upped sticks and went to Uttoxeter. They first lived on Wood Lane. It was a house shared with relatives and overlooked the race course. Bill worked as a car park attendant there on race days, collecting the money in the days before machines. His wife went with him one frosty winter's night.

"Oh look, Bill. I'm so glad I came. I've never seen anything like it. Of course, you wouldn't in Bolton, because of all the smog, but it's so clear here." Bill looked up and, to his amazement, the sky was doing a sort of dance in all sorts of colours, but mainly green and reds, colours streaming and forming various shapes.

By this time Bill had modified his accent as he found that no-one could understand him. "They must be the northern lights. I've never seen them before. Aren't they amazing! I'm really pleased I've seen them. They're something else."

Bill managed to get a job in the local dairy. His lungs improved but he started drinking so much illicit hot condensed milk that it brought him out in boils.

Next they moved to James Street near Uttoxeter Smithfield cattle market. By the outbreak of the war, though, he had got himself a job as a store man at RAF Fauld. They'd had a daughter and son by then, Doreen and Eric.

Monday, 27 November 1944 started off as fine, but frosty. Late morning he decided to come above ground for his smoke break. Then all hell broke loose when the explosion erupted. He was really lucky that he was in the entrance to the mine. He was thrown to the ground but recovered enough to find somewhere to shelter, and that was behind a parked ammunition train, though thinking about it afterwards, it probably wasn't the best place to shelter!

The Day the Sun Disappeared, 27 Nov 1944

Still, it provided some cover and he started shouting out to anyone close by, "Here, come over here. There's a bit of shelter here."

It's then that he saw a woman, screaming and crying quite hysterically. He shouted to her, "Come on lass, get yourself over here." but either she couldn't hear him or she was too hysterical, so he tried to get over to her, dodging the falling clods of earth and alabaster rocks. He grabbed hold of her but she was screaming and shaking and was basically stuck and couldn't move. "Sorry about this lass." And he grabbed her by the legs and dragged her to the relative safety of the ammunition train.

They all survived without harm. Others were not so lucky. He said to another guy with him, "Eh, I reckon smoking has saved my life, chuck!"

At the time of the explosion one of their daughters, Doreen, was working at a grocers in the market place in Uttoxeter. She reported, "All the buildings and the grocery counter started shaking. Mum came running down the High Street. She was in tears shouting that Bill had been blown up in the dump." Of course we were both devastated and completely lost as to what to do.

Doreen reported, "It was several hours of anguish before we knew the truth and that dad was alive. Trying to get information was like trying to get blood out of a stone as the explosion was not something that the authorities wanted to publicise. We didn't know what had caused the explosion. The Allies were fighting their way still through Europe into Germany. An own goal of a large ammunition store blowing up was not what they wanted."

……

Sometime in the late 1940's Bill and his wife moved to a council house, 39 Grange Road, in the area north west of Uttoxeter known as the Heath. Bill was a grandad now, with two grandson's Neil and Keith Wilson, Their daughter, Doreen, had married George Wilson. They lived just up the road in Grange Road.

It was not until the 1950's that Bill received the British Empire Medal, partly for his quick thinking and bravery during the explosion and partly for his service to the community.

He worked as a store man at RAF Stafford until retiring in 1971.

Bill and Maude's son, Eric, married Mary, from Marchington, and they had a son, Paul, who now lives in Uttoxeter.

Their daughter Doreen, and her husband, George Wilson, produced Neil, Keith and Celia. Neil married Janet and they live in Uttoxeter. Keith married Rachel and they had two girls. They live in Yorkshire. Celia, who married David Heede, now lives at Ellastone.

Neil, Keith and Celia's father, George Wilson, was a guard on the railway, supervising many troop and armament trains into Marchington camp and Fauld during the war. Once the train had to be halted as black and white American soldiers on board had started fighting. The fighting continued in the surrounding fields. After that whites and blacks were given separate trains and leave nights in Uttoxeter.

This fighting was quite serious. Presumably soldiers would be drawn from the southern as well as the northern states so there would be varying levels of racial prejudice. Certain white soldiers would resent serving alongside, let alone taking orders from those of African/American origin. As we know, the Civil Rights struggle was intense up until the 1960s and beyond.

……..

The Day the Sun Disappeared, 27 Nov 1944

Mr Philips, a colleague of Bill's (mentioned on page 130) had also been affected by the explosion He was an electrician He was nearly drowned in muddy water after being blown over a bund wall (a concrete or earth wall surrounding a storage tank containing oil, designed to hold the contents of the tank in the event of a rupture or leak). With his eventual compensation, he opened a sweet shop in the Cheadle Road, in the area of Uttoxeter known as the Wharfe. The shop was known by everyone as 'Minty Phillips'. Next to Minty's sweet shop was the sub-Post Office (for the Wharfe area) but one up from that was a 'shop' (little more than a terrace house front) that sold nothing but Staffordshire oat cakes and pikelets (big flat crumpets). It did a roaring trade as these were staples in Uttoxeter during the winter at the time, being toasted or fried with various toppings and, of course, customers would pop next door-but-one to Minty's for something sweet to have afterwards.

As the name suggests, the Wharfe is where the canal from the north had terminated in Uttoxeter, years ago. There is no trace of the canal now except in a few fields as the railway took over for transporting goods.

Bill died in 1982.

The Day the Sun Disappeared, 27 Nov 1944

CHAPTER 23

LEN ASHMORE

Len Ashmore at RAF Fauld. Rear row second from the left

Len Ashore was in the military police, stationed at RAF Fauld. He lived at 31 Balance Street, Uttoxeter, opposite the police station.

On the day the dump went up, he was on a 3-man sentry point.

There was an ominous rumble. I shouted out, "Something's up!" Then there was a blast – a huge gust of wind and everything started to jump around. There was a pressure on my ears, something like that experienced sometimes in a train going through a tunnel or in an aeroplane taking off or landing. This was followed almost

The Day the Sun Disappeared, 27 Nov 1944

immediately by the biggest explosion I could ever imagine. I don't remember much about it, as it happened in seconds, but I felt myself lifted bodily off the ground and being thrown into the air, whoosh. I felt my arms waving around, trying to grab hold of anything, but I was high above the tree line. Then I came down, whack. Ow, I was hurting, but I was alive. I'd landed on a pile of mud, strewn up from the explosion. I tried to get up – everything ached and I couldn't – the mud was coming down, covering me, and as I moved, I was digging myself deeper, sinking in. I started calling out, "Help, help, over here" I looked up, the sky had gone black. I realised it was earth coming down, like rain – rain saturated with mounds of soil containing all sorts of debris from buildings, trees, bushes, big rocks of alabaster. I had to get out of their quickly and find safety. I was calling out for the guys I'd been on watch with. I was going to die there, of suffocation.

Then, to my relief, I felt a hand grab hold of me. Someone had a spade and was digging. Then, with a heave, like a plug oozing out of a barrel, I felt myself being dragged upwards, with the sound of the earth, squelching behind me to fill the gap where I had been.

Finally on my feet, I shook hands with my rescuer, who turned out to be called John Smith. "Thank you for saving my life, sir." I managed to get out, breathlessly. It hurt just to say that.

"I'm just glad I heard you calling out. You'd better go get yourself checked out." He replied.

I staggered back to report for duty, but my commander, on seeing me, sent me back home, to Uttoxeter, on invalidity.

I managed to find my cycle, though my legs seemed to be made of lead, so I walked for a bit using the cycle as a sort of crutch. There was pandemonium and chaos everywhere. I passed by where I knew the other two at my sentry point should be. What I found

The Day the Sun Disappeared, 27 Nov 1944

was one of my team, dead, and a sight I never want to experience again. He'd been decapitated….. Before I knew it, I was throwing up, an immediate expelling of stomach contents – an automatic reaction to the shock. I remember thinking, oh, that so easily could have been me.

My knees had gone to jelly and I just sat down and cried. It's not something that a man should do, cry, but I felt so helpless, and useless and every bone in my body hurt including my jaw – rolling my tongue around, I'd realised I'd lost some teeth.

After a while, I recovered a bit and tried to make my way home. A journey that should have taken no more than half an hour, turned into hours. I couldn't even recognise where I should be going. The fields surrounding the camp didn't exist anymore. In their place was a gigantic crater!

On finally getting back home my family came running to help me. They had all gathered, along with my daughter and grandson, Stewart Allen, who was just four years old. My wife said, "We've been so worried. The noise of the explosion nearly split my ear drums. The whole place was shaking so I made a running jump and hid under the table. I thought the house might come down around me, as it shook so much. Some of the windows are broken and the front door blew open with the force of it. Oh it gave me such a turn and I'm so glad to see you home, Len – we all are."

My wife got a bath ready for me to wash off all of the mud. The warm water was soothing and she rubbed some balm into me, to help with the bruising.

I knew I had been sent home on invalidity, but the next morning, I just knew I had to go back – the rescuers needed all the help they could get. My wife tried to stop me but she could see I was determined. I cycled back to help with the rescue efforts and dig people out.

My commander was surprised to see me but no help was being turned away. He told me that, unfortunately, they had not yet been able to find the body of the third guard.

Letter from Len Ashmore's grandson, John Ashmore:

As he returned to duty Len never received any form of acknowledgement from that day apart from a letter telling him he had been turned down for a medal that he had been put forward for following the explosion!

The Day the Sun Disappeared, 27 Nov 1944

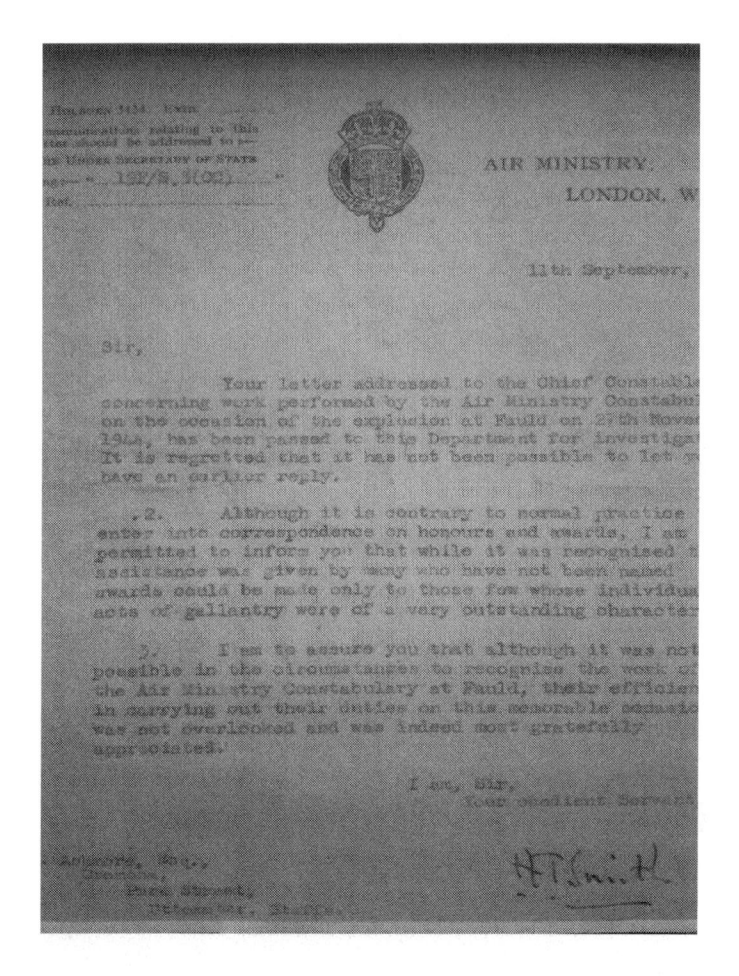

Transcript of letter received from the Air Ministry dated 11th September 1945.

Sir,

The Day the Sun Disappeared, 27 Nov 1944

1   Your letter, addressed to the Chief Constable concerning work performed by the Air Ministry Constabulary on the occasion of the explosion at Fauld on 27th November 1944, has been passed to this Department for investigation. It is regretted that is has not been possible to let you have an earlier reply.

2   Although it is contrary to normal practice to enter into correspondence on honours and awards, I am permitted to inform you that, while it was recognised that assistance was given by many who have not been named, awards could be made only to those few whose individual acts of gallantry were of a very outstanding character.

3   I am to assure you that, although it was not possible, in the circumstances to recognise the work of the Air Ministry Constabulary at Fauld, their efficiency was not overlooked and was indeed most gratefully appreciated.

I am, Sir,

Your obedient Servant.

....

So Len, unfortunately, never got his promised medal.

Len told us that he had already lost most of his teeth and several stump like growths had to be removed from his mouth that they put down to some king of shock or trauma.

He was Mustard gassed at Ypres in the 1^s world war, enlisting slightly before he should have done at the age of just 15 or 16.

The Day the Sun Disappeared, 27 Nov 1944

In 1932 Len started our current Ice Cream business as an extra income as he was struggling to earn enough to look after my Nan and Father. This year is our 90th anniversary of making our real home-made ice cream here in Uttoxeter - quite a change of luck for a man who had a military service like that!

Len rarely talked of such things - that generation just got on with it.

However, grandad told my dad that taking bombs back into the mine after a plane returned, with damaged bombs, or bombs that had not been dropped was a common occurrence, so he believed the theory that they were disarmed below ground against procedure, as it was such a common occurrence.

Regards John Ashmore

Ashmores Ice Cream

The Day the Sun Disappeared, 27 Nov 1944

CHAPTER 24

HARDING FAMILY – After the Explosion

(Continuing from Chapter 10)

On the day of the explosion we were on the morning break at school. We were all queuing in the playground, ready to cross the road, when we heard this terrific explosion. The teachers immediately gathered us all together and we were led to the Anderson shelters for safety. None of us knew what had happened, and there was a lot of noise from us kids, shouting and asking questions, thinking German planes had bombed the area – some of the girls were even crying because a couple of the boys were pretending to be dive bombers, diving their hands through the girls' hair, going "broom, broom, broom" imitating a plane engine. "Be quiet everyone, sit down." One of the teachers shouted out. "We cannot answer your questions but you are safe here. We have books, which I will hand out for you to read." Everyone found a place to sit and things went quiet again, although of course there was still a bit of whispering to the person next to them.

At lunch time we were allowed to go home. I walked up the bank to my house. There was mud and rocks everywhere, and chimneys had smashed to the ground. Nearly every window was cracked or broken. I began to shiver, even though I had my coat and gloves on. I'd never seen anything like this. There was a woman up ahead, screaming. She shouted to me, "If your dad was down the mine, he's dead. I tell you, they're all dead." She ran off screaming out to anyone who could hear, "They're all dead!"

My first thought was yes, my dad worked in the mine….. , then it dawned on me…..that means he's dead. My lovely dad is dead. I burst out crying. I couldn't move, I was in shock. After what seemed like ages, I finally got my legs to move, and ran home.

Mum was there as I ran to throw my arms around her, crying bitterly, "Dad's dead, he's dead."

"It's alright, lovely. Your dad's not dead. He managed to get a message through to let me know he's alright, but he's still there trying to rescue people."

"He's not dead?" I replied, looking up at her, wiping my eyes but with a measure of disbelief at what my mum had said. "But this lady along the way said my dad was dead."

"Oh, now, donna worry, little'un. Yes, a lot of people have died in the explosion, but your dad was lucky. He'd swopped shifts with a colleague of his, so was above ground, working on an engine. Unfortunately, the guy he swopped shifts with got caught in the explosion, and he lost his life. It could so easily have been your dad."

"Where is he? I want to see him" and I went to run out of the door towards the mine.

"You can't see him, Rose. Stop, it's dangerous. We will just have to wait. There's nothing we can do."

I was too wound up to have anything for lunch. We waited and waited with all sorts of things going through my mind, and I'm

The Day the Sun Disappeared, 27 Nov 1944

sure my mum's too. Would he come back safely? Would there be another explosion? Would he be caught up in it?

Finally, dad returned in the evening. He was covered in mud but we both ran to throw our arms around him.

"It's a real calamity, Jane." Bombs in the RAF Fauld dump have gone up. The whole place, for miles, is a mess of dead bodies. A huge crater has been blown skywards. Upper Castle Hayes Farm has gone, buried in the crater. I've been digging and digging, with loads of others who worked there, plus others from farms and the emergency services. We managed to get a few out and they've been taken to hospital. I'll have to go back. Just give me something to eat and I'll be out again."

Dad spent the next 48 hours on the site, trying to find anyone else alive.

....

The daughter of the family above wants her family name kept secret. In her own words she wrote:

It still upsets me to this day that that woman, who said my dad was dead could be so callous. My classmates, some still alive, lost their dads that day. Later, my daughter went to primary school and she too had classmates who never saw their grandads, lost in the dump explosion.

A friend of dad's lost his wife and two children that day. Lots of 'old families' in Tutbury have similar stories and it's still a sensitive subject.

The George Cross was awarded to one guy for his efforts digging out the bodies. He later became the village gravedigger.

The Day the Sun Disappeared, 27 Nov 1944

There has been a constant drip, drip of stories, giving false information about the cause of the explosion. There are still a lot of people alive that had very many sad memories.

It was all a total lack of supervision or training. Health and safety there was poor, workers not obeying the regulations – people actually smoking in the tunnels of all things, while surrounded with bombs!

My daughter's father in law and 4 siblings lost their home and both parents that day. Children went to school that morning and by 11am had lost everything.

In 1938 my grandad, moved up from South London to work for the MOD, first at Hilton, and then at RAF Fauld. His wife, and two daughters, 4 and 1, also joined him shortly afterwards. He was a maintenance fitter working on the engines.

Our neighbour, Mrs R...., lost her husband in the explosion. She returned to Portsmouth after the war.

Mrs P..., who lived in Tutbury, lost her husband too. She'd lost everything, her home, her possessions, her sanity...... She felt she had nothing else to live for - she just walked into the river one day and never walked out. Gone – drowned.

Now the fields plunge back to earth
A massive crater, dead and bare – a crem.
Drowned, broken, gassed, as people mourn
their loved ones, digging, digging to find them.
Now the fields plunge back to earth.

CHAPTER 25

RAF FAULD RESCUE

To the servicemen and civilians alike, there seemed to be nothing unusual about the morning of November 27th. The total issues and receipts for the month was approaching 14,000 tons, but with the hectic days of Overlord behind them, both the Commanding Officer, Group Captain R J Storrar, and the OC HE Mine Area had taken a few days leave.

I, Squadron Leader Anness, was the Acting CEO that day. Flying officer, Joseph Solomon had been on leave for the past week. There was a new guy, Pilot Officer Norman Rollo, who was Joseph Solomon's deputy while Solomon was on leave, but Rollo had only been on site since November 13th. Rollo was allowed one day a week free and this was that day, so I was extra busy.

One Works Department gang had been sent to empty the drainage sumps in the new area and another to inspect the electric light fittings there. For the men underground, it was just a matter of routine. It was a routine day too for the AID men and the servicemen detailed to assist them.

I overheard one of the armourers saying, "The same old job." So, in my mind this indicated that the armourers were bored, not because they had nothing to do but just the complete opposite – they were overloaded with dealing with the bombs, getting them

The Day the Sun Disappeared, 27 Nov 1944

moving quickly - but bored with the same old routine – a bit like a factory conveyor belt worker. Speed was of essence. It didn't occur to me until afterwards that this boredom could lead to slapdash work, and short-corners being taken.

I was still wrestling with the problem of finding enough railway trucks for the regular daily consignment of 4,000lb bombs, which meant I'd have to make my way to Scropton to try to sort that out.

I would meet Flight Lieutenant Giles there, who was the officer in charge of transport.

Whenever bombs jettisoned from an Allied aircraft were recovered, regulations required that they be returned to a Maintenance Unit for repair and re-issue. In theory, all such returned bombs were inspected upon receipt at Scropton, but, taking a cursory glance as I passed by to meet up with Flight Lieutenant Giles, I noticed that the piles of bombs were only being given a quick once-over to check for cracked cases. They should be giving them a thorough checking for internal damage, such as a ruptured CE Exploder (the intermediate charge between the detonator and the main filling). Any broken suspension lugs or bases should be repaired in situ but any damaged bomb would have to be removed to an isolated cavern – the 'exploder bay' for repair.

Still, I didn't have time to spend investigating and reprimanding. Those railway trucks needed to be found.

Just then, at 11.10am, I heard a bang in the direction of the dump. There was smoke billowing over the mine then I saw flames starting to soar up skywards.

Before I could react, there was a second mind-numbing blast, and I automatically covered my ears and crouched down. Tons of earth was rocketing skywards and a gigantic mushroom cloud of smoke, earth and debris had been hurled miles up. I'd never seen anything like it. "God in heaven", I said to myself. The whole top of the bomb dump, covering a vast area was blowing up in a crescendo of noise and a barrage of earth and debris.

I jumped on one of the little trains and drove it back to the mine.

....

John Bell, RAF Fauld's engineer, was making sections at 11.10am on November 27, 1944 when the explosion happened and there were pockets of flames ignited all over.

The electricity power had gone off. He started to shout out orders, "Get those water hoses" he screamed out to his men, trying to get himself heard above the clamour. "Get those fires out." He reckoned there would be just about enough water to last until the fire engines got there. He shouted out to anyone in hearing range, "We need water. Anyone, get down to the billets and bring water. Two people ran the half-a-mile down the road, pinched about half a dozen water bottles, filled them up, and ran back with them. In the meantime John Bell rang all the emergency services.

The firefighters arrived, led by National Fire Service company office, Charles Elliott, from Burton, about 15 minutes after the explosion. "I knew this would happen sometime, sooner or later," he said to himself. His immediate task was to set men to work on the blazing stacks of incendiary bombs.

"Get that hose connected." he shouted out to his men and 800 feet of hose was connected to an emergency supply of water.

Elliott's next task was the mine itself. By now it had become choked with clouds of dust and lethal carbon monoxide fumes created by the explosion. With handkerchiefs held over their

The Day the Sun Disappeared, 27 Nov 1944

mouths, RAF men had been making desperate attempts to get in to search for survivors, but were repeatedly driven back by the fumes.

There was no time to waste. Elliott radioed his headquarters for assistance and ordered four of his men to put on breathing apparatus sets and make their way into the mine.

Despite the many hazards and the lack of information regarding the true positon, the party remained underground until their sets were almost exhausted. They then withdrawn and handed over to the first mines rescue team, giving them valuable information of the situation and what they would find down there.

Wing Commander Kings was in charge of RAF Fauld on the day. At 11.10am Kings was standing in the master provision office. He could hardly believe that the place was still standing through the violent shaking of the walls and smashed windows. He got in his car and drove to the mine, picking up service officers on the way – including Flight Lieutenant J P Lewin. A fire engine drove in front. At the control point b, the mine entrance, two large stacks of incendiary bombs were blazing fiercely and exploding near the mine entrances. King barked orders to the firemen, "Concentrate on nearby stacks of bombs rather than the fires that have gone beyond fighting – we've got to try to prevent the fires spreading to other nearby stacks." He had only been in the mine twice before and, ten minutes after the explosion, went into number two entrance with the civilian storeman, Thomas Mylotte, having just one lamp between them as there were no emergency hand lamps or breathing apparatus readily available. To make matters worse, there were soon signs that deadly carbon monoxide gas was accumulating in the undamaged areas.

COPY

AIR OFFICER i/c ADMINISTRATION, HEADQUARTERS MAINTENANCE COMMAND.

EXPLOSION AT No. 21 M.U. FAULD - DIARY OF EVENTS

1145 Hours, 27th November 1944

Air Commodore Daly rang me up to say that the C.O. No. 51 M.U. Lichfield had phoned him to say that they have just heard and felt a large explosion which they thought came from the direction of 21 M.U. Fauld. I spoke to 42 Group and they had also just heard that there was a fire in the mine at 21 M.U. and had notified the A.O.C. who was at present visiting Corsham. No further details are at present available but the Group are taking energetic action.

1200 hours

Group Captain Honey, 42 Group, rang up to say that he is not quite sure what has happened but it appears that some form of bomb or rocket fell on top of the mine causing incendiaries to ignite. It is understood that there may be a number of casualties and as the telephone line is very much engaged he asked me if I would ask a nearby station to send an ambulance or ambulances in case they are required. I have arranged with 41 Group to get 51 M.U. Lichfield to send an ambulance, and have also arranged with 40 Group to send two ambulances, one from Stafford, if possible, and one from Derby, together with a medical officer.

1430 hours.

Group Captain Honey rang up to say that the fire was now under control. Apparently two sticks of bombs were dropped, total 37, delay action, and these are still going off. The number of casualties is not yet known as personnel are still trapped. Mine rescue squads and teams of the National Fire Service have both arrived. Air Ministry have been informed by 42 Group.

35 M.U. and 61 M.U. have both sent ambulances and a medical officer. Air Commodore Daly, 41 Group, rang up to say that Lichfield have sent an ambulance from Brockton and from one other satellite. He has spoken to the Station Master Lichfield who told him that they were going to send over what they could in

The Day the Sun Disappeared, 27 Nov 1944

the way of ambulances; he also told him that the Americans have already gone over in full force with what they could produce in assistance from their Lichfield Depot.

1500 hours

The Chief Engineer, Maintenance Command, is trying to arrange for Mr. Bryant, the Resident Engineer at Valley, Anglesey, to be flown to Fauld as he knows the place inside out, including the exits and those that had been bricked in. The Chief Engineer had received information that there are 40 R.A.F. and 2 civilians so far unaccounted for.

1600 hours.

Group Captain Honey phoned to say that the acting C.O. 21 M.U. Fauld is of the opinion that nothing was dropped from above to cause the accident; he thought the explosion took place in the mine itself, causing bombs to explode upwards. So far it it believed that there are 20 killed, including Italian co-operators, Service personnel and civilians, and there are 20 missing. The military are now guarding the mine.

2230 hours

Group Captain Honey phoned to say that the Regional Commissioner, Birmingham, had arranged for the supply of water to 21 M.U. Fauld for the next 48 hours, after which it was to be our responsibility. I phoned 40 Group and told them to arrange for up to six water trailers to be detailed immediately. 42 Group were informed.

1000 hours 28th November 1944

Group Captain Honey phoned the following information -

Casualties

Killed 4 - 1 R.A.F. Sgt.; 1 A.M. Constable; 2 Civilian Industrials.

The Day the Sun Disappeared, 27 Nov 1944

Thomas Mylotte had made his way out of the mine. He had been preparing loaded bomb trucks for the journey to the surface and hence to the railway and docks. At 11am, as nothing had happened, Thomas informed his men that he was going to contact the surface to ascertain if the trucks were going to be moved and that they were to touch nothing. He was three minutes away when the explosion occurred.

It was now that Tom's personal training came to assistance. He had been trained by using a blindfold to find his way around and also used the underground railway lines to help him by following the direction with his feet. This had saved his life.

Against doctor's order he returned to the underground chaos,

They made as full a search of the underground area as was possible before they reappeared, gasping for breath at 11.45am. They could do nothing in the dark and, if they stayed any longer, they would have collapsed.

Tom Mylotte was eventually sent home by his fiend, the parish priest.

The Day the Sun Disappeared, 27 Nov 1944

Rock fall on railway tracks - donated by Graham Shaw

Flight Lieutenant J P Lewin had entered the mine on his own, completely under his own jurisdiction soon after the explosion, searching in the underground tunnels.

Roll-call followed. It was unbelievable the RAF Fauld did not have a system whereby each man took a disc with him, for example, when going underground, that he handed back on returning to the surface, let alone a listing of men in the mine!. About 200 workers, including civilians, RAF and some Italian workers had gone into the galleries that Monday morning. A roll-call showed that only 50 escaped.

Kings sent the Italians back to their camp and placed them under guard, "The reason being" so he said, was, "that a few people have been making accusations against the Italians working on site." A direct outcome of this was that the rumours that Italians were behind the explosion (not that anyone ever found a scrap of evidence for sabotage), began at once.

Flight Lieutenant Lewin went down again, this time with Foreman Coker, searching for another hour. By this time the fumes were overpowering and Lewin had to carry Coker out. He only abandoned his searches when the teams from the Mines Rescue Operation arrived.

Kings sent a party of 50 arrived from RAF Church Broughton, with spades and shovels, to Peter Ford's. Flight Lieutenant Lewis joined in with them.

A press reporter had got to the site hitching a lift on the back of a fire engine. He was held at the gate by an RAF officer awaiting orders. King told the officer to tell the reporter, "I do not want the press involved. Tell him that nothing must be reported until the Ministry of Information releases the news officially." He then told the same officer to ring the local press agency representative to warn him against publishing stories. Of course, the press weren't just going to take this lying down and a report of 'a tremendous explosion' at an RAF maintenance depot close to Burton on Trent, went in the Monday late afternoon edition of newspapers across the country.

Joseph Clifford Salt (known as Cliff) had somehow or other managed to get out of his office in the deep gallery of the mines. He was in his office when the explosions occurred and smoke and gases began to fill the galleries. When the National Fire Service arrived, at 12.15pm, under Company Officer Elliott, Salt approached Elliott, "Sir, I am Cliff Salt, not attached to the RAF, but I have detailed knowledge of the mine layout. I am sure I can be of assistance. I had my office underground."

The Day the Sun Disappeared, 27 Nov 1944

Foreman J. O. Salt. **C/O. D. O. Elliott.**

"How did you manage get out, man?" Elliott enquired, quite shocked to find Salt intact, although obviously distressed.

"Well sir, I'd gone along the corridor to check things after the first bang and made my way back to the office. That's when the main explosion happened and I found myself physically blown out of my office, along with Storeman Cresswell and Airman Still. We were alright but the lights had gone out and everything was pitch black. I managed to make my way about 200 yards in the dark to where I knew there was an emergency lamp, so I had light to see my way through and I got out with Cresswell and Still. I could hear voices shouting out for a light, Italians and civilians. Just as we were nearing the entrance though, there was this great blast of air that almost knocked me of my feet again. We found Warder Simpson lying injured and we carried him out. There we met Flight Lieutenant Lewin with a party carrying a stretcher, so Simpson was placed on the stretcher and taken off.

"Well, that's a miracle. Yes, you do appear to know your way around, and thank you Mr Salt for your assistance. All help with be accepted gratefully."

Wing Commander Kings again searched the mine, this time with oxygen sets, accompanied by Mr Joseph Clifford Salt, the civilian storeman, Thomas Mylotte and four firemen and remained underground until their oxygen was almost exhausted.

Volunteer firemen went in to make a human message chain, with orders to get out if they felt gassed.

Kings, Lewin and Mr Salt made repeated attempts to reach military and civilian personnel trapped underground but not having precise knowledge of exactly where people had been working; with not sufficient emergency lighting or breathing apparatus and the carbon monoxide gas spreading even into areas that had been minimally damaged, made the task nigh impossible.

By now the National Fire Service units were soon compelled to withdraw their men from the tunnels and an urgent call went out for specialists from the Mines Rescue Service. However, even the experts found the conditions hazardous and one of their men was lost, overcome by fumes, as he searched for survivors.

Orders were being shouted here there and everywhere, people coughing and spluttering through the smoke, water sprayed at the fires had made the whole area a quagmire. Ambulances on the scene were loading up the injured, their tyres dipping into the mud and squealing as the drivers tried to escape the water-filled pot holes and work their way around the numerous rescuers, their equipment and smouldering boulders and bombs.

Rock fall on top of bombs - donated by Graham Shaw

Although physically shaking after risking life and limb, Mr Salt remained in the mine until everybody in his area had been evacuated. He exited only to return underground, yet again, with Flight Lieut. Shuttleworth and two mine safety men, even though conditions were still dangerous and there were all manner of risks. "I wanted to get to F Loop, trying to get into the New area. I heard someone calling up ahead and we found the janitor, Mr Woodall. He'd been injured by a roof fall so we got him out too."

By this time, following Elliott's telephone calls, civil defence teams from Burton had arrived with more ambulances. In charge was rescue service superintendent, Charles Boyce. They had been clambering over the hillside and realised they were moving directly towards the point at which the explosion had ripped through the surface of the earth. They hadn't recognised where they were as, before the explosion, the area had been one of green fields and trees. Cattle had been grazing in the sunshine and farm workers had been out with their heavy carts and horses.

Now the landscape had changed beyond recognition. Barely a tree or blade of grass remained. Dead and dying cattle were strewn around among the mud and boulders.

At the centre of it all was as Charles Boyce exclaimed out loud, "A huge, damn crater". Boyce looked around him, his eyes widening in astonishment. The crater stretched 300 yards from one end to the other and plunged sharply to a depth of 90ft or so. At the base, between the rubble, were twisted metal tracks from the narrow gauge railway, which had once carried bombs in and out of the mine and large lumps of white alabaster protruding through the mud.

Around, for as far as the eye could see, were hundreds of smaller craters formed by huge boulders, which had been blasted into the air.

……..

Mr Harold Coker, (30, of Alma Road, Doveridge, Derbyshire) had also managed to get out. He had an underground office, like Mr Salt. As he emerged from the tunnel with some other men, and seeing the hail of earth and debris coming down, they stood for a second, wondering what to do. Then rescue workers saw them, and ran towards them to check them out. He told the astonished rescue personnel, breathlessly and coughing, at times violently, trying desperately to rid his lungs of the fumes "The first explosion didn't alarm me much as I was in the underground clearing sheds, (uugh), where we often heard, testing shots. But the other explosion was so violent that we knew something grave had happened. (Trying to breathe in deeply) I organised my party and, after several attempts, in the pitch darkness, (cough) reached the incendiary area. (cough) I knew three of my men had been there and called out, but there was no answer. The fire and fumes were now making it hard going, especially in the blackness and we had to grope our way through the tunnels, to places where I knew emergency lamps were placed.

I had six RAF men helping me and we stumbled and groped through the tunnels to the area where the high-explosives were stored. At that point, one of the RAF lads collapsed from the gas fumes – we managed to drag him out - this guy here – he needs some attention please." Someone called over to the medical people, who came to check them all over. While doing so, Harold Coker continued, "Well, I knew I had to get him to an ARP area where there would be some fresh air and a water supply.

There we soaked our handkerchiefs in water to use as masks against the fumes and the rest of us went back into the tunnels, to look for the others, leaving the RAF man there, We kept going back, soaking our hankies, and going back again, but enough was enough and we had to get out. We just couldn't find the others. My lads have been brilliant though." And he turned towards his team, giving them the thumbs up.

Within 24 hours, 28 excavators, four 500-gallon water tanks, picks and shovels had arrived at RAF Fauld. Civilian mine rescuers had arrived from Midlands' coal pits, to try to search for any survivors.

The Day the Sun Disappeared, 27 Nov 1944

They smelt gas and knew there wouldn't be much hope of rescuing anyone trapped alive underground.

Mr Salt had been down the mine two more times, this time with oxygen apparatus, acting as a guide to the teams, and he continued until he finally had to be assisted out, suffering from the effects of the fumes.

......

Within an hour of the National Fire Service's call for assistance, the first mines rescue teams were on the scene, headed by Mr Robertson, Mr Drinnan and the first rescue teams with their Superintendent, Mr Perry. Mr Robertson took full control of the rescue work. He was only allowing entry into the mines by trained teams wearing breathing apparatus. He didn't want more lives lost.

Section leader Marriott and Leading Fireman Appleby returned to duty.

THE LATE MR. JOSEPH COOPER

The bodies of Joseph Cooper, locomotive driver and Arthur Harris, mine foreman, were recovered from the bottom of the shaft at the plaster mine on Thursday. The rescuers said, "We reached them yesterday, and moved them towards the shaft, but the fumes drove us back. We had to leave them, for we could not breathe."

In the main dump, the bodies of three men were reached. One of them was Corporal A Durose, and the others are two Italian collaborators.

The Day the Sun Disappeared, 27 Nov 1944

Mr Robertson was shouting out orders, "Mr Drinnan – I want you in charge of the underground centre controlling the team. You will lead the first team in with Foreman Salt as your guide. Mr Perry, you shall be in charge of the first team."

"Yes, sir," Perry replied, "I have Alfred Parker, James Beard, Leonard George Snape, Cyril John Whetton, William Slater and John Webb, as captain." Perry's team were attached to the rescue station at Ashby-de-la-Zouch. They had received the call about 11.50am and got to the site about 1pm.

Robertson continued, "I have a tracing map of the mine here, if you could all have a look. I've marked on the map the probable positons of survivors, although we don't know for certain if those people are still where they were working. They may well have tried to make their way to the entrance or even got lost with no lighting. Perry, we want to get down there but no stand-by team has arrived yet to follow-up in face of accidents."

"Our team is ready sir," Perry replied, "We'll start rescue operations immediately."

"Yes", Robertson responded, "There's nothing for it. We can't wait any longer, immediate action is required here - there may well be people inside who can be saved."

They then proceeded to the entrance of the mine.

I, John Webb, as captain, was given a team of five of the men - James Beard (No. 2), (Frederick) William Slater (No.3), Cyril J Whetton (No.4) and Leonard G Snape (No.5, Vice Captain).

"Right team," I said, "I want you to give me the OK when your breathing apparatus has passed the auxiliary test."

Everyone gave me the OK.

The Day the Sun Disappeared, 27 Nov 1944

"OK, each of you, tell me the degree of your fitness."

Each one replied, to the affirmative as fit and well and raring to go.

"Right, we've got a guide and Superintendent Perry will go ahead with a canary, until we reach a point where the canary looks like it is showing some signs that it is failing."

We went through the entrance and only got about 200 yards when Perry indicated the bird was swooning.

"OK men, we'll go back about 58 yards." I then made a chalk mark on the ground and walls.

"This is your safe base, where you know the air is fresh. I want you all now to couple up with your apparatus." Superintendent Perry and I checked each man that their apparatus was on correctly and asked if they were still feeling fit.

"We are proceeding to explore loop 'E' where we will be looking out for falls and possible survivors. I will be chalking our route on the way."

We left the fresh air base at 1.45pm, examining several roadways, eventually getting to a roadway known as E1, which we found to be in a state of devastation. While en-route, I was taking regular checks of each person's oxygen consumption. On the way to E1 two dead bodies were found within a few yards of each other.

At this point, we were all breathing heavily and some of the lads indicated they were getting headaches. "Ok, lads, I think we've had enough down here. We're all beginning to suffer, so I believe we should return to the fresh air base." It would have been about 2.30pm by then. Perry came back with us. "OK, I want Webb, Beard, Slater and Whetton to load the first dead body onto the

The Day the Sun Disappeared, 27 Nov 1944

stretcher. Snape and Beard, you are to take the stretcher and convey the body back."

It was rough going and they only got ten yards when the going proved too difficult trying to lift the stretcher over the fall of rock. Snape and Beard were taking deep breaths, to try to get more oxygen, and this in turn would be using up their oxygen supply more quickly.

Noting this, Perry said, "OK, lads. This is proving too great a risk to recover this dead body and we will have to abandon the body and return to base."

I, (Webb) wrote in chalk on a girder to the effect that the body had had to be abandoned.

There was another fall to negotiate, I climbed over it with Whetton and Slater, leaving Beard and Snape on the inbye side, just five yards apart.

At 2.40pm Slater indicated that Whetton was having trouble, and at the same time, a distress signal was sounded from the inbye side of the fall.

I went to Whetton's assistance and next turned my attention to the inbye side. On climbing over the rock fall and reaching Snape and Beard I found Snape supporting Beard from behind. Beard had his nose-clip off. I'd seen this before when lack of oxygen makes people deranged and they do strange things to try to breathe, even trying to take their breathing apparatus off. He appeared to be in a bad way. I immediately put the nose-clip back on him and sat him down, checking his breathing apparatus. Beard kept uttering, "I'm alright" three or four times, each time less incoherently.

He failed to respond to any treatment and I felt the only possible action was to leave him behind, but before this was done, the mouthpiece and nose-clip of the apparatus were removed and a reviving apparatus securely fixed on. Under the circumstances, I and the rest of the team had to abandon all hope of recovering Beard, we were all having difficulty in breathing, and in our deeply seriously undermined states progressed, as quickly as our legs would carry us, stumbling out to the fresh air base to summon what assistance was available. Superintendent Perry had collapsed, overcome by the gas, and we just about had enough strength to get ourselves out, but RAF personnel at the entrance managed to help him out.

Drinnan's team continued the search until forced back by fumes.

By this time a team from Mansfield had arrived, led by Mr Brown,

On seeing Drinnan's team exiting the mine, in the poorly state they were, Mr Robertson went up to Drinnan stating, "A team from Mansfield has arrived, led by a Mr Brown, so they can take over now. Mr Drinnan, I require you now to concentrate on trying to find a method to combat these damn fumes. We can't continue like this. Teams can only stay down a little while, even with breathing apparatus."

Mr Richardson then directed his attention to Mr Brown, who had actually brought two additional rescue teams.

"Thank you for coming, Mr Brown. I understand you have expert knowledge of mines rescue work. If I could ask you to brief the teams. You'll be assisted by Mr Drinnan."

Mr Drinnan carried on this work continuously for twenty-four hours.

Mr Robertson planned the operations at a control centre, received reports, called up additional teams and apparatus and arranged for the assistance of other technical personnel. He also went

The Day the Sun Disappeared, 27 Nov 1944

underground several times to explore the situation with Leading Fireman Appleby and Leading Fireman Bivens. The party was able to penetrate some hundreds of yards through the bomb storage galleries, and continued in this dangerous and arduous work, managing to bring back several unconscious persons before being checked by a roof fall. On the return journey they searched the side galleries, but without success. They were gradually being overcome by the fumes, which were blowing back towards the shaft. At this point just a few seconds exposure to the fumes, could be lethal. Only the two Leading firemen remained partially conscious. They tried to drag the other three members out, but their strength failed and they themselves were only just able to crawl back to the base and give the alarm.

Before fully recovered from his work in the entrance tunnels, Appleby again entered the mine, this time by the emergency shaft, but without wearing breathing apparatus, trying to recover two people, who afterwards proved to be dead, he was overcome by fumes and collapsed.

Luckily, Leading Fireman Roden came to his aid, bringing him back to the surface. Roden had been directing and assisting his team in the removal of exhausted men and dead bodies at the entrance tunnels. When he was satisfied that further efforts at this positon would be of no avail, he entered the tunnels, this time through the emergency shaft, directing the removal of 4 bodies to the foot of the ventilating shaft. Being almost exhausted by his efforts and the slowly failing supply of oxygen to the breathing apparatus he was wearing, he was assisted up the shaft to the open air. On being revived with oxygen, he again went to the head of the shaft, until removed to hospital suffering from the effects of the gas and exhaustion.

When partially revived by the administration of oxygen, Appleby continued to assist in the work of bringing the recovered bodies up to the surface, until he finally collapsed.

(Taken from the Burton Mail – Day 4: Fauld explosion 60th anniversary and the Supplement to the London Gazette, 10 April 1945)

....

Mr L D Buttle, a Fauld's clerk of works, had been at RAF Sleighford. He returned immediately to Fauld on hearing the explosion, but couldn't do anything until 7.30pm when rescuers asked for a screen to keep air moving through a tunnel entrance. Rescuers were setting up two fans to air the mine. Mr Buttle and a team had the screen in place for 11pm. At 1am, Mr Buttle was told that barricades were necessary to control air in the mine. Work took all night and into Tuesday. He didn't leave Fauld until 5.30pm on November 28, 32 hours after he had begun his shift.

Mr Buttle reported, "I wasn't able to do much else until about 10.30pm, when the Ilkeston Permanent Rescue Brigade arrived. I'd breathed in a lot of gas and my head had been spinning. I had sat down, trying to recover and was just waiting."

Men were walking around with canaries, testing for gas. RAF personnel and civilians were risking their lives entering the mine, penetrating into the labyrinth of tunnels and blocked roadways, passing passageways containing thousands of tons of high explosives, some of it crushed under fallen rock, risking the gravest danger from fire, further explosion, noxious fumes and roof falls.

All day, tin-hatted soldiers and rescue workers toiled without pause in the vast area of desolation up above – of scorched

The Day the Sun Disappeared, 27 Nov 1944

meadows, dead cattle and uprooted trees, of wrecked buildings, craters and mud. It had rained the next day so the tons of earth that had descended from the bomb-blasted fields had turned into a mass of sludge and mire.

All this time, though, I (John Webb) was worrying that the second breathing apparatus I put on Beard, would have been spent, but I couldn't do anything. I'd seen two other teams go in, but Beard hadn't been brought out. Perry finally asked, "Do you think you're fit enough now to lead the Ilkeston team into the mine and recover Beard, as it seemed that two previous teams had failed to locate him."

So, at 11.10pm I went into the mine again with the Ilkeston team and directed them to the point where I had left Beard. We found him about 11.35pm in the exact position he had been left. He was in a sitting positon with the back of his head on a munition box. He appeared to be dead.

The oxygen and reviving apparatus had spent itself out as I so much feared. The light on his hat was just burning out. Try as we may, we could not revive him and we brought his dead body to the entrance.

ON THE SCENE ... a young Frank Lee

A colleague of Beard's arrived, coming direct from his shift at Denisthorpe, Frank Lee, still covered in coal dust, as there were no baths at the mine. He was a member of a trained rescue team, on standby in case of a mining accident. It was dark when he arrived with clouds overhead, black as anything. It was pouring with rain and the phosphorous bombs (two racks of them near the entrance) were ablaze and giving off an eerie yellow light. "By the time anyone realised what was happening, it was too late. I find it hard to describe how fellow mine worker, Beard, died. To me, he was a friend. I asked a colleague, who had been down the mine, how he was."

The reply he got was, "How do you think I am?" He was obviously distraught, "We had to leave Jimmy there!"

"After the death, operations were suspended until we knew how to proceed. Everything was carried out meticulously though, despite the chaos.

People were disinfecting breathing apparatus for the next teams to use – a whole host of activities were being done. The mines rescue squads always kept a trained team employed, available at a minute's notice to go to any mine disasters or fires. Men at the pit, like me were recruited and trained so that we could supplement them and follow up.

Rescue workers sheltered under makeshift cover and half-destroyed buildings. There were about 50 huddled together, trying to keep warm and waiting to be called while the RAF personnel looked after bodies that had been recovered.

In the morning, we were able to look at Jimmy Beard's body.

It was some time that next morning that I was called in with my team. It was a waiting game. A team goes in and could be there for two hours. My team was sent in for the grim task of recovering a body.

Problems with my breathing equipment, meant that I had to use one hand to carry the stretcher and the other hand on the valve of my oxygen cylinder. The body was heavy and I wasn't very big. I was probably not in the mine for longer than an hour.

The Day the Sun Disappeared, 27 Nov 1944

Everywhere I looked was littered with ammunition. Stock had fallen over onto their sides and we initially had to navigate our way around it by following the loco tracks that had been used to haul the bombs around the mine. But then the tracks disappeared, covered in debris and boxes. What I did notice was that there was a stream of water running along the side of the road. I later found out this came from the exploded reservoir.

As I walked away from the mine I heard one official say that there was about 7% carbon monoxide. When you think that 0.5% will kill you, 7% the lads inside there had no chance."

In the meantime, relatives were outside the gates, waiting for any news that could be given them of their loved ones. Mrs Elsie Salt had been in a state of terrible anxiety for many hours, not knowing whether her husband had survived or not. She had felt the blast from their home in Goodman Street, Burton and she had run to the phone box at the end of the road to call Fauld to check all was ok. In her panic, she had called the Burton depot, on Branston Road, where she used to work, by mistake. They reassured her that all was ok. She went home, relieved, but knew something was wrong when he didn't come home at the usual time. She was in despair, wondering what to do, pacing up and down, wondering whether to go to Fauld or not. She didn't want not to be there when he came through the door. Finally he arrived back home, only to collapse in the nearest armchair, having been overcome by fumes and totally exhausted. Mrs Salt went to make him a cup of tea and bring him a bowl of warm water to wash away the grime. By the time she returned, he was asleep. She put a rug over him and let him sleep.

The Day the Sun Disappeared, 27 Nov 1944

Bren gun carriers had helped in clearing a way through the mountains of mud. The explosion had sent the cattle and sheep crazy. They were also shooting badly injured cattle and sheep, some with pieces of shrapnel imbedded in them, dying slowly, in agony. Someone had to tell these soldiers that you had to shoot cattle in the head to kill them. They didn't know. They'd never had to do such a thing before....

One man had a miraculous escape from death. He was working at the RAF station and was hurled high over a tree and fell upright, completely buried by the descending debris, two pieces of which, however, fell crossways immediately above his head, thus preventing him suffocating. His shouts attracted the attention of searchers but it was some time before he could be found.

One of the men who escaped was a Mr T Archer. He told the Daily Mail, "*I had been working about 10 yards from the entrance when the whole of this vast underground store was rocked by the explosion. There was a tremendous glare of light behind us in the heart of the galleries, where many men would be working. I ran for it into a vast cloud of dust and stones, which was pouring out from the galleries in a gale of wind.*

A man near me stumbled and fell. I got hold of him and helped him out. Behind us was just a vast grey wall of dust shot with flames."

About 50 women workers were in a building outside the galleries. Some were hurled through the wooden roof by the explosion, but luckily none had serious injuries.

In the canteen Mrs Lily Flint and other women workers threw themselves on the floor while the building rocked. "Masses of stuff was flying overhead and crashing into the ground," she said, "All we could do was hold tight until the 'earthquake' stopped.

The Day the Sun Disappeared, 27 Nov 1944

Then the wind brought a sandstorm, which covered the gardens with 3 inches of the stuff."

Houses were ruined and about ten families had to find shelter somewhere, staying with friends or family. African/American soldiers were brought in to fix waterproof covers on damaged roofs.

....

Air Marshal Donald, head of RAF maintenance bases, didn't arrive until the day after the explosion. His orders were that everything was to be hushed up. No reporters were allowed in. His main objective was to get the mine operative again, get those bombs moving out to the air sites awaiting them. He had obviously been kept up to date with how the war was progressing and, explosion or not, those bombs had to be got out as this part of the war was critical. General Eisenhower would be conferring that evening with Field-Marshall Montgomery in a third-storey sitting-room of a bleak house near Holland. The object would be to design the final defeat of Germany. Now there was a sense of urgency about the whole business. The armies of General Dempsey were lined up on the west bank of the Maas and of General Crerar, The Canadian Commander, on the south bank and across the Maas.

"There were unexploded bombs down there - government property." was what was on Air Marshall Donald's mind, no matter about how many people had been killed and maimed. This was war.

He'd been advised also that Patton had reached Duran, 10 miles south of Merejig. Downton had earlier wired that rolling northeast along a 40-mile borderland front tanks and infantry made substantial advance toward the river line, at some point fighting among the coal lines and the steel works on Reich territory, striking into Germany's 'black country'.

That day he had been telephoned by Lord Sherwood, Under Secretary of State for Air who had attended a Defence Committee meeting with the Secretary of State for Air, Sir Archibald Sinclair. Lord Sherwood conveyed the following message, "The biggest loss is that of the 1,584 4,000lb bombs, which compares with a monthly production of about 1,800. Our stocks, however, are satisfactory, amounting before this loss to about 17,000 bombs."

What men they could get, what with the wartime shortages of fit men, were put to clearing the railway tracks of mud as quickly as they could under the circumstances. Royal Engineers laid barbed wire along the 1,040 yards of wrecked fencing around the RAF Fauld boundary and put up notices warning civilians to stay clear. The Italians, having no stores to work in, were put to laying a water supply pipe from Hanbury.

The American Army was lending every assistance, both in men and equipment and supplied a giant bulldozer to improve access to roads. The GPO had been busy repairing telephone communications.

At Burton police station calls and telegrams were coming in, one after the other, from relatives of men working in the area. All they could say was, "We will let you know when we have news." *Meanwhile, it is alleged that 'red tape' is keeping relatives of service personnel employed on the dump, in suspense, as to whether their menfolk are dead or alive*

Police at Burton, who have been swamped with telephone calls and telegrams from anxious wives and parents all over the country, state themselves, "This 'red tape' and complete blackout by the Air Ministry on information, is causing a great deal of distress, but we can do nothing about it."

The policemen there were stifled for news, "The blooming RAF– they won't tell us a thing. Their security is so complete and the secrecy so rigid that all we can tell these poor folk is 'Sorry, we can't tell you anything'. It's a flipping disgrace!"

The Aberdeen Evening Express, dated 29th November 1944, printed:

"There is now no hope of reaching the 130 RAF men and workers buried 100 feet below ground in gas chambers at the Service dump hear Burton-on-Trent, which exploded two days ago.

I learn this morning that rescue efforts may be abandoned indefinitely, in view of the insurmountable difficulties facing mines rescue workers from six counties and an 'army' of Civil Defence workers.

The death roll may now even top the 160 figure.

One of the workers at the dump, who escaped with his life when the explosion rocked farm and houses, shook towns and villages fifty miles away, told the reporter:

"There has been no definite check-up on the numbers of civilian and RAF personnel who were in the dump at the time. Six Italian co-operators were working with us. I feel sure there are more than 160 men buried in the chambers."

CHAPTER 26

REPORTS OF SABOTAGE

Reports of sabotage were bandied around, not helped by the secrecy surrounding the explosion imposed by the Air Ministry and Wing Commander Kings.

Buildings for miles around had been damaged, even as far as Derby. People there didn't know what had happened. There were all sorts of rumours going around. This was made worse by the Air Ministry keeping a tight lid on any information being released.

"The German's have let a bomb go."

Others said, "I don't think so, I saw no planes flying over."

The Nazi propaganda machine had seized on the event, and it was not long before Lord Haw Haw (announcer on the English-language propaganda radio programme *Germany Calling* broadcast by Nazi Germany) was on the German wireless, claiming a German V bomb had hit the ammunition dump

Propaganda Minister for the Third Reich, Joseph Göbbels, sent out a fake news broadcast, supposedly coming from Stockholm. "It now transpires from London that this explosion was the result of a bombardment with a German V weapon."

Two days after the explosion, this supposedly 'top secret' ammunition dump and the explosion had got into the German newspapers. An account was featured in the Volkischer Beobachter (The People's Observer). Here is the translation:

**'English Bomb Store Explodes
Hundreds of Dead/V2 the cause?**

More than 200 civilians were killed, according to English newspaper witness accounts, in a terrible explosion in Burton-on-Trent.

The number of soldiers and workers who lost their lives has not been made known.

In the explosion of the RAF bomb store near the Midlands town of Burton, the bomb provision for many hundreds of air attacks was blown up, the military has reported.

The cause of the explosion given was that a smaller bomb exploded and detonated the whole bomb store.

Few people, however, believe this explanation. They point out that bomb stores are, as a rule, laid out in such a way that in the case of part of the store blowing up, the damage is limited to a certain room. It is, therefore, not surprising that the Burton catastrophe is being linked with the V2 (rocket).

The numbers of victims is still not clear. RAF crews put the figure at 200. Local people likewise estimate the same toll.

The explosion could be felt in a radius of 80 miles. One village in the area of the explosion was wiped off the face of the earth.

The Day the Sun Disappeared, 27 Nov 1944

Houses fell over together like cardboard homes and were then blown metres high into the air, along with the people, who could not save themselves in the air-raid shelters, cattle, and farm equipment. The ground around the seat of the explosion trembled and swayed like a severe earthquake. A worker, taking part in the rescue operation, gave the following description of the effects of the explosion: "It was terrible and incredible. The earth swayed as if the ground had been taken from under your feet. A whole hill was swept away and another rose up in its place. It was impossible to get near to the site of the explosion, but we could look into the huge crater."

Great masses of people, mainly women, stand round the scene of the accident, which has been cordoned off by the police, and ask after their relatives. With welding equipment, they try to free the many people who have been buried alive.

A police officer said: 'It is extremely difficult to establish the exact number of dead. Dozens of people have disappeared without trace and no-one knows whether they have been torn into pieces or if they are still alive. That's the position. We don't know where they are, or where they've gone.'

This report had been brought back by a prisoner of war, Mr Gardiner, from Stepenhill, who had been held in a British work camp at Auschwitz after being captured. He pocketed a cutting from the newspaper describing the explosion while fetching medical supplies from a chemist in occupied Poland.

(Excerpt taken from the Burton Mail, November 28 1994.)

The Day the Sun Disappeared, 27 Nov 1944

There were still rumours going around at this time that the explosion could have been caused by Italian sabotage or an enemy air-raid.

"They've got Ities working there. I bet one of them set off one of the bombs to get their own back on us. Maybe he was on Hitler's side and didn't want Italy to change sides?"

"Or it could have been the IRA – I wouldn't put it past them." Other people were saying.

The story that was promoted and didn't seem to want to die, no matter how much people said it was nonsense - was a theory bandied about by Alex Savidge and his father Tom, who survived the explosion.

They were convinced that German secret weapons were to blame.

Alex Savidge was a soldier on embarkation leave in Burton at the time.

He would go from town to town preaching his theories. Ladies would be out in their coats covering their wrap-around pinafores and turbans, hiding their curlers, along with the walking wounded, newspaper men, farmers, shopkeepers and labourers to listen to him speak.

At one event, while standing on his soap box and getting a crowd around him, he started, "It is my belief," he said, "that this talk of the civilian armourers and RAF being to blame for disregarding regulations, is just a ruse, using them as scapegoats to cover the fact that the explosion was detonated by enemy action.

I have it on good authority that V2 bombs have been launched by the Germans from bases across the Channel. These fly supersonically and you don't know they are overhead until they land on their targets. I believe the explosion was the result of an attack by a converted Ju 88. I know this as advancing American forces found Ju 88s converted into flying bombs with a 7,700lb warhead. They are flown to the target by an FW190 fighter on a superstructure built over the Ju 88, where the pilot would lock them on and disengage them at up to 32,000 feet.

For those not in the know, these Ju 88 bombers were originally built to withstand dives of up to 400mph and could easily have reached more than supersonic speeds in its 17km dive on the target. What's more, at 32,000 feet, our radar defences wouldn't be able to pick them up, the attacking aircraft can easily fool Allied defences."

There was a lot of heckling at this point from total non-believers in his theory. Someone shouted out, "We all know these V2 bombs can't get as far as Staffordshire."

But Alex shouted down the hecklers.

"To support my theory", he continued, "I know that survivors of the explosion have reported the ground rising up about a foot underneath them, just before the big explosion."

Alex' father, Tom, standing at Alex' side, then spoke up, "I myself witnessed smoke from an explosion, rising from the hillside around the side of the disaster, several seconds before the main underground detonation occurred. This, I believe, is an event consistent with a supersonic attack."

Alex returned to his soapbox, "But why, I ask you, has there been this cover up? We've all heard talk of a possible atom bomb being developed – a bomb to end the war. I don't know how far we or the Americans have got with this, but they're obviously looking at developing it. The War Office, the Pentagon and the Allied

The Day the Sun Disappeared, 27 Nov 1944

General Staff want to keep this secret, but secrets have a habit of getting out. What if the Germans have infiltrated the Americans, got their secrets, and even reached such a degree of progress with remote-fired weaponry or that the Allies already understood that such long range weapons might have the capability to deliver an atom bomb."

"A lot of 'what ifs", someone shouted out in the crowd.

"Ah, but what if?" Alex replied. "You know what the War Office is like, everyone kept hush hush – but we all knew about this ammunition site, so there's no reason to think the Germans didn't know about it and the other bomb sites around. Which one is going to be next?"

Alex even appeared on the wireless to promote his theory and even came up with a more outrageous notion that it could have been a uranium bomb! He had based his theory on the report of a farmer, John Bowley, who was interviewed on the same wireless programme, having bought a Geiger counter at an auction and, plying it over his field, it began to tick violently.

There was some discussion in the programme and basically ended with the producer stating, "Yes, a Geiger counter would have found iron from the bombs scattered across the land, but Geiger counters are very poor at detecting uranium, so that blows your theory out of the water. Also, I have consulted military intelligence and Germany is nowhere near making a nuclear bomb and there is nothing to back up this theory."

The Day the Sun Disappeared, 27 Nov 1944

Now the sun has been blanked out.
Underground, in pitch black, bereft of light
Blind men crawl and choke for air.
Above, rescuers surveying the blight.
Now the sun has been blanked out.

CHAPTER 27

CORPORAL ARMOURER, L.W. POYNTON

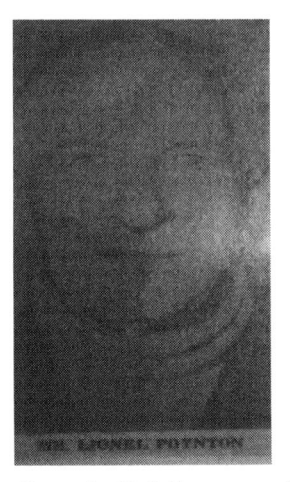

I, RAF Corporal Armourer, L W Poynton had been posted to Fauld from RAF Kirkham in July 1944. For three years I had been an instructor at Kirkham and had a detailed knowledge of bombs.

I was concerned about the flagrant disobedience of orders when dismantling bombs that I asked for my immediate superior, Sergeant Stanley Game, to come with me on a visit to the mine, so that he might alert senior RAF officers. I didn't feel that the Commanding Officer, Group Captain R J Storrar to be knowledgeable enough in bomb disposal to assist in this matter and Squadron Leader L H Anness, who I'd met in the canteen, had only been on site for less than three months and he was extremely busy as acting Chief Equipment Officer, in the absence of a permanent replacement, so not the right person to ask. I arranged to meet Sergeant Game on the morning of

The Day the Sun Disappeared, 27 Nov 1944

November 27th, as I knew Group Captain Storrar was going on leave that morning. I met Sergeant Game to show him the mine. "I am really interested in viewing the workings of the mine, corporal. It is my first time down in one of these MU complexes." Sergeant Game was saying.

"Yes, sir. I don't know how interesting you will find it but I am concerned about work practices and would like you to have the opportunity to observe where the various RAF personnel are working and what their duties entail." I replied.

At about 10.15am I was taking Game through the small arms area. "This area is known as the 'new area', sir. You can see here two Aircraftsmen working on 1,000lb medium case bombs. Their job is to remove the nose and tail plugs, where possible, and remove the exploder container complete."

"You say, 'where possible', corporal. What if this is not possible?"

"Well, sir. If the Aircraftsmen get into difficulties, so to speak, they have to remove the composition explosives from the exploder pocket and collect it in an ammunition box. As it happens, it looks like one of the LACs is actually engaged in chiselling out the composition explosives as we speak. As this is a dangerous task, the work is carried out under the supervision of the Ammunition Inspectorate Department."

We talked to the LACs for a few minutes and an AID Examiner, Mr Saunders came up to join us. The lad chiselling out the CE (composition explosive) from the exploder pocket was called Thomas Bailey. He was a young lad, just 23-years-old. He was working with another Leading Aircraftman (LAC), Henry Charles Fairbanks, who looked in his late 30s.

The Day the Sun Disappeared, 27 Nov 1944

Then I led Sergeant Game back to the 'old area'. I heard an anxious voice calling out for the lamp lad. I believe it was Saunders, an AID examiner – calling for extra light. My thoughts were possibly he and Nicklin (AID viewer) had found something strange when inspecting the bombs and required a bit of extra light. A young lad, about 15 years old, answered the call. I then saw him disappear towards the 'new area'. I'd seen him before – his name was Lewis Frow, a trainee electrician.

On carrying on we came across a gang of Italian former prisoners-of-war, supervised by a Leading Aircraftsman as they stencilled small arms ammunition boxes. Then we carried on to another group of Italians who were working near the main line.

"Ammunition boxes are stacked up to the roof, sir and, as you can see, this has left the entrance very narrow. You will have to walk sideways to get through into the gallery, sir."

As we exited the gallery of the 'new area', Sergeant Game turned back to speak to the LAC. Just at that moment there was a loud boom and a terrific blast of warm air. I was physically picked up and catapulted against the wall, in this blast.

When I landed I found myself on the main road, underground, but the sergeant, who had turned back, was still in the entrance to the gallery. Then the lights went out and there was another even greater explosion and I was thrown to the ground.

There were ammunition boxes flying around like flies. I put my arm out to try to prevent myself being hit by the boxes and hurriedly got to my feet. I couldn't see a thing. It was complete blackout.

"Sergeant Game, sir. Are you there, sir?" I called.

The Day the Sun Disappeared, 27 Nov 1944

There was no answer, so I called out a couple of times more. I could feel myself sweating. I was completely disorientated. The hair on the back of my head was standing up. What direction was I facing? I had no idea. I stretched my arms out but could feel nothing, no walls, just boxes of ammunition. I tried to walk, but stumbled against crates of ammunition that had been blasted out, and fell against them. I got up on my knees. The ground was the only contact I had with anything. I had never imagined being blind before, or how a blind person gets about and I was scared. I kept calling out, but no-one answered me. All these questions kept running around in my thoughts. Had everyone been killed? Was I the only one to survive? Was there going to be another explosion – would that then be the end of me?

I started coughing, there was a lot of dust swirling around. I started crawling around in the darkness, pushing the boxes aside as I came across them. I knew I was about three quarters of a mile inside the mine. I crawled around trying to find Sergeant Game, in the direction I thought he might be, but the dust was thick and I was finding it difficult to breathe, so I about turned and headed in what I hoped was the direction to get out.

The Day the Sun Disappeared, 27 Nov 1944

(Alabaster broken amongst ammunition boxes. Image: donated by John Cooper)

I suppose I had gone about 150 yards, although I had no way to judge, just reckoning on two shuffles on my knees for a yard. Just then I heard a voice, someone calling out. I was so relieved.

"I'm here." I called out into the blackness.

"Is that you, Poynton?"

"Yes, it's me."

"I recognised your voice. I heard you calling out for Sergeant Game."

"Stay where you are," I said, "I'll try to make my way to you." I got up and immediately fell over a pile of ammunition boxes in front of me. I fell back onto my knees and somehow or other

The Day the Sun Disappeared, 27 Nov 1944

managed to find the railway track. I knew if I followed the track, I'd be going the right way.

I eventually found the other man, Ken McLeod, and put our arms around each other in relief. This was no time for formalities. "I'm so pleased to find someone alive. I thought I'd die here."

"We need to get out of here but, don't worry, all we need to do is follow the rail."

We were standing, trying to follow the railway line in the pitch black. Then I heard Ken stumble.

"Blast in hell, that hurt! I've gone down on the rail, bashed the side of my knee. Hold on a minute, I've got to try and find something to wrap round it." Then I heard what sounded like ripping of material. Getting down on his knees with a few grunts issuing from him, he began feeling around. "Aw, I must have tripped over a lever to change the points. Oh damn, that means we've been going the wrong way all this time."

"We'd best turn back then, Ken and start crawling, if you can manage on your busted knee. We don't want either of us to fall and injure ourselves even more.

So, we turned round. When we had got our bearings, we decided to hold onto the other person. Every so often, especially when the rail made a turn, we were calling out, "Anybody there?"

Whispering, McLeod was saying, "I don't know about you, but I heard this sort of 'crump' sound and I was thrown against a wall. Then this was followed by a huge explosion which threw me to the ground. Then there was a terrific rush of air whooshing me out of the cavern into the main railway line area. We were all pulled down and blown out of the cavern like leaves. Then the lights went out and it was pitch black. I could feel dust and grit blowing about.

The Day the Sun Disappeared, 27 Nov 1944

I got a few minor scrapes from the alabaster, but nothing worse, apart from my knee that is."

"Yes, the same with me."

Ken continued, "I'd heard someone call for the lamp lad. Obviously they wanted to inspect something they'd found unusual in the bombs."

"Maybe a detonator had been left in one of the bombs, or one of the bombs was corroded".

It was the boy, Lewis Frow, I saw answering the call for more light. I saw him go down the slope to the 'new area', about 100 yards away."

"I think that must be the end of him and everyone else down there."

"I was working with four Italians and two other airmen, in the small arms ammunition area. The Italians were doing the donkey work, feeding us boxes of ammunition down the conveyor belt, while we inspected it to see if it could be used again. Those Italians and airmen must be dead."

Ken continued, "Thing is, Lionel, just a day or two ago, I saw four 1,000lb armour-piercing bombs on a truck in a siding. They were all jumbled up in a mess and covered in mud. They should have been inspected as soon as they arrived. I've an inkling they weren't, or not checked over thoroughly, what with everything having to be done on the quick, so to speak."

"You may well be right, Ken, and look what's happened. I dread to think how many others have been killed."

"Hold on a minute, Lionel. Did you hear that? I thought I heard voices. Hey, we're here." Ken shouted, fairly softly, fearing a possible rock fall. Several yards on they came across three or four more airmen. One of them was Leading Aircraftman Michael Watson.

Michael told us that five minutes before the explosion, he had gone in search of the correct skids to load four 4,000lb bombs onto the railway trucks, to get them out of the mine.

One of the others was LAC Gibbard. He told us his story. "I'd been working labelling ammunition boxes, lifting a box up, when this massive gush of air blasted through, and a thud. I was lifted off my feet and pinned to the roof with the force of the blast. It was a horrible feeling. I had no control – just suspended there, hanging, like in the Wall of Death, at a fairground. A second or two later, although it seemed like an eternity, I found myself falling back down. I landed with a thump, bashing my knee against something and my elbow feels pretty tender. Thing is, I didn't hear an actual bang."

We all agreed we'd had the same experience.

Young airman, Malcolm Kidd was in that group too. It had been he, who had warned Squadron Leader Anness of the dangerous methods being used in the mine, had been working in the old mine. He managed, breathlessly, to tell us, "I felt a blast of hot air through the old mine tunnel, followed by a blast of cold. Then everything went black.

I'd been working in a big cavern off the main line, quite a massive cavern, about 100ft by 50ft and that's probably what saved my life, the force of the explosion went up the main avenue.

Malcolm Kidd, as we were groping in the dark, actually walked straight into a big, heavy locomotive, that's how pitch black it was. Imagine, a huge locomotive, but being black, and not a glimmer of light anywhere, the locomotive could not be seen. We were all relying on touch alone. We kept walking and walking then, just then, someone shouted out, "I can see light, just a pinhole of light, but it's definitely light." We all peered into the distance. "It must be the main entrance."

"Yes, but it looks like it's had a rock fall around it. As it happened, a driver had actually left a locomotive with its light on, which helped as we could see vaguely where we were going and actually stand up. We're getting there, lads." and a whispered cheer went up, again keeping any noise to the minimum. "Ay up, I smell gas," one of us said. We all sniffed, and he was right. Gas was creeping up on us. So, we all tried to up our pace.

Malcolm Kidd started panicking and I put my arm around his shoulder. "Look, there is another light up ahead. Looks like a torch," one of them said. As we got nearer, it turned out to be Mr Higgs the AID viewer and, with the aid of his torch, we were able to scurry out, just in time before the gas hit us. The pin-hole of light we saw was about a foot-and-a-half in diameter, so we could just about squeeze through to get to the outside.

On finally getting out, we could see the shockwave had set off boxes of incendiary bombs and they were blazing away. Malcolm Kidd was the first to scramble out of the mine and, there in front of him, found the body of a policemen. Half his head had been blown away (that may have been the policemen colleague of Len Ashmore). He turned him over. He screamed, "I thought he was just leaning out of the sentry box but no." Then Malcolm just ran.

"I don't remember screaming, but I think I must have," he told PC Mackay, "and I just ran, anywhere to get any from that grizzly sight. I suppose I was in such a state that I didn't know what I was doing. In fact I nearly got shot by the RAF Regiment by mistake. I think they must have been out shooting cattle. A stranger physically stopped me, sat me down and spoke calmly to me. I don't know who the stranger was but he gave me a drink of whisky from his hip flask and directed me to report back to camp."

.....

The rest of us, on finally getting out, ascertained it had been about three quarters of an hour since the explosion.

That wasn't the end of the danger though. As soon as we got out we were being rained on by bits of incendiary bombs. There was mud, water and dead bodies here and there. The smell of the explosives was overwhelming and we started coughing and choking.

The first thing we saw was the dead Ministry of Defence policeman, who Malcolm Kidd had seen. He had obviously been on duty at the mine entrance. His head had been blown off.

In the yard outside of the two main entrances to the ammunition dump, before the explosion, air ministry policeman, Constable Leslie Inger, was among a number of officers who had been on duty that day.

From a small hut, a tannoy operator had been directing traffic in and out of the mine.

At the moment of the explosion, Inger was standing beside one of the hut windows.

Another air ministry policeman on duty near the mine entrance had his stomach ripped open by the force of the blast. Two more of Inger's colleagues, who were standing near to each other, were struck by the shock waves – one was killed.

The Day the Sun Disappeared, 27 Nov 1944

We were all given a shot in the arm and I was taken to the American military hospital at Sudbury, where I spent three days, then sent onto the RAF Cosford Hospital. One of the other airmen was in a very shocked state. Eventually I was sent home on sick leave. I then attended the official court of inquiry and the final inquest.

I found out that I was the last man to get out of the gallery alive. Three days after the explosion, the bodies of Sergeant Game and some six Italian ex-prisoners of war were found buried under tons of ammunition boxes. The body of young Lewis Frow was never found.

Thomas Bailey, the lad we had talked to inside, was probably blown to pieces. His body was never found. The AID probably wasn't paying much attention as it looked like young Bailey, against protocol, had probably picked up a brass chisel and a hammer as he was having such a problem getting the explosive out.

"Sergeant Game was the unluckiest of the lot" I said at the inquest. "He had never been in the mine before – this was his first visit."

The section of the mine where the sergeant and others perished has remained sealed and, because of the potential danger of some unexploded bombs still being there, it may remain so forever.

Even in Ken McLeod's shocked state and on sick leave, he volunteered to help with the rescue, going back that night with two others. He was lucky as he got out with just a few grit marks.

"The nurse at the First Aid post gave us face masks soaked in disinfectant. Each man then collected a shovel and went down into a tunnel, where we were met with the biggest load of thick slime I have ever seen. It was right up to the roof of the tunnel, and the smell was dreadful. We were only allowed down there for about 20 minutes, then others took over while we got some fresh air.

He was up all night with the rescue work. He noticed that the guy he spoke to, asking for volunteers, had obviously had to claw his way out, as his nails were torn off.

We were told that the duty nurse desperately needed clean water, so I and a few others collected water cans and took them to the first aid room, where the injured were and a few dead bodies.

"We had to help carry a body out, carrying him on a stretcher along the lip of the crater. There was only about five inches of slimy mud to walk on. I will never forget losing my footing and slipping down into the crater with the body on top of us. As I moved him off me, he moaned and I thought he was still alive, but it was just the air coming out of his lungs. It was terrible. I'd had enough. It was all just too much to take.

A few days later we took the body of one of the airmen that had been killed to Derby Train Station, where he was put on the overnight train back to his mother in Crieff, Scotland. That was LAC Deuchars.

The next day our task was to go to somewhere where debris had fallen to see if we could find any bodies. We had long sticks and I was prodding about with it. I felt something soft, and I held my breath, expecting the worst, but it turned out to be a soft pillow.

McLeod, in his report to PC Mackay, said, "I think I kept sane by keeping busy for a long while after. One thing I am still nervous about though, is going to the toilet on my own. I think it is being on my own in a small confined space - I start shaking and have to have all the lights on.

The digging and searching for bodies went on for about three weeks, clearing up the mud, but no further bodies were found. Every evening when I went to see my girlfriend, the family would ask me if there was any new of Lewis Frow, the brother. Later he was declared dead. We had a church parade in memory of those who died.

The one thing that disappointed me on the station was that a commendation certificate was the only award made to the nurse in charge, an elderly lady, who worked all hours of the day for almost a month. How she kept going I will never know. She was a wonderful woman and deserved the George Medal, but they went to the Officers – one of whom was on leave at the time.

I stayed at Fauld until my demob in 1946.

Someone tried to explain why I had been saved and the others hadn't. I seems that, as there was a long and narrow passage from the new area – where the explosion occurred – to the old area, this prevented an explosion of even greater magnitude. Indeed, in the old area, there was probably about ten times more high explosive, which fortunately was not detonated.

Had the detonation wave spread to this area, it was reasonable to assume that the resulting explosion and devastation would have been at least ten times greater. Burton itself might well have been badly hit by the blast.

The explosion produced some freak results. Although I escaped with shock and minor injuries, another man, a mile away, was killed. And despite the tremendous explosion, only one glass window in the RAF main building at Fauld was broken, yet windows were shattered over a wide area, even as far afield as Coventry."

What actually appears to have happened was that one bomb exploded, and the rush of air acted as a detonator for all the bombs in the dump, causing an earthquake effect to be felt many miles' away. This is why people were saying there was a first explosion in one area, followed by the massive explosion of uplifted ground and the mushroom cloud effect, some distance away.

"When I'd properly recovered I returned to help shift all the bombs that were still intact from Fauld to RAF Tatenhill. There was no let-up in those days. I was put on night shift and sent back to inspect all the remaining bombs to see which were serviceable."

Information taken from Burton Mail, November 28 1994

Ambrose Patterson, George Powell and Frederick William Slater were among those named who did not make it. The body of Sergeant Game was found later that day, beneath boxes of ammunition.

The bodies of Caporale Rocco Novello and Soldato Salvatore Trovato were recovered on 1 December and those of Caporale Luigi Scuto, Soldato Emilia Di Paolo, Soldato Aldo Lanzoni and Soldato Salvatore Ruggeri were discovered eleven days later on 8 December. They had been buried under tons of ammunition boxes and blasted rock.

No trace of the men working in the 'new area' were ever found, - Leading Aircraftmen Bailey –next of kin was his father, living in Wednesbury

The Day the Sun Disappeared, 27 Nov 1944

H Fairbanks – leaving a wife, living in Battersea, SW11

AID examiner Thomas Sander,

AID viewers James Brassington and Frederick Nicklin. Electrician's mate Alfred Shipley – leaving a wife, living in Burton

Trainee electricians Frederick Campbell – leaving a wife, from Harehill.

Lewis Frow – next of kin was his father, from Tutbury

Charles Hogg – leaving a wife, from Tutbury

Gerald Mahon – next of kin his mother, living in Newborough

Albert Mellor and Bert Stanley of the Air Ministry Works Departments.

The Day the Sun Disappeared, 27 Nov 1944

CHAPTER 28

LEWIS FROW

(Taken from the Burton Mail, 28 November 1994)

Fifteen-year –old Lewis Frow had just left school and started work as an apprentice electrician up at the dump. He was living with his family in Castle Street, Tutbury.

At 10.50am on the day of the blast, he was called underground to replace light bulbs.

Lewis' sister, Joyce wrote that at about 11.10am the whole place where she was started to shake. We all thought bombs had been dropped. We went outside onto the fire escape where we could see this huge dark cloud a long way off. When the tremors stopped we were told to go back to work. We found out a little later it was 21 MU at RAF Fauld that had blown up.

Lewis Frow, four years before he was killed

My first thought was my brother, Lewis, knowing he worked there. I approached the foreman, "My brother is working at RAF Fauld. I'm very worried for him. Could I have permission please to go?"

He agreed and I got on my bike, after seeing that mum was OK, and cycled there.

The Day the Sun Disappeared, 27 Nov 1944

"Could you tell me if Lewis Frow is safe, please?"

The officer looked through a series of names on a listing, while I impatiently waited, twiddling my thumbs nervously.

"Ah yes, Lewis Frow is safe and will be returning home as usual."

I was so pleased I jumped on my bike again and cycled home to await his return. My sister, Mary, had arrived home too.

Lewis' normal hour of return came and went. Mum and I were getting frantic. "Where is he?"

"This isn't right. Something happened."

It was dark now and had started raining. We sat up all night. Every time we heard a noise, a car door or people talking, we went outside to investigate. We could see emergency vehicles going by regularly.

"Oh, I feel so helpless. We haven't even got a telephone to call anyone. I'll go and try the phone box", Mary said. She came back, "I think all the lines to RAF Fauld are down. I just couldn't get through."

"That officer was useless, telling me that Lewis was safe." I moaned.

It wasn't until a few days later that we got a telegram, which read, "Your son, Lewis Frow, is missing and must now be presumed dead,"

Mum snatched the telegram off me, whimpering, "I don't believe it." and, in her distress, threw the telegram onto the fire.

We wanted to send a telegram to dad, who had just been transferred to the Ministry of Defence in Scotland but, because of the clamp down on information, we were not able to get a telegram

The Day the Sun Disappeared, 27 Nov 1944

to him for another two days. We wanted to put, "RAF Fauld explosion, Lewis missing" but all we were allowed to say was, "Come home, Lewis missing." We weren't allowed to put anything about the explosion or RAF Fauld.

Lewis' body was never found, the youngest of the 18 bodies never to be recovered, their graves a bog of mud, from the overnight rain.

We heard later that Ken McLeod, a young Scot posted to RAF Fauld about 18 months earlier, was inspecting ammunition in one of the underground caverns in the old area of the mine, when he heard an anxious voice calling for the lamp lad. "I saw Lewis answer the call and walk to his death. Only the teenager's belt, coat and lunchbox were ever found. McLeod's sergeant, Sergeant Game, who was with McLeod at the time, just moments before the blast was also killed. McLeod got trapped underground after the explosion but he managed to find his way out of the mine, with other airmen.

Five months later, on 8 May 1945, Ken McLeod met his future wife at a dance held at the RAF station at Fauld, held to celebrate VE day – his future wife was Joyce Frow, the sister of Lewis Frow.

Ken McLeod didn't have the heart to tell, Joyce, the sister of Lewis Frow, and who he was now engaged to, that he had seen Lewis just before the eruption, in the heart of the explosion and there was no chance of him being alive. It was just too heart-rending for him to bring up the subject, and he didn't want this to lead to a rift in their relationship. The subject didn't come up until years after their marriage - it just wasn't spoken about. Ken also didn't tell Joyce that he was at the Court of Inquiry, but, to him, the explosion was as clear as day and the memory had not faded.

CHAPTER 29

PETER FORD'S UNDERGROUND MINING

The Air Ministry were surveying various areas underground, for storage of huge quantities of bombs, what with the prospect of war on the horizon, and came across Peter Ford's underground gypsum mines – land that was owned by the Duchy of Lancaster. These mines were 90ft below ground level and the Air Ministry considered they were preferable to some places they had surveyed, which were liable to land falls and flooding. So the Air Ministry bought them from the Duchy of Lancaster in 1937. To start off the Air Ministry stored 10,000 tons of bombs there, but realising war was imminent, they increased this to 24,000 tons.

There wasn't that much to do to convert the mines, just the construction of a 50ft barrier to separate the incendiaries from the high-explosive bombs and a 110ft barrier to isolate the detonator store. However, although the high-explosive bombs were stored under a ceiling of 90ft of ground, the incendiary storage area only had 60ft of ground above and the detonator storage area (the most sensitive of all), had just a depth of 40ft above it.

Peter Ford's already had a single railway line to Scropton, to transport the gypsum, plaster and plasterboards, but the Air Ministry decided it was necessary to build a further line leading direct from the underground storage direct to the railway sidings at Scropton. In the mine, this narrow-gauge railway branched off to service the individual storage locations.

The Day the Sun Disappeared, 27 Nov 1944

In June 1941 the Air Ministry purchased an adjacent mine from Peter Ford's – the two areas were known as the 'old' and 'new' mine areas. This was not ideal and basically contravened the safety regulations at the time, however, in view of the urgency of the situation, the rules regarding the proximity of operational quarry workings, that would otherwise have precluded the use of Ford's mine, were disregarded.

The Air Ministry agreed to construct a blast barrier (varying from 15 to 50ft in thickness) to protect Ford workers against a possible accidental blast. They also left a 100ft pillar of unmined gypsum (the Castle Hayes Pillar) and constructed a 100ft artificial barrier, to separate the 'old' and 'new' mine areas, which they thought would provide enough safety should there be an incident. Two tunnel entrances, gave access to the 'new' area. one of which was constructed through the 100ft pillar of unmined gypsum.

After the wall, the mine branched towards the working, 140ft below Hanbury Fields farmland.

There were emergency exits and ventilation systems for those working underground.

By 1942 sufficient space had been allocated to provide storage of up to 30,000 bombs and explosives and Fauld became the largest munitions storage in the country.

The Day the Sun Disappeared, 27 Nov 1944

Getting ready for blasting - Donated by Graham Shaw

A party of miners had gone down the gypsum mine that morning, 27th November. It was quite a large party – twenty one miners. It was warm but not too stuffy down there as there was a ventilation shaft that exited into Hanbury Fields Farm, owned by Mr Woolicroft. This ventilation shaft was shared by part of the RAF munitions dump and could act as an emergency exit, if necessary. They ignored it as they passed by, as they passed it every working day. It's like the chimney in the house, you ignore it until it decides not to work efficiently, then you know you've got to get a chimney sweep. So, they knew the ventilation shaft was there but it had become part of the everyday working life.

Fred Bowring started humming, "Heigh ho, heigh ho, it's off to work we go" from a song he'd heard on the wireless that morning from Snow White and the Seven Dwarfs. Some of the others joined in with him. They were all in a good mood. It wasn't all that cold, it was a bit frosty outside, but the mine was warm.

The Day the Sun Disappeared, 27 Nov 1944

They were walking through an underground road, which ran parallel to the ammunition storage (the RAF new area) with their wicker food baskets flung over their shoulders attached to pieces of string. The walk would take about 25 minutes. The wall between the two had been reinforced to ensure it was blast-poof. They were following the rails for getting the loaded trucks back to the surface.

Some of them were talking about the weekend football results. Someone else started changing the words to the Seven Dwarf's song. –'We dig dig dig dig dig dig dig dig up everything in sight and 'We pass pass pass pass pass pass pass pass the alabaster white'.

When they reached the gypsum-face, one hundred and forty feet below the Hanbury Fields farmland, the miners split up into groups. Fred Bowring, was from Hanbury. Just that morning he had been seen walking across Hanbury fields, that covered the mine, to the mine entrance. He was saying to Joseph Cooper, a loco driver, "Mr Woolliscroft, from Hanbury Park Farm, wanted me to stay to do his milking this morning, as he's been ill, but I wanted to be here with my pals. Anyway, I think he managed to get the two lads from the cottage close by Top Farm to help. I believe they are John and Fred Ford. They normally work for Bert Hardwick at Top Farm, which is next to Wooliscroft's farm."

Jack Gorton, who lived in Tutbury, was the leader of one group. He was a big guy but, like Geoff Capes (voted one time as the world's strongest man, but who actually owned canaries) was really tender and caring. George Shepherd and Charlie Gibbs (a 39-year-old blaster and loader) were part of his team. He was a nice looking guy – straight nose and strong chin.

They were ¾ mile from the mine entrance.

The Day the Sun Disappeared, 27 Nov 1944

They were chatting away, general chitchat about what their various wives and children had got up to. "He's a right little youth my Charlie", Charles was talking about his son, Charles Gibbs Jnr, "The wife tells me he's been playing truant again."

"You can't really blame him, Charlie," George Shepherd replied, "I wasn't one for education. I was bored stiff. It all went over me 'ead. I wanted to be out playing footie with the lads."

"Ay, and look where it got yer, down pit. I donna want my lad to end up down here. There's no controlling 'im though. If he goes home there's no-one there as the wife's looking after old Mrs Deauville, so he does his own thing. I'll tan his hide if I find he's been pinching stuff."

Jack Gorton started to say about his eldest daughter, Eileen. "My 11 year old, Eileen is off school with peritonitis. She's at home with the wife, who's looking after the baby. My little Linda's as cute as a plum, just 7½ months old now.

Others were talking football. Not much to talk about as all league matches had been postponed because of the war. Still there had been an international friendly on 14 October 1944 England versus Scotland. England won 6:2.

"That was some match" George Shepherd was saying.

"Yes, the Centre Forward was Tommy Lawton. He scored three of the goals - a hat trick. I bet those Scots were fuming!" Jack Gorton commented.

"Yes, they probably thought they had a chance, what with scoring the first goal."

"They didn't have a hope in hell, though, once Inside Forward, Horatio Carter, and Outside Left, Leslie Smith scored their goals

The Day the Sun Disappeared, 27 Nov 1944

for England. Oh, they had a good try near the end of the game with Scotland getting another goal, but it was just too late. If I can remember, I believe it was Milne and Walker got the Scottish goals."

"No competition!"

The back-breaking work stopped at about 11am as it was time for a tea-break.

At 10 minutes past 11 o'clock everyone felt a dramatic judder that lifted them off their feet, like a lift going down with a thump.

"What was that? the foreman, Arthur Harris bellowed. Just then, there was a second explosion a lot greater than the first. It even lifted the wagon containing almost four tons of gypsum. Everyone was thrown about. Then the electric lights went out.

"Has a bomb gone off?" Charlie Gibbs shouted through the darkness. Let's have some candle-light here from the emergency lamps."

The foreman said, "I think the air shaft should be checked."

Harris (the foreman) went to check and came back, "There's nothing in the air shaft just a barrowful or so of soil" Then said, "Perhaps it's one of Hitler's new-fangled pilotless V bombers."

"I doubt it, gaffer." Charlie Gibbs replied, "They can't get this far. It's probably the other team, blasting the alabaster at their end.

"Well, we seem to be ok, so back to work everyone."

William Watson (the loco driver) then arrived in his loco to where Fred Bowring and Percy Priestley were, to pick up the last load of stone. "What's with the lights?" he asked.

"Didn't you feel the tremor, Willy?"

The Day the Sun Disappeared, 27 Nov 1944

"Well, I was about a mile out from the main entrance, on my little loco, when I felt my loco waver, but she makes too much noise to hear anything. Then the lights went out."

"Well, we were all chucked around here, some of us were sent flying into the rock face. Don't know what it was but I know I'm going to have some fair bruises."

Anyway, they all carried on working and, by 12 o'clock, they had already mined over four tons of gypsum and this had been loaded onto the narrow gauge trucks ready to be hauled by William Watson's loco back to the surface. William Watson was about 46 and had lived in Hanbury all his working life.

Unknown to them, the explosion had breached the concrete barrier which separated the dump from the access tunnel along which they had travelled earlier that morning. A cloud of carbon monoxide gas was working insidiously towards them.

A few of the miners then decided to try to find out what had caused the tremor, including Fred Bowring, who lived in Hanbury (his brother Tom worked at Ford's, on the surface). "Right, I'll go along and investigate." Harris said, "You others stay here." He went along with Harris and Percy Priestley. They were about three-quarters of a mile from the mine entrance and one hundred and forty feet below Hanbury Fields Farm.

We carried on loading while we were waiting.

Percy Priestley came back a little while later, it must have been about 11.25am, and told us that the loco wouldn't be able to pass through as the 'gobs' had gone (that is a pit term referring to dirt compressed into holes where the alabaster had been removed, to add support). The 'gobs' had blown out and covered the track.

The Day the Sun Disappeared, 27 Nov 1944

This was about 11.25am. "Bowring and Harris have gone on towards the main entrance on foot." Priestley added.

Some of the others - George Smith, Joseph Cooper, Harry Shepherd, Jack Wright and Herbert Morris with William Watson (the loco driver) then followed Fred Bowring and Arthur 'Massey' Harris (the foreman) making their way back along the tunnel, passing the air shaft after about 250 yards. Harry Shepherd was the oldest miner there, still working at the age of 73 and had lived in the district all of his life. George Smith was 61.

The air shaft, with a series of escape ladders, looked to them like it was blocked, with the door to the shaft being damaged, so they decided to proceed to the entrance. Had they looked more carefully, however, they would have realised that this escape route was in fact intact.

Jack Gorton and Charlie Gibbs had been among those who had stayed behind, along with James Treadwell and Percy Priestley.

After a while Charlie said, "Hey, Jack, what's keeping that group who went to check things out? They should have been back by now. Do you think we should investigate?"

"It's strange," Jack said, "Yes, go have a look."

So Charlie went off, holding a lit candle. All few minutes later, he returned, "There's gas, I smelt it. Smells like burnt sugar. I didn't want to go further but I think the others must have got caught up in it. We need a rescue party.

So, Charlie Gibbs and Jack Gorton joined the rescue party along with James Treadwell and Percy Priestley.

. . . .

The Day the Sun Disappeared, 27 Nov 1944

Unbeknownst to them, the explosion from the bomb had released deadly carbon monoxide gas, which was filtering stealthily towards the miners.

…………..

In the group that had gone ahead, they realised there was gas but had to carry on to try to find Fred Bowring and Massey Harris and try to get out. The fumes were beginning to get to them though. Their eyes were stinging and Willy started wheezing, trying to get more air.

About 250yards past the air shaft they found Fred Bowring. He was lying on his front by the side of the track. Willy turned him over and undid his shirt in a futile attempt to get him air, but at that moment, Fred's head just slew to one side. He had died at that moment….

Realising there was nothing that could be done for Fred, Willy Watson looked up from the dead body of his work colleague then, even though his eyes were stinging and watering, he spied something ahead and exclaimed, "I can see a light from a lamp just a little bit further on. There's someone else not got very far. You others go on, I'll have to rest up here a little."

"I'll stay with you," Harry said, "My legs don't seem to want to carry me and I feel dizzy." So, Joseph Cooper and Jack Wright went to investigate, as neither Willy nor Charles had the strength to go on. Joe Cooper called back, "It's Massey (meaning Harris, the foreman) …..and he's dead…".Then Joe started coughing violently. "Come on, we need to get out of here," and started on again towards the tunnel entrance. Wright came staggering back, but then, uttering, "It's got me, it's got me," collapsed. The others could just about see Cooper struggling on ahead to get to the outside, coughing and spluttering. He was staggering, weaving from side to side, then they saw him fall – the gas had got him.

Willy Watson had seen enough. Joseph Cooper was dead. He appeared to have got some distance to safety, together with Harris, but they were overcome before they could cover the last few yards. He shouted to Harry Shepherd and George Smith "Come on, let's get out or it will have us." Herbert Morris grabbed hold of Jack Wright to give him a helping hand to get out.

They made their way back towards the entrance, Willy Watson with Harry Shepherd and Smith behind him, crawling to keep as low as possible, away from the gas, every inch of their bodies aching. It was the only way out as, to all intents and purposes, the air shaft had been blocked.

They hadn't got far, about 40 yards… just 40 yards but every movement was causing excruciating agony, like climbing Mount Everest without oxygen. The tunnel was spinning and their heads felt like they were bursting with the pain. They felt woozy and nauseous, coughing and gasping for breath, trying desperately to rid their lungs of the toxic gas. Willy Watson just couldn't go any further and, try as he might, his legs went from under him and he collapsed, but, amazingly, he continued to crawl, down on all fours, such was his desperation, his hold on life, in trying to reach safety. He just couldn't make it, though – the end of the tunnel was out of his grasp, just 70 yards past the air shaft towards the end of the mine, and he eventually lost consciousness….. but, somehow or other, through his frantic desire to live, his eyes flickered open. George Smith, Harry Shepherd and Fred Bowring lay dead near him. He couldn't move and he was still wavering in and out of consciousness.

The Day the Sun Disappeared, 27 Nov 1944

In the gloomy passage, just lit by their torches and passing the vent, Jack Gorton and Charles Gibbs, from the team that were following on behind, came across a body. "Hey, it's Willy Watson, the loco driver." Charlie called out. He was lying on the ground. Charlie checked him out, called his name and tried to sit him up, working his arm like a pump. "Hey, see that, his eyes just flickered – he's alive - looks like he's out cold though. Here, grab hold of him. Let's get him back through the relief door, as they'll be fresh air there."

Charles Gibbs and Jack Gorton carried on, looking for the others, covering their mouths and noses with handkerchiefs to try to keep the gas out but they were coughing, trying to catch their breath. Their faces had taken on a red hue from the gas inhalation, but they were going to save their friends, if it cost them their lives. None of them had gas masks on them, having left them up on the surface. They never thought that gas would get to them down in the mine. They passed through two pockets of gas. They found Harry Shepherd – dead, then they saw George Smith ahead and all of a sudden they saw him collapse, unconscious.

Jack said, "You two youths, go and see if you can clear the air shaft. We need to get these men out to the fresh air." Alfred Page and Fred Lowe went back to try to clear the air shaft of soil, which they managed to do, then got up the ladders to run for help. Jack Gorton had carried on.

Jack Gorton's vision was blurring by now and the mine seemed to be spinning. He felt ill. A piece of rock dropped down on his hand, that's when he realised he hadn't actually felt it, a sure sign that the gas had got to him. Jack decided to go back to the air shaft to get a bit of fresh air. He then collapsed. He was dragged back to safety, half unconscious.

The Day the Sun Disappeared, 27 Nov 1944

After a while, in the fresh air, Jack began to feel better. He wasn't going to give up though and went back down again. He knew there was an emergency door leading to the adjoining mine, that belonging to J C Staton & Co. He had worked for them before and thought he could find his way through their mine, dragging any still alive colleagues he could with him.

Jack went with a few of the others and burst the door open, but it was totally black as well. He realised he had no idea where to go and didn't recognise that part of the mine. So he went back to the air shaft.

Jack was in no fit state to walk by then and the rest of the crew, with Charles Gibbs dragged Jack Gorton and George Smith back, crawling with them slung over their backs and got them up to safety, hoisting them up on their backs and tying ropes around them that their rescuers had thrown down from above. Jack had collapsed on the third platform of the shaft and was taken to Burton Infirmary and detained for thirty six hours. Watson went with him. There were eleven men at the Burton Infirmary, on 28th November, suffering from the effects of the disaster, but none were in danger. Jesse Simpson, of Tutbury, had head and other injuries and Harry Gibson, of Draycott-in-Clay, was slightly hurt.

There was a farmer at the top of the vent, calling down to them, with two RAF men, who commenced hauling them up. Jack never found out who the farmer was, as he was too out of it, but believes it could have been Bert Hardwick of Top Farm, Hanbury, who was also a Civil Defence worker.

Those helping to bring out the workers were Corporal Rock and Corporal Peter, who repeatedly went down the ladder to bring out survivors. Flight Lieutenant J P Lewin had also made his way there, even though he had already spent hours in the RAF mine, attempting to rescue people.

The other miners had been so overcome with the gas fumes that they were too weak to climb unaided up the 80ft of iron ladders, which led to fresh air, but a system of pulleys had been set up. Another farmer from Hanbury was there, 52-year-old Leslie Shotton of Knightsfield Farm (Chairman of the Parish Council), hauling on the pulley with the others. He continued to work, untiringly, to help and succour the stricken relatives, and he helped the police in very many ways.

Willy Watson roused back into consciousness at 1.20pm – 70 yards past the air shaft towards the end of the mine. Around him were the dead bodies of George Smith, Harry Shepherd and Fred Bowring. A few minutes later he found himself being lifted up the airshaft, on a stretcher, by the RAF and Firemen. He was the last to be brought up the shaft. He exclaimed to his rescuers, on looking around him, his voice trembling, almost crying. "What's happened? There are just heaps of mud and huge craters. What's happened to the fields I walk over every morning to get here? I don't recognise anything. What way is home? What's happened to the Goodwin farm – it's all gone?" On being told he was the last to be brought out, he told his rescuers, "It's no good going back down there. The others are all dead."

The gas had claimed the lives of five of the miners. If only they had stopped work after the explosion, and made their way out then, they would have been saved. The toxic gas had permeated through the air vent shared by the RAF dump and the Ford's alabaster tunnels..

Charles Gibbs went back with the rescue party the next morning to direct them, although he was suffering with gas inhalation, as the police and fire service asked him to return to help them. However, the canaries they had with them, died immediately. It wasn't until the Wednesday that the gas had cleared and the dead bodies could be removed from the mine. He didn't go to any of the funerals. He had lost all of his mates. He never got over the loss of his pal, Fred Bowring.

Company Officer Elliott arrived there some time later with his men. They had been down the mine earlier and handed over to the first mines rescue team. They went down the shaft for several hours, with breathing apparatus, bringing up bodies, until their oxygen had depleted.

……..

The carbon monoxide gas had killed five miners:

Harry Shepherd from Tutbury – the oldest at 73 years old – he left two daughters.

George Smith from Tutbury -61 years old – had three sons serving overseas and two married daughters.

Arthur Harris, the mine foreman – left a daughter, Esme. His son, William, also lost his life that day, on the surface.

Fred Bowring – left a widow and seven young children

Joseph Cooper – 48 years old - left a widow and eight children, four of whom were still at school. His wife, Mary valiantly managed the morgue, even though her husband was the first dead body to arrive.

Those who were rescued via the air shaft were:

The Day the Sun Disappeared, 27 Nov 1944

Jack Gorton, George Shepherd, Fred Rowe, Alf Page, Jim Treadwell, Percy Priestley, Charles Gibbs and Willy Watson.

In Memory Of
Civilian

JOSEPH COOPER

Civilian War Dead who died on 27 November 1944 Age 48

At Peter Ford Works, Fauld, Staffs.

Remembered with Honour
TUTBURY, RURAL DISTRICT

COMMONWEALTH
WAR GRAVES

COMMEMORATED IN PERPETUITY BY THE COMMONWEALTH WAR GRAVES COMMISSION

The Day the Sun Disappeared, 27 Nov 1944

CHAPTER 30

INTERVIEW WITH JOE COOPER

I interviewed Joe Cooper, son of Mary Cooper in February 2023, along with his nephew, Graham Shaw.

According to Joe Cooper, one of Mary's sons, both his mother and PC Mackay were given £5 apiece for the work they undertook. "That was a fair bit of money in those days."

Joe Cooper knew PC Mackay. He was 11 years old at the time of the explosion. I asked him what PC Mackay looked like.

"He was a very nice chap, a solid sort of bloke, a good six foot but big with it. We called him Mackay actually, not the Scottish version of Mack-eye. Ron Thompson was Mackay's sidekick. They worked together. He was a very useful bloke Ron Thompson. He could look after himself and you. Mackay was a bit like that an' all. You got to understand, it was war time and they got all sorts about – if there was anybody kicking muck up, they were there. They never backed off. They couldn't afford to.

Joe, seemed to think that PC Mackay lived in police cottages in Tutbury – both he (from 1950 to 1954) and Thompson – at two police houses at Fishpond Lane Police Station. The police station was at No. 15 Fishpond, with police houses and 16 and 17. Graham Shaw stated, "I had worked with Thompson when I had just started in the police force. He was a very handy bloke when there was a mess in a pub or such like. You didn't argue with Ron. He was an ex-miner, a Bevan boy."

The Day the Sun Disappeared, 27 Nov 1944

I found out later, from Rob Minchin at the Tutbury Museum, that the by then, Sergeant Mackay, was resident at 17 Burton Street, (at least by 19.8.50, and still there 9.5.54) and marrying off his daughters. Ronald Thompson was witness at one of the marriages in Tutbury.

Joe continued, "A lot of them down the mine never went back. I worked at Peter Ford's for 25 years, ending up as foreman. My brother, John Cooper, was a mine engineer. I worked on the face when I first went there, working with Hurst Priestly to start with. You worked in pairs and you worked in what they called the 'heading', which was a face. You worked in twos. It was like working for yourself actually. We were on piece work. Clock work was about 1s an hour when I worked there and then you got paid on tonnage on what you did. So you had to blast your own rock and load it by hand. The locos were diesel, made by Ruston & Hornby. They only had two of them, and would drop a truck off and the trucks were solid wood – I mean you can imagine. They were about 6ft long, 4ft 6in wide, I would think with big solid buffers on them. They used to make their own there. They were rimmed round with steel to stop them getting knocked about. You lifted a big lump of stone, the biggest you could lift and stacked them on the side and all the middle was filled up with bits and bobs of anything you could tuck in. You built them up. We used to stand on the buffers to check they were just the right height, otherwise you would have lost the top. There was round about 5-6 ton the loads, depending on the quality of stuff you were loading. They weren't pattern-mining then. It was like a rabbit warren when we were down there. We followed the stone, not going in a straight line. We took the bulk of it.

When the explosion happened, the gas didn't go all over the mine as some people think. I talked to the blokes that came out, Charlie

The Day the Sun Disappeared, 27 Nov 1944

Gibbs was one, who had been working at the face. He was only short, about 5ft tall. They kept loading until 2.30-3pm. The time to knock off was 2.30pm and you walked out around 3pm. You started at 7 in the morning."

I asked Joe about the rescues.

"I was at Tutbury at the time, at school – I was 11 years old - and I only heard one explosion. It went up like a big mushroom – it looked like the atom bomb dropping – a big mushroom cloud with tons and tons of stuff up in" the air."

The Yanks came and rescued people out of the reservoir flood. Mrs Nellie Ford was one. She was up to her neck in mud. Harry Hill and Bill Ford lived at the Purse Cottages. They used to walk up to the Cock."

Graham Shaw (Joe's nephew) added, "People wouldn't have known at the time that it was like Hiroshima because Hiroshima hadn't happened at that point. Now you can reflect on it and say it was."

Joe continued, "It was the biggest explosion that they had had until Hiroshima. It was felt on the continent, on a seismograph in Geneva. The men down the pit were that used to blasting that they thought it was just a good'un (a blasting in another part of the mine). It didn't perturb them and they carried on working. It was only them that were wandering about or were close to it, where the gas got to.

Ida Harrison's mother was Clara in the house opposite the village hall – No relation to Dorothy Harrison, who lived at Fauld Cottage. There is no trace of Clara Harrison's house now, nor Fauld Cottage or Jim Heathcote's farm. Gypsum took it all down, not that long ago. The big house, that used to be Gypsum's

The Day the Sun Disappeared, 27 Nov 1944

headquarters on the right – that's still there. Jim's farm backed up to that, the barn and the cow sheds. The big house was incredibly untouched. There might have been the odd window broken but, apart from that, it wasn't touched. It was the way the blast went, caught the ridge. It flattened the board works. That was where a lot of the people were killed. They wouldn't have stood a chance. It was flattened. The Hellaby house would have had broken windows but their house was intact. I'm talking from memory now. Even the village hall, that's all different. They opened the new one in 1962. Botham's farm was right down the bottom of that lane".

Joe then continued about the alabaster mine.

"The locos: there was one coming out, which my dad (Joseph Cooper) drove, one fetching the stuff out of the faces and taking the trucks back and my dad got a string of trucks on his loco and took them outside. But dad had come back down the tunnel and wasn't able to get out. He came back and wouldn't know what was cracking off. The tunnel entrance had blocked, had caved in.

My dad trammed out and old Bill Watson used to fetch them out of the faces. They knew how long it would take them. Someone would ask 'how long will you be done' and he'd reply, 'Gee's an hour, 20 minutes' for them to load it and then they'd come back, fetch it out and bring another. So, they'd always got a truck, you see. Most of them did three a day.

You did your own railway tracking – put your track down as you went forward with the face. There were rails placed on the side that were then put down. We never put sleepers down, just dropped some short rails down on the end of the original track, so you could take the truck a bit farther, make it handier. But you could only go, perhaps, two or three foot. You'd have to have a

The Day the Sun Disappeared, 27 Nov 1944

day every now and then to do the proper tracking, put sleepers down. These tracks were then permanent. When you were blasting you had to stay well back, round a corner, if possible, as rock would be blasted on top of the rails, but you would clean that off as you went, until the end of the road. They were only doing about six shots at a time. Now they do about 30-32 shots at a time. It's a different ball game now. We used to do what they call 'selective shooting'. Now it's pattern- blasting. They put a grab in on the runners now and go forward about 10 foot. We had small electric diggers, made by Armco. You used to run in, load it and it would rock up and throw it into a trailer. All electric. They were brilliant little tools. Me and my pal Dabber used to do 1500 ton on a good day, picking about 7 ton up at a time. Now they have the massive Deutsch engine scoops. You could feel the air pressure as they went by. All the alabaster is then sorted and graded outside, using water pressure. The light stuff they wanted, would float, and the hard-arse, as we used to call it, fell, and that was tipped out after. The pure alabaster would be used to make plaster. Anhydrite was the hard-arse, pure crystal white and that was just cement stone rubbish in other words.

There were no telephone lines down there. Peter Ford's was electric lit and they worked with electric in the faces and they fired off electric. Whereas Staton's worked with candles and carbine lights. Staton's at the time would use an old-fashioned way of blasting. They'd put a straw in the black powder, then light it. You knew how long it was going to take to burn to hit the powder, so it would give you time to get out of the way. Every time someone blasted the carbine light would put the light out. If the lights went out, the only way to get out was to keep one foot on the track.

We didn't have many accidents, very few. You've always got the idiots, no matter what job you're on. One lad got himself stuck in a conveyor belt! That would be self-inflicted as most of the belts had guards round, on the drive edge but you couldn't guard the belts.

Joseph Cooper, my dad, had medals from the First World War but also had a special medal received getting people out who were trapped in a fort. He was only a teenager then 18 or 19.

People are not on piece work now. They are paid members of a team.

Those local to the airshaft went there, naturally, as that was the way out and that's where the gas was going up the airshaft. There's a spiral steel staircase in there. It's still there but the airshaft has been blocked up as people were going pinching cable."

CHAPTER 31

ABOVE THE AIR SHAFT

Up above them, Joseph Foster (Peter Ford's Works Manager) was with me, PC Mackay. Joseph had told me that there was an air shaft on Moat Farm (Hanbury Fields Farm) and, as this was still visible, I went there to try and contact the miners working below. The entrance was covered in mud so we started digging until we uncovered the step ladders leading down. I started calling out, over and over "Hello, can anyone hear me?" But I got no response.

By this time others had arrived - Bert Hardwick of Top Farm, Hanbury, who was also a Civil Defence worker, Corporal Rock and Corporal Peter.

Bert Hardwick managed to set up a system of pulleys to hoist the miners up the 80ft of iron ladders.

Flight Lieutenant J P Lewin had also made his way there, even though he had already spent hours in the RAF mine, attempting to rescue people.

Another farmer from Hanbury appeared, 52-year-old Leslie Shotton, of Knghtsfield Farm. He was also Chairman of the Parish Council. (He continued to work, untiringly, to give help and succour the stricken relatives, and he helped the police in very many ways).

The Day the Sun Disappeared, 27 Nov 1944

"We'll have to get down there." I said, there's got to be men down there. They may be in difficulty, not knowing the air vent is free now, and be wandering to try and get out another way. We will need ropes and lamps." I sent the RAF soldiers back for ropes and lamps.

When they returned, Joseph Foster took his turn in hollering down the air shaft as loud as possible. "It's quite a way down to the mine, three tiers of ladders." Joseph told me.

At last we heard faint calls from below. "Thank goodness", I said as we heard footsteps on the ladders. Alfred Page and Fred Lowe succeeded in climbing the shaft.

"The vent was blocked, we didn't know we could get out, so others are trying to make their way to the entrance. But there's gas down there," Alfred said, "and it's pitch black. Some have succumbed already to the gas, collapsed. I believe they're dead, but there's a few others down there that need help.

"Right, get down there", Joseph ordered the two airmen.

They'd got someone and tied ropes around him. "Haul away" one shouted from below, so we all began pulling. That turned out to be Jack Gorton. He had just about collapsed but the fresh air luckily brought him round.

Corporals Rock and Peter repeatedly went down the ladders to bring out survivors, coming up for air - then immediately descending again.

William Watson, the loco driver, was the last to be brought up. So terrible was the scene of desolation all around him, where huge craters overlapped on another as far as one could see and all the familiar landmarks had disappeared that, when recovered enough to speak, looked round, and observed, eyes aghast, "Where am I,

The Day the Sun Disappeared, 27 Nov 1944

what's happened? I don't recognise anything. I don't even know the direction to Hanbury, where I live!"

The Day the Sun Disappeared, 27 Nov 1944

CHAPTER 32

MACKAY AT THE MORGUE

Doctors were on hand but there was little they could do as either the casualties coming in were dead or had nothing much in the way of injuries, such as Mr Foster from the Peter Ford mill, who had a finger trapped and might lose the nail – apart from that, not a scratch on him, especially as the mill is now a tangled and crumpled wreckage. It is difficult to realise that anyone could have emerged from that holocaust unscathed. I spoke to him and how he felt at the time, "I didn't feel anything really. One second everything was normal, and the next, everything was coming to pieces. I, and a young lad of 17, who had been working with me, went to help the injured and I suppose it was the fact that our attention was kept busy helping people straight away, that kept our thoughts off ourselves."

Mr Foster carried on, "I went to our mine entrance and saw the reservoir had disappeared and that there was a huge gap where it had once been. I then went on towards Upper Castle Hayes Farm and saw the huge crater, where the farm had been and the countryside for a mile around was torn up into unrecognisable shapes. It was only seeing all of the destruction that I realised that the explosion had taken place at the RAF Station."

While we were working together, Mr Foster enlightened me a bit more, "It's strange. The reservoir didn't actually burst. It sort of just disappeared and the water came pouring into the workings. They have drained most of it away now. I believe there is water trouble at the main dump too and, this morning, the Civil Defence has fixed up a hose from the main road to pump the water out onto the fields, what's left of them, of course."

One by one, bodies were brought into the mortuary. On 3rd December the first recovery was made, another on 12 December and another on 19th December but, from then on, victims were recovered at intervals until finally the last one was recovered on 5th February 1945. One victim only was never recovered from this works yard, a tribute to the work of Mr Mur and his men.

The morgue was an awful place to be, seeing these mutilated, even bits of bodies coming through. The doctors recommended I put camphor-soaked cotton wool up my nose as the days went on, as those bodies had been down there over a month. The worst part was when a wife or family came to identify a body. Some were naturally in tears, some in hysterics, some even showed no deep sorry at the time, placing a tender kiss on their loved ones, but I knew, in these instances, the shock would set in and tears would come later, in torrents.

I did what I could to help, making a list of the names, trying to keep the place clean, and keeping the fire lit.

I was helping the coroner with identification of the victims and, with the passage of time, this became a very difficult task. Too often the body was unidentified and identification became possible only by small intimate possessions in their clothes such as a penknife, cigarette case and lighter. Most of the bodies were those of working men, and the nature of their work called for old clothes and a minimum of attire. Some even changed into old working clothes at the Works and carried practically nothing in their pockets, so that, at times, identification was virtually impossible. Bodies came in quickly, at first, then slowly as the

The Day the Sun Disappeared, 27 Nov 1944

diggers were trying to find those deeply buried and in the RAF mine. Searchers had to wait for the bombs to be cleared out before they could enter the mines to retrieve the bodies. I took meticulous notes as to evidence of cause of death in each instance.

Joseph Foster (works manager at Ford's) was able to help considerably. I said to him, "We've been working all night here, trying to compile lists, but the trouble is that scores of people have simply disappeared and, until we can check up on them, we are unable to say whether or not they have been blown to bits, or are still alive. That's the position – we don't know where they are, or where they've gone."

Mr Foster told me, with a sort of smile, to try to lighten the situation, but not really succeeding, "I keep a black suit in the car ready to change into, as there are so many funerals to attend."

That black suit stayed in his car for two months.

. . . .

Mr Auden's inquests were attended by my Police Superintendent H.G Heath from Burton, Superintendent Vodrey, from Uttoxeter, Sergeant Haywood, from Burton, the vicar of the parish and Mr R F Furner, clerk to the Tutbury Rural District Council.

Those bodies brought in on Tuesday, 28th, were that of Samuel Pickering, 36 - killed by multiple injuries in the plaster mine. Mr Joseph Foster, the works manager at the plaster mines and mills, identified Pickering and others. He was unsure about Pickering, though, as the body was in such a state. All he said, when asked if he could identify the body was, "To the best of my ability."

Samuel Pickering

251

The Day the Sun Disappeared, 27 Nov 1944

Mr Joseph Foster also identified Lawrence George Cockayne, 49, blacksmith – his back had been pierced by his anvil.

Richard Bell, glassmaker of 25 New Street, Hanbury, identified George Smith, 61 - a, plaster pit worker – killed by fumes

Frederick Charles Bowring, 39, plaster pit worker was identified by his wife, Mrs Olive Rosina Bowring. He had been killed by fumes. That was awful as his wife was deeply distressed. I got a chair for her and made her a cup of tea.

Henry (Harry) Shepherd, 73, plaster pit miner, was identified by his son-in-law, Charles Arme, of 16 Burton Street, Tutbury – Harry had been overcome by fumes.

George Edward Page, 58, plaster pit worker, was identified by Thomas George Page, The Green, Weston, Stafford. He had been killed by fumes.

Other bodies brought in were:
George H Powell, age unknown, of 7 Church Street, Tutbury. He had multiple head injuries
Frederick William Slater aged between 40 and 50, of New Road, Draycott-in-the-Clay - multiple head injuries
Ambrose Patterson, aged 40, of 96 Green Lane, Tutbury- general mutilation but could only be identified as he had a previous injury leaving two fingers missing from his right hand.
John William Skelett, 48, of 19 Smallholding, Knowle Hill, Rolleston - multiple injuries
Sgt Stanley Gordon Game, 36, RAF – fractured base of skull – his next of kin was his wife, who was based in Colchester, Essex.

The Day the Sun Disappeared, 27 Nov 1944

James Beard, 51, of Hill View, Tamworth, Ashby de la Zouche – killed by fumes
Sydney Chawner, 50, asphyxiated. He was identified by his wife, Mrs Violet Chawner.

Two of the Italian victims were brought in: Corporal Rocco Novello (27) had multiple injuries and Private Salvator Trovato died from the fumes. Both were identified by Lieutenant Luigi Silvestri.

John William West (23) farm labourer, killed by the blast, was identified by Thomas George Page; and George Priestly (63) gypsum miner, died of multiple injuries, was identified by his son, Percy John Priestley.

Another body was recovered on Sunday, and still another from the plaster mine on Monday, that of William Ford (57), a fitter. The coroner opened the inquest in this case. Evidence of identification was given by George Wetherill, carpenter, and it was stated that death was due to multiple injuries.

Other civilian victims included:

John Henry Appleton
Harry Hill,
Joseph Cooper (Mary's husband)
Arthur Harris
William Gent
Percy Cooper,
Philip Page
Norman Worthington
William Ford
Thomas Hudson

The Day the Sun Disappeared, 27 Nov 1944

Ernest William Gustave Daniels, aged 35. A body had been found in a standing position with his arm guarding his face. He'd literally been buried alive. When the man's head was clear, two fellow workers stated they thought it was someone they recognised, Bell, the work's accountant, and the man's widow was advised. However, when the body was eventually recovered, after two hours work, it was found to be a Mr Daniels, as they recognised him from his hobnail boots and corduroys trousers. He was identified by his wife, Jean Daniels by means of his driving licence and other articles. His body had been completely mutilated.

Oma Alma Gilbert (61), had been a bricklayer. His body was recovered from the RAF depot.

The lower half of a male body was recovered on Friday, the identity of which is believed to have been definitely established.

John Henry Appleton, of 16 Watson Street, Penkhull, had originally been listed as missing. He had been a sales manager at Peter Ford's cement firm. He lived with his two sisters, Emily and May. I spoke to Emily, "John left for work, as usual, on the Monday morning, and when he did not return in the evening, and learning of the news of the explosion, May and I immediately made enquiries. Burton police told us that the offices had been destroyed and that our brother was officially listed as missing." May interrupted, "But at least we have his body and can bury him. I understand that many still have not been found." She added, "He was so popular – he had won a number of trophies at tennis and badminton and, until last year, he was an enthusiastic playing member of Trentham and Basford tennis clubs and, for many years, had been the Secretary of the North Staffordshire badminton association, representing Staffordshire on a number of occasions. He had also been church warden at St Barnabas Church, Penkhull and was also an air raid warden."

I commiserated, "Such a loss to you both, and to the people who knew him. He will be sorely missed." and I thanked the two ladies for their information.

Frederick Harrison's body finally came into the morgue on Boxing Day. He was 58 and had lived at 8 Wyggeston Street, Burton that had got bombed a while ago. Wyggeston Street was close to the Burton Police Station and I knew him. We'd often see him, after work at the local and have a chat. I felt really sad, actually seeing the body of someone that I knew fairly well. His body was identified by his wife, Mrs Leah Harrison, mainly from various articles found on his body, as it was otherwise impossible to recognise the mutilated remains that lay on the table, having been in the ground for so long. Mrs Harrison had obviously known for some time that her husband was dead but, still, the site of his body, was traumatic to her. She finally managed to say, through a few tears, "He was a good man, Mr Mackay. He'd worked with the Prudential for 30 years and was a well-known church worker at Horninglow, where he had been a church warden." I tried to calm her, "I know this won't help but your husband would not have felt anything, Mrs Harrison. He would have died instantly."

His funeral was to be at St John's Church, Horninglow, on Saturday at 2pm.

On the following Wednesday, the Coroner opened the inquest on Mrs Sarah Louise Hill, aged 54, and wife of Mr Harry John Hill, who is still missing. LAC William Charles Hill identified the body and it was stated that death was from multiple injuries.

Auden wrote of PC Mackay, after the inquest was over, 'For 72 days, without rest, he has carried out the removal, cleansing and identification of bodies in every state of mutilation and decomposition. In addition to this, he has kept me informed and done most of the clerical work of which there was a considerable amount daily. At no time has he shown signs of nerves and his cheerfulness has helped everyone through an exceedingly difficult period.'

Mary Cooper's work did not go unnoticed as, early in 1945, John Auden, the coroner for East Staffordshire officially recognised her unstinting work.

The Day the Sun Disappeared, 27 Nov 1944

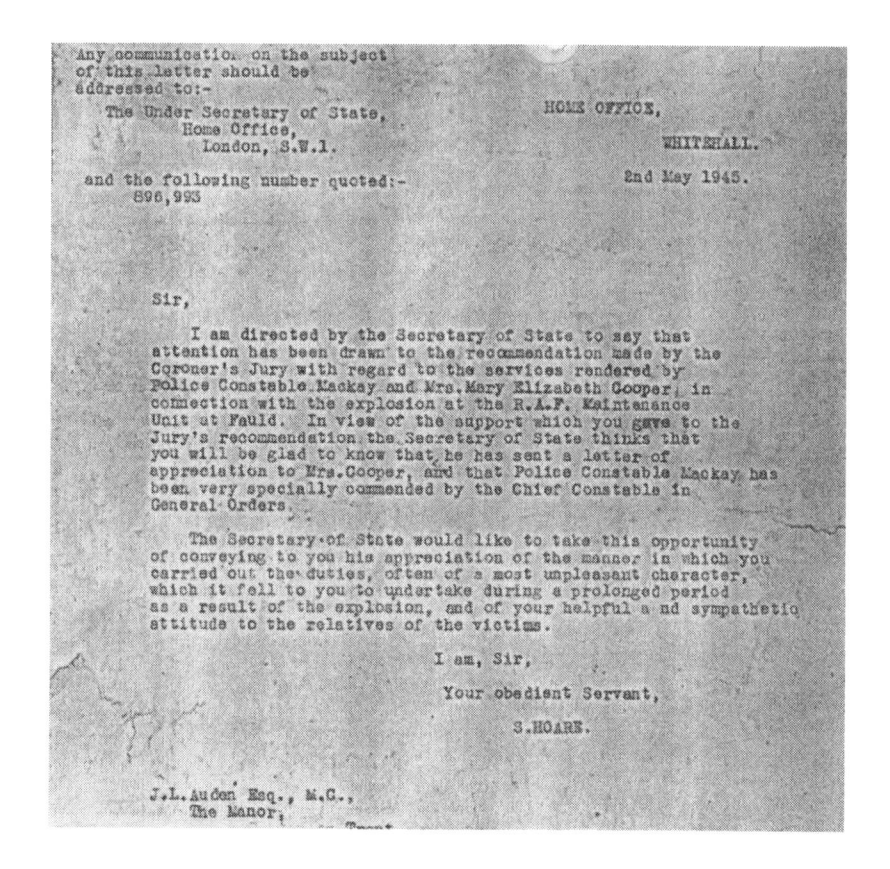

> Any communication on the subject of this letter should be addressed to:-
> The Under Secretary of State,
> Home Office,
> London, S.W.1.
>
> and the following number quoted:-
> 896,993
>
> HOME OFFICE,
> WHITEHALL.
> 2nd May 1945.
>
> Sir,
>
> I am directed by the Secretary of State to say that attention has been drawn to the recommendation made by the Coroner's Jury with regard to the services rendered by Police Constable Mackay and Mrs. Mary Elizabeth Cooper, in connection with the explosion at the R.A.F. Maintenance Unit at Fauld. In view of the support which you gave to the Jury's recommendation the Secretary of State thinks that you will be glad to know that he has sent a letter of appreciation to Mrs. Cooper, and that Police Constable Mackay has been very specially commended by the Chief Constable in General Orders.
>
> The Secretary of State would like to take this opportunity of conveying to you his appreciation of the manner in which you carried out the duties, often of a most unpleasant character, which it fell to you to undertake during a prolonged period as a result of the explosion, and of your helpful and sympathetic attitude to the relatives of the victims.
>
> I am, Sir,
> Your obedient Servant,
> S. HOARE.
>
> J.L. Auden Esq., M.C.,
> The Manor,

Auden wrote: This woman, of her own free will, has cleaned and scrubbed a very gruesome temporary mortuary every day for 72 days. The work has been indescribable. She has helped with the undressing and also the washing of clothes removed from the bodies. One of the first victims that she had to deal with was her own husband. In most cases, that would have been sufficient for a middle-aged woman to undertake without volunteering to continue the work with all the remainder. She survived the wrecking of a farm at which she was looking after an old lady, and it is probably due to her action that the old lady's life was saved.'

I was there when Chawner's body was finally discovered, at about 1.50pm. Rev Crook discovered him and with the assistance of an Italian, they managed to dig the body out of its half-buried position. He lay head-first between the ruins of Mr Goodwin's farm and Mr Botham's farm – he had been working for Mr Botham. He also found the body of a horse, some 30 yards away and fragments of a cart about another 30 yards away. Rev Crook arranged for diggers to dig up the mud, but still they couldn't find Rock's body. Rev Crook had the unenviable task of telling Sydney Chawner's wife, Violet, in Anslow, that her husband's body had been found and taken to the school room. This had become almost a daily task for him, notifying relatives of bodies found and giving comfort to the bereaved.

Rev Crook worked on at the school to help clear it ready for the reception of causalities and worked on until the last of the bodies was brought from the pit. He told me. "You police have been wonderful and so have the RAF personnel and the Americans. One cannot speak too highly of you all."

I, PC Mackay, continued to make searches of the area around Moat Farm (Botham's farm), in many directions looking for any trace of Rock. I again made a search on 13 January 1945, with three other police officers and thirty Civil Defence personnel, a search of a 100 square yards, pacing and digging foot by foot over the ground, but there was still no trace.

The Day the Sun Disappeared, 27 Nov 1944

CHAPTER 33

Others had their stories to tell:

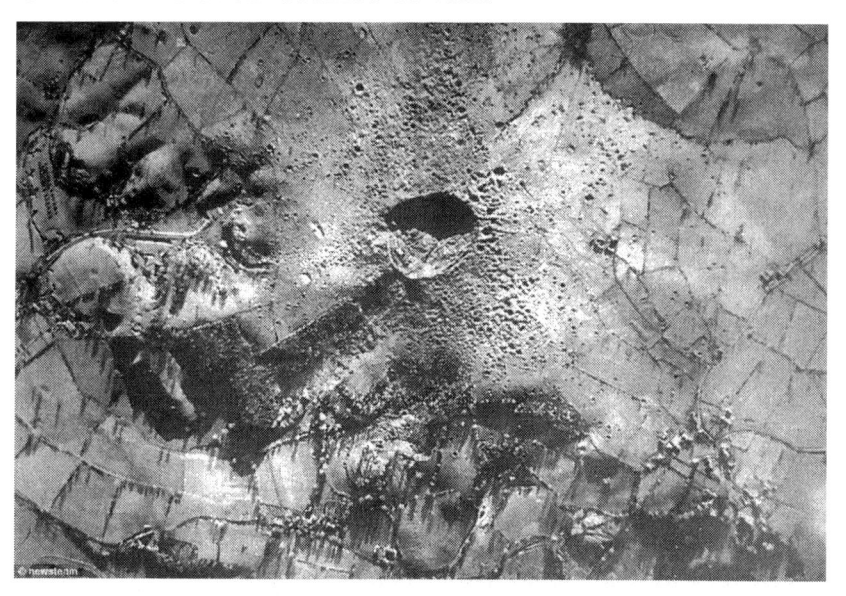

Aerial view of the Crater - Donated by Graham Shaw

Seventeen-year-old Roy Gregson was working in fields on his father's farm, Church Farm, near Hanbury's village church. Like everyone else around, he knew that the 21st Maintenance Unit at RAF Fauld was an underground munitions dump, and that bombs were stored in the disused gypsum mine. But still, his first thought when he heard that sickening explosion, was that a plane had come down.

The Day the Sun Disappeared, 27 Nov 1944

"I'd been working with a horse and cart, carting cabbages for the cattle. I remember it suddenly went dark, when the ground gave this enormous shake. The horse ran away, with me coming after it. … it was like gusts, gusts of boulders moving up into the sky.. rolling up. Soil was being sent skyward. I threw myself to the ground on and off. I saw a gigantic piece of alabaster, about ¾ mile away. It must have weighed about 20 tons, just hoisted up into the sky as if it were a piece of foam rubber. Mature trees had been plucked out of the ground and strewn about, their roots landing upwards in a tangled mass. The soil continued coming down for about 20 minutes and the backs of the cattle were covered in soil.

It was only when I got back to the village where all the tiles were off and there was a hole in the road with water pouring out of a burst main that I knew my worst fears were realised: the whole dump had gone up."

Afterwards, Roy went to help with the rescue mission from the mine shaft, taking bodies to the mortuary at the school hall that Mary Cooper had set up and would help Mary, where he could (information received from Ian Gregson, Roy's son).

Vivienne Hill stated that her father-in-law and 4 siblings lost their home and both parents that day. Children went to school that morning and, by 11am, had lost everything! There are still families scarred by that day.

Helen Gibson wrote that her dad was driving down Burton Street and saw the dump go up - trees and all! My aunt Muriel, who was only 17 at the time, was working at the ordnance depot at Branston. They guessed what had happened and sent her off to cycle home to Tutbury – to see what was left.

The Day the Sun Disappeared, 27 Nov 1944

Rose Jones wrote. "I am a health care assistant on a hospital ward, often elderly patients ask me where I live. When I say Fauld, they usually exclaim "Ooh where the dump went up!" Some tell of being in school in Burton or surrounding areas and hearing it, chimneypots rattling etc."

Michael J W Goodwin wrote: "I did a lot of research when I found a distant cousin had died in the incident. Maurice Goodwin (known as George) was married to Florence Knight (1897-1987) in 1934 at Hanbury Church. They had no children.

In 1939 George was a gardener, living near Grebe Farm, Hanbury, where his mother Polly, a widow, worked as a domestic.

On 27 Nov 1944 he died at Moat Farm, Featherbed Lane, Hanbury, where he worked at the time. There was no burial but he was remembered in the cemetery at RAF Fauld and at the war memorial in Hanbury Church, dedicated to all those who lost their lives in the WW2 explosion. He had no children and left £346 in his will.

Frederick George Goodwin (1904-1944) was the eldest son of Mary Ann (Polly) Goodwin, who was one of my grandfather's elder sisters! All from Stramshall, near Uttoxeter – farmers' children.

Frederick George Goodwin did not work for the Goodwin family who perished in the flood. He was employed by a farmer in Hanbury, Croft Farm, I believe, not 100% sure. Both Fred and his wife were members of the Hanbury Church Choir. I remember seeing a photograph of them in the Burton Evening Mail.

The Day the Sun Disappeared, 27 Nov 1944

In about 1953 a Company, from Southampton, I believe, were tasked with exploring the explosion crater in a search for bodies. Some bits and pieces of a horse-drawn cart were found but nothing of the horse or my relative. They had been vaporised!

It was then decided that the site should be a memorial to the dead, fenced off and trees planted.

'George' Rock, was the verger, working for Harry Botham of Hanbury Fields Farm (aka Moat Farm), and also sang in the choir. George perished in the crater – aged just 40 years old, although he looked younger. He was handsome, slim with thick, dark hair, parted on the left and some may say, slightly protruding ears. His body was never found. He had a brother, Edward John Rock (1906-1986), who was a policeman in the Sandwell area, Staffs. He never married and had no children.

Andrew Black: My grandmother was a bomb-examiner up there but she worked on the surface as she had been told women were not permitted to work in the mine. On that fateful day she was unwell so had the day off. My grandmother's name was Betsy Wooldridge. She continued to work up there until she retired, in the early 1960s. Yes, she was very special but, because it was wartime, many women took on such jobs. She once told me no bomb went back in the mine, but was put in storage on the surface as it would be too dangerous. But the impossible did happen, sadly. From what I remember having read the report when it came out, the operative was removing cordite with a brass chisel instead of a copper one. This came from the chief eye witness in the area, who survived due to the blast going away from him. Copper is a soft metal so the chances are it will not cause a spark, whereas brass is a hard alloy and if struck, the casing would explode.

The Day the Sun Disappeared, 27 Nov 1944

Sarah Corbishley: My mother, who has recently passed away, was at school in Kingstone the day of the explosion and all the glass shattered in the school windows.

Fred Seabury: I can't remember any Italians being at Flaxley Green POW camp, but I know that there were plenty of Germans. I used to go when I was young in the late 1940s with my Uncle Joe, in his van to collect 2 German POWs, Heinze and Fred. They worked in my Uncle Joe's Radio shop in Hednesford.

Stefano Martini. Flaxley was Italian POWs under control of the US military. The German POW camp was on the A51 just before Wolseley Bridge, where the Staffordshire sewage works are now.

Glynn Davies, Museum Guide at Moira Furnace Museum and Country Park – lives in Oakthorpe.

My father was at a barracks awaiting travel orders to visit home in Oakthorpe. He had come back from India. When he went to his superior officer for a pass, the officer saw that his address was Oakthorpe, near Burton on Trent, so on the fact, that he lived near Burton – 9 miles away, he got a week's leave.

Sarah Corbishley: my mother, who has recently passed away was at school in Kingstone the day of the explosion and all the glass shattered in the school windows.

Derby Evening Telegraph 26 November 1994

A few miles away, in Tutbury, a class of children at Richard Wakefield Infant school was just coming in from their break.

One of them, Richard Whitebrook recalled: "We were in the playground and I remember hearing the bang and everyone turning to look towards Hanbury. The teacher said 'The dump's gone up' and, as we were staring, we saw Tutbury move up, actually rise about six feet as the force of the explosion passed through. We saw it roll out towards Rolleston on Dove."

His school mate, Dennis Shaw, was just nine when the disaster happened.

"I was back in the classroom, and all the desks had shifted into the middle of the room. One chap told me he had been sitting on his doorstep and the force blew him across the road. We didn't know what it was, what had happened, but, going home, all the chimney pots were down, it was a mess."

"My younger brother Arthur was ill and had been kept home. When it happened, he went out through a gap in the fence into a field and saw the cloud rising above Hanbury. But we still didn't know, not until the next day, the full extent of what had happened."

Ryan Kirk Locker: My great, great uncle, John (Jack) Redfern, of Marchington Woodlands, died in the explosion. William Lovatt of Uttoxeter was at the Ford works that day. He saw John Redfern at work at about 8.40am but they didn't exchange any conversation as John was hard at work. He was a skilled craftsman, working as a stone-dresser, carving alabaster. John's body was never found, or never recognised.

The Day the Sun Disappeared, 27 Nov 1944

In Memory Of
Civilian

JOHN REDFERN

Civilian War Dead who died on 27 November 1944 Age 32

At RAF Fauld, Staffs.

Remembered with Honour
TUTBURY, RURAL DISTRICT

COMMONWEALTH
WAR GRAVES

COMMEMORATED IN PERPETUITY BY THE COMMONWEALTH
WAR GRAVES COMMISSION

The Day the Sun Disappeared, 27 Nov 1944

The Way We Were: Your letters

Fauld tragedy killed our pals

MADAM, After reading the article in The Way We Were about the Staffordshire explosion at Fauld I've needed to write in to say that I remember it very well.

I was 16-years-old at the time and my family lived at Mill Cottage, Cubley.

We knew the West family at Mill Farm.

I remember the tremor as being like an earthquake and there was a large black cloud as we looked towards Sudbury.

John and Steve West both worked at Castle Hayes Farm, and John was married and lived at Hatton. His body was found on the day of the explosion and buried at Hatton.

Steve West's body was not found until 1947, when he was brought to Cubley to be laid to rest with his family.

Jack Redfern, our cousin, was also killed in the Fauld explosion.

JOAN BURGESS (NEE REDFERN)
Manchester

DEVASTATION: Left, the explosion left a crater 400 yards wide by 35 yards deep, the size of six football pitches.

266

The Day the Sun Disappeared, 27 Nov 1944

CHAPTER 34

H J PAYNE

These are my personal memories of the event.
(From information received by Graham Shaw)

As a 16-year-old in 1944, I had started my working life in the laboratory at Nestles factory in August of that year and, as a junior, had to perform many of the menial tasks which including opening cans of Condensed Milk for someone to come along and taste to assess the quality.

Whilst washing my hands and can-opener in the laboratory sink, the laboratory floor, which was at first floor level, suddenly began violently to ripple as in an earthquake. This occurred at approximately 11am and lasted for at least 10 seconds.

From the laboratory window, which faced the Hanbury area, I could see two long V –shaped columns of black smoke. A member of the laboratory staff shouted, "My God, it's the Dump".

Everyone's first reaction as that it had been hit by a V2 rocket – a weapon being used by the enemy at the time.

My immediate concern was for my father, Reg Payne, who was employed by the Air Ministry as an Inspector and worked along with other team members in the mine engaged on quality controlling and validating bombs and ammunition before despatch by rail for wartime purposes.

The Day the Sun Disappeared, 27 Nov 1944

Reg Payne was the landlord of The New Inn in Ludgate Street, Tutbury, until 1940.

At the onset of war in September 1939 pub trade hit a recession and trade became very slack. Beer supplies were short and it was necessary for him to bolster his income with a second job. So, for a short time, he worked part-time across the road for Webb & Corbett glassworks in the acid-dipping department. This eventually started to affect his health. My mother ran The New Inn whilst he was at work in the glassworks.

An opportunity arose when the Ministry of Defence opened the unit at Fauld to change his job. A position of a Munitions Inspector was available and he decided to leave the New Inn and work full time there. A home move was made to a house in Park Lane, Tutbury before starting his new job.

At the time of the explosion I knew my father would be in the vicinity of the mines in which the bombs and ammunition was stored and I asked to be excused from work, got on my cycle and pedalled towards home.

At this time, my grandmother also lived in Park Lane, at a bungalow named Oaklands, which I had to pass before getting home.

At the gate of the bungalow stood granny and mother, along with my 3-year-old sister, waiting for news of what had happened. In my haste I remember braking too hard and skidding, owing to the icy condition of the road that morning, and coming off my bike.

I told my mother and grandma that I would go down to Fauld to see what information I could get and, as I pedalled along Park Lane, I vividly remember at almost every gate there were people

The Day the Sun Disappeared, 27 Nov 1944

who had come out of their houses, standing on the pavement, looking up and down the road, anxious for news.

On arrival at Fauld gate-house, I was stopped by Security Guard, Mr Cross, who I knew, and he told me that I should go home again. He was obviously in a state of shock and didn't react when I pedalled past him and towards the mine.

Some way up the road I saw dad, sitting on a boulder at the side of the road, smoking a cigarette. When he saw me he told me to go home and tell mum he was OK, and would be home as soon as he could.

I remember seeing further up the road a greenish-yellow glow in the side of a hill, which I assumed was fire inside the mine.

After relief, knowing that dad was safe and apparently well, I turned back for home, to meet my mother walking alone along the road towards Fauld. After reassuring her that dad was OK, and unharmed, we both waked tearfully back home. A small thing that I remember is that, on the way back, she asked me if I would like a cigarette. Although I was a secret smoker, I didn't think she knew, but I accepted.

Until the time he died in 1979, my father never ever expressed an opinion on how the explosion occurred. The only information he gave was that he was extremely lucky to have survived. He had been called out of the mine to another job only minutes before the explosion. Some years after the event, in the 1960s, he was interviewed in a TV documentary, but even then would not be pressed to express any opinion.

A most-lasting memory of this disaster was during a visit to Tutbury Parish Church a few days later, to see that several pews

The Day the Sun Disappeared, 27 Nov 1944

at the back of the church had been removed and the floor space occupied by rows of coffins containing victims of the tragedy.

Some weeks after the explosion, I had the opportunity to fly in a Wellington bomber aircraft over the site of the damage.

Being a member of the Air Training Corps, I occasionally went to the airfield at Church Broughton, which was staffed by Australians, and ask if there was any chance of a flight. More often than not, there was. The flight, usually with crew under training, would last between 30 minutes and 3 hours and, on one trip, I was able to view the massive crater caused by the disaster.

H J Payne 13.5.1999

CHAPTER 35

Story by Gary Smith – son of Nancy Smith

Nancy Smith was working in the cashier's office at Marston's brewery in Burton when the explosion happened. Everything shook, desks rising off the floor and papers being scattered about. Even the large, heavy safe in the office skidded across the room.

They all rushed to the windows. "Has something exploded in the brewery?" Nancy asked.

"Don't know, it could have been a 'buzz bomb', someone answered. Some of the staff had sustained minor injuries, having been thrown against walls and desks, but luckily no-one was badly injured.

A member of staff went into the grounds of the brewery to check. He returned to say it was an explosion on the way to Uttoxeter. Maybe a bomb had dropped there.

There was talk of a huge crater and numbers of people being killed.

Her parents lived in Anslow, (to the west of Burton upon Trent and south of Tutbury). They were Eva and George Bentley of Hopley Road. She needed to check that they were safe and made her way there.

She remembers giving her parents a hug as they opened the front door, "So glad you are safe."

The Day the Sun Disappeared, 27 Nov 1944

"Yes," her father replied, "but have you seen the damage that bomb has done, just come inside."

Nancy went in and was taken upstairs. "Just look at those huge cracks in the ceiling." George Bentley indicated. "And look here, large chunks of the ceiling have come down. Lucky your ma was in the kitchen and I was in the parlour. If we'd been upstairs we could have been nastily injured. We'll need a new ceiling and roof and I'm darned if I'm gonna pay for it. Someone's responsible." Nancy looked around at the mess, bits of the beams and plaster covered the bed and her dad had put buckets around to catch the rain, just in case it did.

"Ay, it's freezing up here too. Where are you sleeping, you can't sleep here?

"Oh, your ma's made up a bed downstairs. You'll have to stay downstairs with us, if you're staying."

A number of days later Nancy decided to go for a walk from Anslow to the crater. She found the roads towards Hanbury resembling ploughed fields. She passed a half-demolished farm, where an unopened bottle of milk stood undisturbed at the front door. She recalled wondering if Mr Weston of Anslow had delivered the milk around the area on his horse and cart and hoped he hadn't got caught in the blast.

On getting to Hanbury, what remained of the roofs of the houses were covered in thick soil. Most of the trees had had their branches blown away, leaving just bare tree trunks. Others had been lifted out of the ground with the roots uppermost and the branches buried in the mud.

Climbing over the heaped-up remains of a stone wall into what once was a field, she gasped audibly. There spread out before her,

The Day the Sun Disappeared, 27 Nov 1944

where once there had been cows grazing peacefully, were the rotting bodies of those same cows.

The Day the Sun Disappeared, 27 Nov 1944

CHAPTER 36

JAMES BRASSINGTON

(Information from Burton Mail, November 28, 1994)

Jean Brassington was 13 years old and living with her grandfather, James Brassington in Monk Street, Tutbury. He was in his early 50s and had taken on her care as she had no-one else. Her grandfather was everything to her, all she had in the world.

Before the war he had worked at Ganes Ironmongers in Tutbury and the local council but had gone to join the RAF Fauld works, as an AID viewer, after the war had started, as so many people were needed there.

I was at school in Tutbury when the explosion happened, having a science lesson on the first floor. The Bunsen burners were lit on the desks.

All of a sudden we heard a thud – it felt like an earthquake and it rocked the whole of the school. All the class rushed to the windows, looking toward Fauld, trying to peek through the paper crosses that had been stuck to the windows to prevent flying glass should a bomb explode nearby. There were no houses in between so we could see straight over the fields.

There were flames rising up, like a gigantic bonfire with huge pieces of whatever rising up out of it.

The Day the Sun Disappeared, 27 Nov 1944

Everyone was shouting out, "What's happened?" with those not able to see, pushing their way eventually to the front by the windows.

"Hush now, children," the teacher shouted, just about managing to get her voice heard above the ruckus we were making.

"We do not know what has happened. You may not be safe by the windows and you must get under the desks, as you have been ordered to do in an emergency such as a bomb being dropped. Now, everyone, get under the desks – NOW!"

So, we got under the desks. "Is it a doodlebug?" someone said. There was all sorts of whispering as to what it could be.

Eventually, the head teacher came to our class and dismissed us all. We were allowed to go home.

On getting outside, I looked around. There didn't appear to be any damage to the school, although I could smell burning and there were bits of trees and earth floating in the air. I couldn't see so well on the ground floor as I could upstairs in the classroom but I knew something drastic had happened. Everything had gone dark. I knew my granddad was working at RAF Fauld and I was hoping he was safe.

I made my way home quickly, going along Duke Street, and was being passed by a number of Army Green Goddesses. As I got closer, I saw men, caked in mud, wearing gas masks and safety hats. In Ludgate Street there were a pile of ambulances with so many people shouting orders, taking orders, dealing with badly injured. The scene that greeted me was one of chaos.

Nearly home, I knew from the raised voices around me that the explosion had occurred in the Dump. I stopped. I couldn't go any further, my legs just wouldn't move. I gasped and my hand went

The Day the Sun Disappeared, 27 Nov 1944

to my mouth. It had dawned on me that my granddad was working at RAF Fauld - we'd spoken about his work and that he worked in the 'new area' of the mine, examining bombs that were brought in for repair and reissue. As realisation struck home I knew my granddad could be badly injured – he could have been killed! I started to cry.

I got home, but have no real memory of doing so. I have no memory of who told me that my grandfather had been killed in the explosion. It all seemed a blur.

Granddad's body was never found.

The massive crater, caused by the blast, is his grave.

In her own words, Jean said, "No-one will ever really know what happened, but I can't understand why they let a bomb with a detonator go back into the mine. I always thought the detonators were supposed to be got out before going into the mine, because it was the detonator that set the bomb off. The bombs were stored, without detonators attached before being taken by rail down to RAF Scropton and then from there, by road to different airfields."

Jean speaks from experience of handling bombs as eight years after the tragedy she worked at Fauld, where detonators were examined for the RAF. She inspected the detonators to see if there was any corrosion.

"It was 15 years before I could bring myself to visit the crater. In the company of my husband, Ray, and our two children, I ventured to the bottom of the crater, where I saw pieces of bombs and the fin of one sticking out of the ground. The memory of that momentous day still brings back tears, although its most painful moments have been blotted from my mind.

The Day the Sun Disappeared, 27 Nov 1944

I feel the true facts of the events on that winter morning have not come to light."

The Day the Sun Disappeared, 27 Nov 1944

CHAPTER 37

PC MACKAY'S REPORT - From Day Two

Gradually order came out of chaos, but the night after the explosion, the weather changed and rain fell heavily, turning the hundreds of acres of devastation into a horrible bog, reminiscent of 'No-man's land' of the 1914-18 war. You know what the edge of a bomb crater is like. Well, the ground was like that for an area of over a square mile – not even grass left. There was a gigantic crater at least 250 yards across. I was unable to recognise people standing on the other side of it. I knew a house had been there, but it had disappeared so completely, that it was impossible to say where exactly it had stood. Mud was feet deep, and dead or dying cattle lay all around. Many more were buried with perhaps a foot or a head or even just a horn of a cow showing.

On the following day the RAF sent an aircraft over the area to photograph the devastation. It was a huge crater, about eight hundred feet long, three hundred feet wide, and about one hundred and twenty feet deep. It was on the crest of the Stone Pits Hill bluff on the south side of the valley of the river Dover. To the west, just over a mile away from the crater lay the village of Hanbury, the buildings of which had suffered severe damage. Upper Hayes farm, which had lain on top of the mine storage area, had totally disappeared, engulfed by the crater. Nearby Hanbury Fields farm was buried under the debris. The plaster factory of Peter Ford & Sons was almost totally destroyed, and much of Brown's Coppice and Queen's Purse wood, along the summit of the bluff, had disappeared. Many smaller craters – from thirty to sixty feet across – had appeared on the northwest, southeast axis around the main crater – fumaroles caused by gases forcing their way to the surface and impact craters formed by falling rocks and bombs.

The explosion had occurred in the smaller, 'new area' of the mine, completely destroying it. Serious damage was done to the stocks in the larger 'old area', which lay to the east of the new.

Veterinary surgeons had been called for, and mercifully shot those animals that were still alive and suffering. So chaotic was the scene of destruction that it was utterly impossible to recover the body of any such animal.

Two days later a young heifer was found alive in the area. It was a brown colour, and had remained utterly still, and unobserved against the background of the destruction. This animal and one other slightly wounded cow were the only two animals which survived.

For health purposes, it was necessary to dispose of the dead cattle and, to this end, American bulldozers attempted this job, but speedily became bogged down in the mud. Later, Royal Engineers did this job, and buried more than a hundred head of cattle, where they lay.

By 29th November rescuers in oxygen masks burrowing into the gas-filled underground pits, realised they would not to find anyone possibly alive, but they had to make the mine safe. They couldn't make headway though. They were driven back time after time. They tried to penetrate areas filled with fumes and carbon monoxide gasses, using coalmine gas-masks. Some of them came staggering out again, after being in the galleries only two minutes. James Beard of Tamworth Road, Ashby-de-la-Zouch met his end

The Day the Sun Disappeared, 27 Nov 1944

on Tuesday, 28th, overcome by fumes in the main dump. It was going to be a long and dangerous mission. He was 51 years old and left a wife, Emily and three children. He had become a member of the Mines Rescue Brigade at Ashby some years ago. In early life he frequently played cricket.

George White was with the rescuers as he'd worked in the mines all his life and knew his way around. He went down the mine, with rescue teams, to show the way around. He also acted an unofficial first aider. His day job was to look at water piping and plumbing. He'd use a steel pipe, take it off somewhere where it was no longer needed, and attach it where it was needed, put taps on and you were away again. He lived in Fauld cottages. George survived.

Tarpaulin sheets were brought by American Troops, who quickly lashed them over gaping holes in the roofs of damaged houses in Hanbury village, and builders men commenced to remove dangerous masonry and generally to tidy up. No water, gas or electricity remained, but the authorities quickly arranged for water containers to be brought, and mobile canteens arrived with voluntary helpers to provide meals for those so sorely in need of help.

The recovery of victims outside the RAF station was commenced by the Royal Engineers, who made a magnificent effort, under appalling conditions. Mr T Hall, an Electrical Engineer from Burton Corporation was, with his assistants, rapidly getting current through to some parts of the village. Electric cables were laid and work performed unceasingly for two days, then the Staffordshire County Surveyor, Robert S Murt, OBE took over the task. Bulldozers, mechanical diggers of every type and dumpers appears in ever increasing numbers and the works yard of Messrs Peter Ford and Sons became a scene of heart-breaking toil.

The Day the Sun Disappeared, 27 Nov 1944

Fauld remains by Mark Rowe

In bitter weather, work went on. Many of the survivors of Ford's were employed in this work and all engaged were grimly determined to recover the bodies of their comrades as only two had been recovered immediately after the explosion.

The Works Manager, Mr Joseph Foster, who was in his 70s, attended daily to advise Mr Murt upon certain details, and to him fell the duty of identifying the bodies as they were recovered. Foster had worked at Peter Ford's all his life and knew most of his men intimately. Some had worked with him all their lives, and it was a grim task and a distressing one for him to have to identify the pitiful remains of his life-long friends. Many burdens fell upon him during those dark days, but he never faltered and earned for himself the admiration and respect of all who came into contact with him.

The Day the Sun Disappeared, 27 Nov 1944

Mr Foster himself had had a miraculous escape from death and had helped to liberate a trapped workman just in time to save him from being drowned by the water from the reservoir. An hour later, the spot was covered with six feet of debris.

Everyone was helping everyone who required it, doing whatever they could, even if it was only comfort. This was a caring community but PC Mackay noted that none complained during those terrible days. "Most of the villagers had lived in the quiet of an English village all their lives, and war had seemed very far away from them. Nobly they faced up to disaster, and went quietly on, obeying instructions. Many of them too had lost someone dear to them, but this did not deter them from boldly facing up to the trials, perils and difficulties of those dark days."

What PC Mackay had heard though was people were telling him that bombs were being returned to Fauld, still in their dromes, with the fuses and detonators still in them. This should never have happened, but these live bombs were sent back into the mine. It only needed one of them to be dropped or mishandled, and it would have exploded.

…..

This never came to light though until PC Mackay's papers were published in 2006

The Day the Sun Disappeared, 27 Nov 1944

CHAPTER 38

REPORT OF DAMAGE CAUSED

/http://www.helenlee.co.uk/Tutbury/images/fauld/aerial1.jpg
Aerial photographs courtesy of Barry Wright

John Pittaway (PC Mackay's father-in-law) was reading the newspaper on Thursday, 30 November 1944. It was the Yorkshire Evening Post. He had got all the papers he could obtain. He read a few pieces out to Constance Mackay.

The Day the Sun Disappeared, 27 Nov 1944

Reported in the Daily Herald, Wednesday, 29 November 1944

Burton-on-Trent, Tuesday Night:

Sixty dead; 110 entombed and missing and all hope abandoned for them; 200 injured.

This is the latest casualty list given me here tonight by tired rescue workers at the RAF maintenance depot where yesterday's explosion, the biggest of the war in Britain – devastated the countryside five miles from this town and changed its entire contours.

Thirty-one men are dead beneath the ruins of a plaster works on a hilltop. Six bodies have been recovered from the tangle of wreckage and machinery.

Twenty-three other bodies have been taken out of the ammunition dump. They include 16 RAF men.

Miners and Troops

As darkness comes down over this panorama of horror and wreckage of hillside churned into quagmires of fields pitted and pot-marked like any no-man's land on the Western Front, of villages battered and torn, the order has been given "Suspend rescue work."

For 26 hours this work has been carried on by miners' rescue teams called in from six countries.

The men, wearing oxygen apparatus have fought unceasingly against swelling gases and thousands of tons of fallen earth.

One of the rescue workers died from gas. He was Charles Beard, aged 51, of Ashby-de-le-Zouche.

The Day the Sun Disappeared, 27 Nov 1944

Hundreds of troops and civil defence men, who worked in Fly-Bomb Alley have been on the job, too.

Tonight, all hope has been abandoned of reaching any of the entombed men alive.

Before darkness closed in over the nearer villages, I ploughed almost waist deep in mud over the hills to see this stricken stretch of countryside lying like a tattered burnt-out carpet below me.

All the time, as you walk, the mud sucks at you. The grass has vanished and the pitted ground has become a morass.

Bombs of all calibres and shells have been spewed up out of the dumps and have crashed down to tear open the earth, to blow farms of the face of the earth, to smash homes and to send a tornado blast across the quiet countryside.

The Daily Mirror reported on Wednesday 29 November 1944:

Gas peril stops bomb dump rescue work

Gas has stopped the rescue work at the gigantic explosion at the RAF depot near Burton-on-Trent. Many of the rescue men have been working in peril of suffering the same fate as James Beard. It was decided last night to close the galleries of the depot for twenty-four hours to try to clear the gas away. Much of the rescue work yesterday had to be done by men wearing masks. At the time of the explosion several men who escaped from the wrecked plaster works near the dump, ran into a pocket of gas and died. It is expected that, when the final count is made, it will show that a total of eighty people – servicemen and civilians – were killed and injured.

All day, tin-hatted soldiers, rescue brigades from the Midlands and other parts of England had toiled without pause in a vast area

The Day the Sun Disappeared, 27 Nov 1944

of desolation – of scorched meadows, dead cattle and uprooted trees, of wrecked buildings and great bomb craters.

"There is little hope for the entombed men," said one of the rescue workers.

Bren gun carriers had helped in clearing a way through the mountains of mud and uprooted trees.

Staffordshire Advertiser 2 December 1944

A Seizemologist, J J Shaw, of West Bromich, which is nearly 40 miles from the scene, stated that his instrument recorded a violent explosion. "The vibration lasted about three minutes and the earth was shaken by violent jerks for the whole of that time, chiefly in the north and south directions. It is undoubtedly the heaviest explosion I have experienced in the whole of my 36 years as a seismologist." Convoys of ambulances and all available doctors were rushed to the scene. Parties of rescuers with gas apparatus, Civil Defence workers, ARP personal and American troops battled to rescue people from under the debris. The latest information from Sir Archibald Sinclair, as stated in the House of Commons last Thursday is that 7 Air Ministry people have lost their lives with some more 20 missing. In addition 16 have been injured and have been delivered to hospital. Plus, amongst civilians living and working in the area, 9 have been killed and 23 are missing, believed killed.

The Air Minister's Statement

In the House of Commons today, Sir Archibald Sinclair, Secretary for Air, replying to Mr Gretton (C., Burton), made a statement on the disaster which occurred at an RAF maintenance unit near Burton-on-Trent on Monday.

The Day the Sun Disappeared, 27 Nov 1944

'If the primary impression that it was not due to enemy action is correct, then compensation to civilians for the loss of life and property will be the responsibility of my department. In the meantime, officials have been sent down to give help and payments to those who have suffered and urgently require help.

I do not know that I can do more. I have sent officials down there with money in their pockets and they will ensure that payment of compensation, which is due, is made promptly.'

"So, Olive, the Air Ministry will be arranging compensation."

"I hope it comes quickly as it is desperately needed," Olive replied.

Elsewhere, John noticed Churchill's name and read the passage out to Olive:

"A court of inquiry has been ordered to investigate the circumstances....

Mr Churchill, who was received with cheers and acknowledged them by commencing, 'I thank the House very much indeed for its courtesy and kindness," and said that it would seem, in accordance with broad justice, that through whatever channels this relief was administered, the result should be practically the same to the victims.'

He was not able to say straight away whether that was the way in which the existing regulations would work, but they would go into the matter and, if there was a discrepancy, it would be for the House to express an opinion.

Mr Thorne (Lab. Plaistow) asked whether, if the inquiry proved that workmen were responsible for the explosion, the Government would be responsible.

The Day the Sun Disappeared, 27 Nov 1944

Mr Churchill: I do not know that we should assume that anyone was responsible. These dangerous explosives have sometimes spontaneous action.'

"So, Olive, as I thought, there's going to be a court of inquiry. There had to be. We'll find out then what really happened."

………

From **"Largest Wartime Explosion" – Fauld, Staffordshire. Issue No. 18 "After the Battle", November 1977.**

There was no trace of Upper Castle Hayes Farm and, so complete was the change in the landscape that no-one could accurately pinpoint the site.

A letter was sent by T H Brooks, Group Officer, A Group, No. lll Region, Burton-on-Trent to Mr Bowler, No. lX Regional Officer on 1 January 1945 concerning the Goodwin's farm.

"After making a careful reconnaissance of the crater and farm area, the following has been found:

1. Red and blue bricks found over a wide area 100-150 yards from the rim of the crater. Red bricks of the same type have also been found in the valley towards the Ford's factory.
2. The Goodwin's car may have come from the farm area into this factory.
3. A portion of a pig (leg) found 100 yards from the crater.
4. An oak beam 9" square found 60 yards from the crater and broken in two. This was part of the house.
5. An oak stack in Dutch Barn – pieces of iron work, twisted in straw, wheat straw and oak straw, also pieces of roof asbestos have been found in the straw.
6. The position of the farm marked by police with a red flag, is 30 yards inside the crater.

7. An iron bedstead has also been seen inside the crater. A few bedclothes were also found 50 yards from the rim of the crater.

It is possible that some of the farm has gone down the valley towards the Ford's factory, some of it in the field which is covered with earth and mud, and very possibly some has gone back into the crater, due to the suction of the blast wave.

I feel sure the only means of making sure that no bodies are in the field is to clear the area with mechanical means."

R A Youll, Principal Officer, reported in January 1945:

"I feel it is time to abandon the search for bodies. The number of persons missing at the present time is as follows:

Peter Ford & Sons – 3 bodies

Hanbury Fields (Botham's Farm – 1 body

Upper Castle Hayes (Goodwin's) Farm – 4 bodies

There is very little hope of any bodies now being recovered, unless a very comprehensive scheme of clearing the fields surrounding the farms if undertaken. As the depth of superimposed clay and debris ranges from about 30 ft to zero and covers an approximate area of one square mile, this would be a long and tedious process. In due course it may be necessary to carry out this work for agricultural purposes, and while it is understood that the County War Agricultural Committee is at present considering measures to this end, it is not known when the work will be put in hand.

The Day the Sun Disappeared, 27 Nov 1944

The Day the Sun Disappeared, 27 Nov 1944

At Botham's farm, a farmhand was heard talking approximately ten minutes before the explosion and no-one is able to give any indication of the work he was doing or the direction he may have taken during that period. A thorough search has revealed no sign of the missing man. Another labourer on this farm was killed and his body, minus legs, was found, almost completely buried, head down. It is generally felt that the missing man may have suffered a similar fate.

Goodwin's Farm: As the site of the farm is in the crater, it is generally felt that the four missing persons (one woman and three men) must have been blown to pieces with the rest of the farm at the time of the explosion. In support of this theory, a lower leg with kneecap attached and some fragments of flesh severed at the ankle and knee have been found near the site of the offices at Peter Ford's and it is assumed that this fragment probably reached the spot in the condition it was found by the considerable force of the explosion.

All bodies recovered from Peter Ford's offices and works have shown no signs of any violent upheaval. 22 bodies have been recovered and only three remain to be found.

The destruction and depth of debris was so great that accurate plotting of the location of many parts of the Peter Ford's Works was impossible and the forward surge of the debris had carried everything before it so that no spot could be overlooked in the search.

One man who survived had been cutting a field of roots on the edge of a wood. He reported that he watched as the entire topsoil from a square mile of land went up and came back to earth up to 11 miles away. Also 2.5 acres of woodland went up into the air and out of sight. Some trees returned to earth, being hurled so deep

The Day the Sun Disappeared, 27 Nov 1944

into the ground that farmers ploughing their land came upon them roots first.

First a path to the Works had to be cleared. A huge piece of gypsum stone was encountered in this path. It weighed approximately 20 tons and, presumably, had been blown there from the crater half a mile away.

Huge trees had also been blown there and presented a serious obstruction. Often they were half buried in thick mud and could not be dragged out. Steel Hawsers snapped like cotton and saws had to be used before the trees could be dragged clear.

Three other farms Hanbury Fields, Hare Holes and Croft Farm had been extensively damaged; a Dutch barn and cattle sheds at Stalford's buildings were flattened and, throughout the affected area, a total of two hundred cattle had been killed.

Mr Maurice Goodwin's farm, of about 200 acres, is described as "out of commission for at least a year."

Another farm has only three acres which are fit for use.

Mr Botham's farm is in a similar condition.

Fields of cabbage needed for winter keep are buried by the earth thrown out of the craters. Not a cabbage is now to be seen.

Hay stacks and straw stacks have been destroyed, or rendered unusable and a considerable amount of farm tackle was wrecked by the collapse of the buildings in which they were housed.

"You can say without fear of contradiction that anything between 600 and 1000 acres of good land have been rendered derelict at least so far as next year's crops are concerned and some will be useless for much longer than that" said a local farmer.

"For instance, I should have been able to turn ten heifers into that field over there for the winter. I shall be lucky if I get anything into it before next August."

It is hoped that bulldozers will supply the answer to the problem in some of the less battered fields.

Fate of animals. The RSCPA made a thorough search in connection with dispatching animals humanely and the People's Dispensary for Sick Animals staff, with their well-equipped van, rendered first aid to those animals with a chance of recovery.

Many domestic pets fled to the fields and woods, terror-stricken at the explosion.

Much humane work was carried out by local veterinary surgeons and slaughterhouse men from Burton.

....

Flight Sergeant Bill Allen and four others, had the unspeakable task of going around the outer area of the mine, to find maimed and dying cattle and sheep, and to put them out of their misery.

Walking around an area of railings, Bill came across a sight he never wished to see again. A horse had been lifted up bodily in the explosion and had come down upon the railings, impaling it. It was still alive! Bill was so shocked at the sight that he immediately threw up. One of the others went to see he was alright but he raised his hand to ward him off and, as a gut reaction, through tears that were running down his face, turned his sten gun at the beast and emptied its contents into the horses head. He then

The Day the Sun Disappeared, 27 Nov 1944

fell down on his knees in the mud and hung his head, silently weeping.

....

In Hanbury village, where few buildings had escaped the blast, the Cock Inn had been damaged beyond repair and the village hall was flattened, with its chairs and piano scattered everywhere. The earth tremor had displaced the upper section of the church tower. Both Hanbury and Tutbury villages had suffered a complete breakdown in public services. Water mains had been shattered, telephones put out of action and overhead power-lines brought down by falling debris.

Neither were the effects purely local; the explosion had been heard and the tremor felt at distances of over fifty miles and, at Burton-on-Trent, five miles away, there were reports of minor, structural damage to about a hundred and fifty older-type houses.

The explosion had killed sixty-eight persons, and injured a further twenty-two. Twenty-six had died at 21 MU, including all of those working in the new area and six Italians and a member of the Mines Rescue Service. In addition to the five Ford's employees who had died in the gas-filled mine, another twenty-seven of their men had been killed in the surface buildings. Nearby, at Purse Cottages, two civilians had been killed by the flood. Five farm workers and members of their families had vanished without trace at Upper Castle Hayes Farm and another had been killed in the fallen buildings at Stalfords.

....

Peter Ford's plasterboard works were never rebuilt and the gypsum mine, presently worked by BPB Industries Ltd. is the largest in Europe. The whole landscape north of the crater remains a wilderness, although part has been used since 1973 by Staffordshire County Council for refuse tipping. The council did try to get permission from the Ministry of Defence to tip household waste in the crater itself (which it is estimated could hold 20 years' rubbish) but objections were raised by the relatives of those whose bodies were never recovered. The posts from the sluice gates for the old Ford reservoir can still be seen on the hillside, as can odd pieces of brickwork and narrow-gauge railway track. The two rear emergency exits to the present RAF Fauld mine can be seen close to the modern BPB works buildings.

The crater and the distorted hillside at Fauld survive today as a permanent reminder of what it meant to one small village to have been part of a war zone.

As to the St John's Church, Horninglow and Christ Church, Burton, St John's has been repaired, but the graceful, tapering spire of Christ Church was rendered quite unsafe.

Blocks of stone were loosened and steeplejacks began work immediately, surrounding the tower and spire with a network of steel scaffolding.

About a third of the spire had been taken down when it was discovered that the rest of the masonry had been shaken more than had been feared at first. A Zeppelin bomb had fallen near the church in 1916, which demolished the Mission Room while a service was in progress and killing a number of people, while damage was caused to the fabric, including the tower.

The Day the Sun Disappeared, 27 Nov 1944

John Pittaway read from the Burton Observer, dated 7 December.

Dump disaster – 68 killed or missing

Less than 4,000 tons bombs lost

Relief measured in Burton District

Exaggerated estimates published in some of the national newspaper of the death-roll caused by the two explosions last Monday week were fortunately not confirmed when the official figures were announced in the House of Commons on Thursday.

These showed a total of 68 killed and missing- two more than were mentioned on good authority in last week's Burton Observer. The official officials were as follows.

Killed – 16

Missing believed killed – 43, Missing – 9, Inured 13

....

On 1 June 1945 Mr MacDonald, in charge of the steeplejacks' operations was in communication with Mr G Moncur, the Borough Surveyor. He stated that he was not satisfied as to the stability of the remaining portion of the spire and that there was a certain amount of danger which necessitated the taking of precautions.

Mr Moncur immediately informed the police authorities and portions of the streets in the immediate vicinity were closed to traffic and pedestrians, prominent notices being displayed and officers put on guard.

Barricades were erected at the junctions of Moor Street and Dukes Street; New Street and Orchard Street; and Uxbridge Street and Park Street.

Uxbridge Street Church before the explosion cracked it

As an extra measure of care, the railway crossing near the church was closed, the steeplejacks having found that the passage of trains set up a certain amount of vibration.

A third of the spire had to be taken down and, because of the possibility that the remainder might collapse, portions of the street in the immediate vicinity were closed.

It was decided not to replace the spire because of the high expenses involved in restoring it.

The Day the Sun Disappeared, 27 Nov 1944

CHAPTER 39

BRIAN JOHNSON

(Developed from excerpt in the Burton Mail, November 28 1994)

When war broke out and Hitler was raining bombs down on London and the major cities of the UK, children from those cities were being evacuated to the countryside. Some went to Wales, others such as Brian Johnson and his sister, Shirley, were evacuated from Birmingham to the comparative safety of Hanbury. No-one knew then what was going to happen.

They were waiting at a station to be picked up by an allotted family. All they had on them was a little brown case each containing a change of clothes and packed lunches that they had already eaten. Their mother had also packed some tinned food and a huge bar of Cadbury's chocolate intended for their host families. Where mum got the chocolate from was anyone's guess but they just couldn't resist it, not having tasted chocolate for so long, so the bar hadn't lasted long.

They wore labels around their necks indicating their names. There were a few others, waiting there patiently for someone to call out their names and take them somewhere safe, to a new family. They were not excited and in fact quite worried as to what they could expect. Shirley was shivering with anticipation, holding on tightly to her brother's hand. They had left their loving parents back in Birmingham (where they had been living in their two up, two down terraced house), a major city with loads of people coming

The Day the Sun Disappeared, 27 Nov 1944

and going about their business, to go to a place they had never been to, to rolling green countryside that they had never seen to such a great extent with fields, little white-painted cottages and farms. It seemed all like a different world to them.

"Will they like us?" Shirley asked her brother.

"I'm not worried if they like us or not. The thing is, will they treat us like slaves, making us do all the dirty, hard graft that no-one else wants to do. I've read this sort of thing in Dickens, 'David Copperfield' and such like – and they'll make us live on leftover scraps that you wouldn't feed to a pig."

"Oh, mum and dad wouldn't send us to a place like that. You're just trying to upset me, you're a rotter you are, Brian."

Then Shirley had another thought, "Oh Brian, I hope they are not going to separate us. What if these new families only have room for one child? Oh, you're all I've got here Brian. Even though you're horrid to me sometimes, I'd rather we were together."

"We'll just have to wait and see, Shirley. Even if they do separate us, I'll make sure I get to see you regularly, don't worry."

Anyway, they needn't have worried. They were both taken in by a nice family and both settled down in their new school.

By November 1944 Brian was 13 years old. He was either in the science room or craft room at Tutbury School on 27 November. The class had only been in progress about 10 minutes when suddenly there was a most horrendous noise. The building shook, the walls seemed to go in and out twice, as if they were made of cardboard, and the glass in the windows broke.

Everyone was screaming things like, "There's been an air-raid."

The Day the Sun Disappeared, 27 Nov 1944

"We'd had regular air-raid training and this was always preceded by a warning siren, an extremely loud, whirr, whirr, whirr. But there hadn't been a warning siren.

The air was filled with a terrible roaring and rushing sound, even minutes after the loud explosion."

The headmaster, Mr Stevens, appeared and gave orders, "Right everyone, teachers and children, everyone, into the playground, Now." I was flummoxed. Why into the playground. All the bomb training we'd had had directed us to get under our desks. Anyway, we all headed into the playground.

We could see over in the direction of Hanbury and Fauld two columns of grey smoke and flames rising up to the sky. I thought we'd be ordered from there into the air-raid shelters but no – instead the teachers organised all of us pupils to line up and we were told to run all around the perimeter of the playground, in two lines!

Children started coughing, as bits were coming out of the sky, bits of earth and debris. Right against the school railings was a dead cow. Girls started crying and anyone looking up, their eyes were soon filled with dust. My eyes were stinging. We stopped running. Through blurry sight I looked towards Tutbury – we all did. Everywhere we looked we saw damage – houses with gaping holes in the roofs, chimney stacks gone. Out in the fields, all the cattle were dead.

All this time, smoke was pouring into the sky from Fauld and flames were rising.

I heard one of the teachers say, "Looks like the RAF ammunition dump has been bombed or been blown up."

The Day the Sun Disappeared, 27 Nov 1944

I looked skywards but there wasn't a sign of a single aeroplane, so where had the bomber disappeared to?

Rumour after rumour went round the school that day. I heard that Hanbury village had been destroyed.

At last the headmaster gave orders that we could go home early, so staff and pupils could get to their own villages to find out if we still had homes and families.

On the bus, with Shirley, looking out of the windows, we could see scenes of devastation everywhere. There were large lumps of white gypsum rock planted in mud, broken trees, houses and farm buildings damaged, everything covered in a white powder from the gypsum mines.

Getting back to "auntie and uncle" who had taken us on during the evacuation, we saw that their roof had sustained damage then, going inside, discovered that the force of the explosion had cracked the wall of the house.

(Brian was going to write a book of his experiences, but unfortunately, I cannot find if this book ever got into print.)

The Day the Sun Disappeared, 27 Nov 1944

CHAPTER 40

VISIT BY THE BISHOP OF LICHFIELD

A steady downpour of rain from a leaden sky cloaked the area as groups formed outside. People enquired about relatives and friends and consoled each other. Near the door lay the shattered remains of stone pinnacle blasted from the top of the tower.

It was only in the last minute that people were able to have the service in their own church. On Saturday, it was still pronounced unsafe but workmen 'splinted' the damaged tower in scaffolding.

Crowded inside with the villagers were off-duty rescue workers, members of the RAF, men from the dump, NFAS, WVS, officials and members of the rural council and officials and directors of the works; Mr John F Gretton, MP for Burton and Mrs Gretton were present, with the Mayor and Mayoress of Burton (Coun. And Mrs A Fidkin).

They heard the Bishop of Lichfield describe the dead in the disaster as a genuine part of the war casualties. "They would never have had to give their lives if it had not been for the war, and especially the chances of war that brought that vast munitions dump to this corner of England.

Conducting the service with the Bishop was the vicar, tired and haggard-looking from his ceaseless efforts to help others since that day when he himself miraculously escaped injury. The Bishop praised him for his self-sacrifice and devotion. To add to his worry his wife has collapsed just yesterday and was very seriously ill.

The Day the Sun Disappeared, 27 Nov 1944

Just then, news came that another body had been discovered from the debris. It was the body of William Ford

"It was part of the sacrifice of war. The price that has to be paid". These were the words of the Bishop of Lichfield, when he preached yesterday at the memorial hall service, at the shattered little village, near the scene of the bomb dump which plunged the district into mourning. If not for the war effort, Nazi tyranny, the world would have entered into a dark age, which might have lasted 400-500 years.

The Bishop suggested that, as well as a memorial service, it was a thanksgiving service for those who were spared.

On 29 November, the Bishop of Lichfield, Dr F S Woods, toured the devastated district. He was covered in mud and dirt, and hatless, but went unceasingly to the homes of those who suffered most and offered condolences. He had recently returned from a tour of the battle front in Italy and Malta. He was interviewed by a Burton reporter, "It is the worst scene of desolation that I have seen – worse than anything I saw in Italy. I will hold a memorial service at the village on Sunday."

He spoke to those following him.

"The bodies recovered will be buried in their respective parishes and on Sunday morning we are arranging a memorial service for the dead and a thanksgiving service for those who were rescued. The joint service will be held in the little parish church.

Someone in the crowd asked, "So many men have died here. How will their families survive? Will there be a relief fund for the dependants of the victims?"

The Bishop replied, "I deeply regret this disaster and recognise the grief that you are all suffering and will suffer in the future following the loss of your loved ones. Let it be known that I will do my utmost to bring the possibility of a relief fund under consideration. I will be in contact with the Mayor of Burton-on-Trent and the chairman of the Rural District Council concerned.

I wish to add that Councillor Fidkin, the Mayor of Burton has received messages expressing sympathy with the bereaved from the American Consul at Birmingham, Mr Samuel Sokobin, and from the officers and ship's company of HMS Savage, which I have been made aware of is the town's adopted destroyer."

On Sunday morning, in the village church, Hanbury in front of a crowd of mourners, helpers and well-wishers that filled the church, including the Hon. Mr and Mrs Gretton, the Mayor and Mayoress of Burton, representatives of the RAF, both British and American, representatives of various rural councils, Civil Defence, NFS and WVS, the Bishop conducted a service of remembrance. I, PC Thomas Mackay and my wife, Olive, were there, along with many of the people who had been rescued, Jack Gorton, rescued from Fords mine; Bert Hardwick from Top Farm; Miss Farden, the school teacher, Tom Bowring from Peter Ford's works, Joseph Foster, the Works Manager were there, to name but a few of the many who attended.

The Bishop started his service. "The deaths of these good folk are an integral part of the war casualties – part of the price to be paid in a great and worthy purpose."

The Day the Sun Disappeared, 27 Nov 1944

The hymns especially chosen were:
How bright these glorious spirits shine
Oh God our help in ages past
Through all the changing scenes of life
Put though thy trust in God, and
Jesus still leads on.

The psalm read was the 91st.

Whoever goes to the Lord for safety,
Whoever remains under the protection of the Almighty,
can say to him
You are my defender and protector
You are my God; in you I trust
He will keep you safe from all hidden dangers and from all deadly
diseases

He will cover you with his wings
You will be safe in his care
His faithfulness will protect and defend you
A thousand may fall dead beside you
Ten thousand all round you
but you will not be harmed
You will look and see how the wicked are punished

God says, "I will save those who love me
and will protect those who know me as Lord
When they call to me, I will answer them;
When they are in trouble, I will be with them.
I will rescue them and honour them.
I will reward them with long life;
I will save them."

The Day the Sun Disappeared, 27 Nov 1944

I whispered to Olive. "The Bishop has chosen that psalm wisely. It is certainly pertinent and I trust in the goodness and mercy of God that he has indeed got our dead people under his wings."

A minute's silence was observed in memory of the dead.

The Bishop addressed those assembled there, "On this sad and memorable occasion, I am not surprised to see this church filled to the doors with a large and representative congregation. It has been a sudden and tragic happening in your midst.

I come in the name of the Father, our God, to all the folk in this county and half of Shropshire and I should like to assure you all, especially the inhabitants of these parishes, of the depth and sincerity of the sympathy, which has been evoked by this unforeseen and unprecedented disaster.

I have personally received many messages of sympathy, some of them of money and offers of hospitality, and I know I am not speaking just for the members of the Church of England, but for all throughout this place. I am glad that our service should be of a united character.

I pay tribute to the vicar of this parish for the self-sacrificing way he has devoted himself to the succour of those who need it, and I know that sympathy goes out to him at this time, when his wife has been stricken with a serious illness.

We are all in the hands of God. These things come and, in these days, I suppose all of us – those who fight and those who serve – are used by now to looking death in the face.

We have faced that for six years. Here we stand in the sixth winter of the war, and, thank God, there is no flagging of the spirit of courage and patient endurance. We have never flinched from the sacrifice.

The Day the Sun Disappeared, 27 Nov 1944

It is more and more clear that, if it had not been for our standing up to that ghastly Nazi tyranny, the world would have entered upon a dark age, which might have lasted four or five hundred years.

We have faced sacrifice to prevent that, and to make it possible to build something better, to open the door of Christian civilisation to Europe and the world. It is for this that we and our Allies have faced death, have given lives. Now, this call to sacrifice has come right home to this part of the world. I pray that, in these days we shall feel something of that consolation.

While they died in the Lord, the converse is true. We live in the Lord. This should be also a service of thanksgiving for those who are spared.

Yet here we stand today, in sight of victory....but at the same time we must think of the difficulties of the post-war condition, the confusion and disorder in Europe, of the stupendous task of economic and political reconstruction. These things could only come to pass if they learned to love the Lord their God and neighbour as themselves.

Relative to the offertory, the vicar of the parish has explained that it would be devoted in the relief of those who need it, when all other relief is exhausted. Help has been very generous and the expense of the funerals have been and will be borne and other help has been given."

There was a smattering of talk among the congregation. I gave generously but there was much delving into pockets to retrieve what small change people had. I whispered to Olive, "People can't contribute, no matter how much they want to. They've got their

The Day the Sun Disappeared, 27 Nov 1944

own ruined places to sort out, some haven't even got places to live anymore and are relying on the kindness of others. It's a bit much passing around the offertory to people who have gone through so much loss. They should get money coming to them from the Council and charities."

Olive agreed. "I'm just glad we weren't damaged beyond repair and can help out. People here are helping out others all they can, helping people repair their houses, helping with food and clothing. It's not as though most people here have any money to spare anyway. I do hope some recompense will be forthcoming soon."

....

However, the offertory managed to raise £85. A fund was set up and by the end of December 1944, the fund stood at £1,220.

The fund soon reached £4,500 which included £635 from the Mayor of Burton's Fund. By the end of 1945 the Fund reached its maximum amount of £7831. At Christmas of that year each child to the age of 16 years bereaved by the explosion had a gift of 10s.0d. and being "Victory in Europe Year" each widow and dependant adult was given £5. During 1945 the sum of £504 was distributed.

....

John Pittaway, Olive Mackay's father was reading the paper, as ever. "Well, that's a bit of good news Olive. It says here:

Work for the workless: An official notification was sent out that the plaster employees rendered workless as a result of the corporation and who desire will be found employment by the firm concerned.

The Day the Sun Disappeared, 27 Nov 1944

It was also definitely stated that, as far as these workers and the relatives of all their dead comrades are concerned, all steps are being taken, and will be taken to alleviate any possibility of financial stress.

A word of praise and thanks is due to the WVS and NAAFI for vans which have plied the rescue workers with free hot drinks and light refreshment from early in the morning to dusk. There is little comfort for those men in their gruesome task, but these ladies have done everything they could – and so cheerfully."

"Well the poor families need so much help. I'll have a rummage through and see if there are any old clothes I can take for the needy. That's the best I can do and we haven't got any food to spare, what with the rationing. It looks like everyone's doing their bit, coming together to help in any way they can and at least jobs will be offered to those out of work now."

Olive returned a bit later, with an armful of clothes. "Barbara has grown out of these and I've found some old baby clothes in the ottoman upstairs. And there dresses of mine, well, I've lost so much weight with only having the minimum to eat that these dresses are swimming on me now. I suppose I could take them in at the seams but they'll never look the same, so I think they can go too. There are these jumpers and cardigans too, that have seen better days. I suppose I could unpick them and knit knew ones, but people need them now, so I'll see how my clothes rations stretch for new wool and knit some more. I'll get the bus to the Women's Voluntary Service. It's a shame you can't walk too far, dad, otherwise you could have helped me."

"Sorry, Olive, but my legs are just not up to it. I feel so sorry for the mites who have lost their fathers. It's a terrible situation,

The Day the Sun Disappeared, 27 Nov 1944

awful. Tom's doing his bit though. We've hardly seen hide nor hair from him in these past weeks."

"Yes, he just comes home, has a bite to eat and a wash and off to bed for a few hours shut eye, then he's out again early doors. I make sure he's got his snap though, to take with 'im. He's not wearing his uniform, because that would be ruined with all the mud, but he puts on his wellington boots and overalls, with an old jacket – just wears his police helmet to identify him. "

CHAPTER 41

FUNERALS

Funerals of the victims of RAF explosion – Burton Observer, Thurs 14 December 1944

The funerals of six victims of the explosion at the RAF maintenance depot near Burton-on-Trent, took place at a parish church in the district.

Family mourners, friends and comrades of the deceased filled the church to overflowing.

The congregation included many branches of the services, and many who, in various capacities, had rendered gallant assistance in rescue work.

The vicar of the parish and other clergy from the district took part in the choral service, which included the 23rd Psalm and the hymns, "All ye who seek for sure relief in trouble and distress" and "Peace, perfect peace."

The Bishop of Lichfield, Dr E S Woods, in his address, spoke of the volume of sympathy evoked in this untoward and unprecedented disaster.

As the oak coffins, each covered with a Union Jack, were borne from the church, the Dune Dimittis was sung.

At the interment prayers were offered by respective clergy, and in each case the committal was made by the Bishop.

The Day the Sun Disappeared, 27 Nov 1944

The late Mr G Smith (61) a married man with three sons serving in the Forces, had lived in the district all his life and had been employed at the plaster works. Two of his sons are serving overseas.

Mr George Lawrence Cokayne, aged 50, one of the victims, had lived in the district all his life and was employed as a blacksmith at the plaster works. He lost his wife about seven years ago, and his only son is service abroad.

Corporal Durose, who would have been 24 last Friday week, leaves a widow and baby daughter. The interment took place at Burton Cemetery of Corporal Alan Sydney Durose, RAF.

He enlisted on May 25th 1937 and served in Iraq untl May 1st 1942, after which he was transferred to England. He was authorised, subject to confirmation, to wear the 1939-1943 Star.

RAF members were the bearers and formed a guard of honour.

Mr Samuel Pickering was a single man, a victim at the plaster works, was an only son, and his father was one of the rescued at the same works.

He had served in the Army during the present war and had received his discharge.

The Day the Sun Disappeared, 27 Nov 1944

Mr William Henry Shephard, a married man, with no children, employed as a plaster worker, is one of the missing in connection with the RAF dump explosion near Burton on November 27th. He is the only son of Mr Henry Shephard, a 73 year old plaster miner, who lost his life in the explosion. William Henry Shephard is a popular member of the Tutbury Bowling Club.

Mr Ambrose Patterson, (47), who leaves a wife and one daughter, came to work at the RAF depot from Sunderland about four years ago. He served overseas in the last war.

In several cases, workmates acted as bearers.

Mr George Henry Powell, (37?), who leaves a wife and two daughters, had served for over 18 years with the North Stafford shire Regiment. His four brothers have also seen Army service.

He was a worker at the maintenance unit, was a member of the Old Comrades Association and the Druids Lodge. Home Guard comrades were bearers.

The funeral of Mr George Priestly (63), a plaster miner and victim of the recent explosion, took place at a parish church in the district last Wednesday. He had been employed at the plaster works for about 41 years. Interested in football, he had been a member of the committee and a trainer of the local club. He had also been a keen supporter of the local silver prize band. He leaves a widow, seven sons and two daughters. Five of his sons are serving with HM forces overseas.

The work of excavation at the scene of the explosion, is proceeding under conditions of considerable difficulty.

The Day the Sun Disappeared, 27 Nov 1944

Five more bodies had been recovered up to Saturday, those of Lac W Deuchers, of 71 King Street, Crieff, Scotland and four Italians. Deuchars had multiple injuries.

Mr J L Auden, East Staffordshire coroner, opened the inquests on them.

The funerals finally took place, on 19 December of Mr William Maurice Goodwin and his wife, Mary Goodwin of Upper Castle Hayes Farm – the farm that had disappeared into the crater. The funeral was held in the local Methodist church and was packed out by mourners. Mrs Goodwin's body had been found on Wednesday 17th December, and her husband's the day after. The funeral was conducted by the Superintendent Minister. I had gone along to pay my respects. The Minister referred to the irreparable loss sustained by the church, where Mr Goodwin had been a steward. Mrs L J Shotton accompanied the hymns on the organ as the congregation sang 'Rock of Ages' and 'Oh love that will not let me go'.

They were buried in the same grave in the churchyard.

The funeral took place on Thursday of Mr Joseph Bell, a plaster mine victim of the recent explosion, whose body was recovered on Tuesday. He was buried at St Mary's Priory Church, Tutbury, although with no known headstone.

A single man, aged 39 years, he lived with his father, Mr Eli Bell, a retired plaster miner. He has two brothers, serving abroad, and a brother who has been missing for two years. The service was choral.

....

The Day the Sun Disappeared, 27 Nov 1944

(Burton Observer, 28 December)

St John's Church, Horninglow, the spire of which was damaged as a result of the explosion, was used for the ordinary services on Sunday. At Sunday's Christmas fair, the Vicar, AGF Barker, was able to announce that the steeplejacks had given their assurance that the church was safe. The spire is strongly supported by steel girders, which it was ascertained rendered the possibility of the structure collapsing, very remote.

Christ Church, Burton, was also open on Sunday again for services, the steeple having been pronounced safe.

Up to date the Staffordshire Explosion Relief Fund Committee has received £1,084.2s.11d. This is made up mainly of small donations received from all parts of the country.

CHAPTER 42

CORONER'S REPORT ON DEATHS

The rumours were rife about the number of people killed. These rumours even got into the Algerian newspapers. The Depêche Algerienne, dated 28 November 1944, stated that 220 people had been killed in an RAF munitions depot in the region of Burton.

Yes, the numbers killed was greatly exaggerated but, so much for the RAF trying to keep information under control, as this report clearly stated that the explosion came from the RAF ammunitions storage.

The Daily Mirror reported on Wednesday, 29th November,

The Coroner, Mr J L Auden, sent a letter to the Burton Daily Mail, issued on 2nd December 1944. He was outraged

He had addressed the court at the inquests yesterday on two of the victims. His letter stated:

Even after the Coroner's letter, **The London Daily Mail on 29 December** still reported that 50 had died, then later amended that to 200 killed. What the London Daily Mail did report was that 'Two distinct explosions were heard. According to the people in the district, the first, it is believed was comparatively slight, killing one person and injuring several.

The second occurred, some distance from the first, and apparently caused great damage and the bulk of the casualties.'

The Day the Sun Disappeared, 27 Nov 1944

The explosions were felt 60 miles away and were heard in several Midland towns. Houses in Leicester and district were shaken; damage to houses in Coventry was also caused; and farms were wiped out, with hundreds of cows being killed.

The Coroner, Dr Auden, reported on 14 December that the number of dead and missing may now be considered to be about 70.

Three more bodies were reported recovered on 4 January 1945, five more on 8 January, another on 15th.

The Hampshire Telegraph reported on Friday, 26 January, 1945 a notification from the Coroner, Mr J L Auden:

"More than 50 bodies have now been recovered from the site of the RAF depot explosion near Burton and it is expected that another seven will be reached during the next few days at the cement and plaster works. Mr Auden has stated that it is probable that no figure of the casualties will ever be exact and that at both the depot and the near-by works were some people who possibly will never be known. The Coroner is waiting for the result of the latest effort of the Civil Defence rescue parties before asking the Home Secretary for permission to presume that the remainder of those known to be missing, are dead."

The Coroner, J.L Auden Esq. had been in contact, back and forth, with Mr Gretton, MP, who was trying to get an answer as to when an inquiry could be held.

A letter, dated 24 January 1945, to Mr Gretton stated,

The Day the Sun Disappeared, 27 Nov 1944

"I am being pressed to hold the Inquest as soon as possible but do not intend doing so until the first week in February, as my Coroner's officer is quite confident that two or three more bodies will be recovered by then.

It will not be sufficient for me to just bring in a verdict of Accidental Death on these numerous people, as I understand that I am to be asked many questions to which, I think it would be a great mistake to give ambiguous answers. I gather I am going to be asked:

1. *Whether the accident was due to sabotage*
2. *Whether the Italian Co-operators were in any way involved*
3. *Whether blasting in a neighbouring works was the cause, and*
4. *The likelihood of a repetition of the disaster.*

If I could give the general public some ideas as to the cause it would be most helpful, but if, for security reasons, this is impossible, I should be very much obliged if I can definitely answer the first three questions. As to the fourth, I intend to evade this as best as possible.

I quite believe, and I am sure you will agree with me, that the more the public are allowed to know about this matter, the sooner will the many rumours be crushed. I wonder if you could see the Minister for Air and ask him exactly how far I am or may not go at the Inquiry."

The Day the Sun Disappeared, 27 Nov 1944

*Now's the time to consider
Where the fault lies, who is taking the blame.
Repairs are made, but not hearts
of families: - recompense – not the same.
Now's the time to consider.*

CHAPTER 43

VILLAGE WAITING FOR AID

People were gathered in the Village Hall. Is was now the end of January 1945. They were up in arms and voices raised in protest at the delay in getting any offer of compensation.

They had read in the Daily Mail on 31 January, under the title 'Village waiting for aid'. In their report they stated that Nine weeks have elapsed since the disaster. Temporary 'first aid' repairs have been done to the least damaged houses in Hanbury and the local lanes have been cleared for traffic, but final compensation arrangements have still to be made.'

The Vicar, Rev Crook, was saying,

"We are still very much dazed as a result of the explosion. I have sent many letters to our MP, Mr John Gretton on the question of adequate compensation for the dependants of men who lost their lives and people whose homes have been shattered as a result of the RAF bomb dump explosion.

My understanding is that there have been talks taking place between Mr Gretton and Lord Sherwood, Under-Secretary for the Air Ministry."

The Day the Sun Disappeared, 27 Nov 1944

Someone shouted out in the crowd gathered there, "That was nine weeks ago, nine whole weeks and we've had nothing. People have lost their family, their homes, their belongings and the Air Ministry keeps us waiting. The Bowring family have been left fatherless – he left 7 children, all at school age, one a baby in arms. They are relying on hand-outs from friends and family. Then there's the Cooper family – Joseph Cooper had eight children, four of whom are at school. Mary, his wife, set up the temporary mortuary and has slaved every day since - and what are you doing for her – nothing! These families would starve if it wasn't for their friends. Do you want more deaths on your hands?"

Someone else shouted out, "These poor people are relying on the friendship of neighbours and family. Most have no income coming in now as the main breadwinner was killed in the damn explosion. We demand recompense, NOW."

Another voice shouted out, "Is the Air Ministry trying to deny the disaster was their fault, as we're all damn well sure now that it was one of their employees who created the explosion?"

The Vicar was trying to keep order, trying to raise his voice above the multitude thronged there.

"Ladies and gentlemen, please let me continue.

First aid repairs have been carried out, where possible, on damaged cottages; a few of the churned-up roads have been made usable; and people who lost their homes are now accommodated elsewhere but I wholeheartedly understand the aggression that is now being felt, that no compensation seems to be forthcoming. I have been told that the Air Ministry is giving the question of compensation urgent consideration – everything should be settled in not more than six weeks."

The Day the Sun Disappeared, 27 Nov 1944

There was a hushed mumble in the hall but someone else shouted out, "What are these poor folk supposed to live on in the meantime?"

The vicar responded, "I understand that emergency grants have been made to cover eight weeks, of 32s for a widow and 11s for each child – with a ruling that each family should not get less than £2.10s weekly.

"The same voice shouted out, "But that's no great amount in comparison to the £6 and £7 weekly, which the 21 breadwinners of the village were bringing into their homes before they were killed!"

Another voice shouted out, "We're in the middle of winter. People need money for heating. Where's that money coming from? These poor people are enduring extreme hardships. Something must be done to help out these people, and quickly."

Rev Crook continued, "I agree that is no great amount …. But the Air Ministry seems to be terribly slow in getting things settled."

The secretary of the Distress Fund then stood up, "The grants received now total nearly £5,000, unfortunately, and I am very aware this is to everyone's great misfortune, only two small grants have been made. We do not, in any way, want to hold the money back from anyone really in need of it, however, the trustees are waiting for the Air Ministry to adjust the compensation question, and then the money will be distributed among the most needy."

There could be no further come-back on this. Everyone in need would be looked after, but as to compensation, they would have to wait another six weeks.

The meeting closed with a lot of disgruntled voices as people left the hall.

The Day the Sun Disappeared, 27 Nov 1944

(Reported in the London Daily Mail, 31 January 1945)

"Sir Archibald Sinclair, Secretary for Air, told Mr John Gretton, Conservative MP for Burton, in the Commons today, that compensation would be paid on the basis of the awards which those concerned might reasonably expect in a successful action for damages under the Fatal Accidents Act, the Law Reform Act, or at Common Law. All reasonable legal costs would also be paid.

It wasn't actually until October, as reported in the Burton Daily Mail on 29 October 1945, that the Air Ministry agreed to pay £41,686.10s damages to relatives of 22 members of the Transport and General Workers' Union killed in the RAF bomb dump explosion. Following negotiations with the Treasury, the union's legal department reported that the individual amounts range from £1,196.16s for a widow and six children to £325 for a married daughter not dependent. The union was also dealing with 16 personal injury claims, half of which had been satisfactorily settled, and stated the remainder will probably have been adjusted before the end of the year.

As an example of the deliberations in cases brought forward, the case of Miss Edith Fell, of Hoar Cross, was cited in the Burton Daily Mail on 1 August 1946. Her brother had been killed at the Peter Ford & Sons mine, where he worked. The Air Ministry, had assumed liability to dependants of the victims and had aided Miss Fell for a year, but then declined to do any more for her, on the ground that, being only a sister of the deceased, she had no claim. Action was bought under the Workman's Compensation Act, against Peter Ford & Sons Ltd. Miss Fell claimed that she was entirely dependent on her brother, being his housekeeper. Her solicitor submitted that the brother was made to work in a place especially exposed to a certain peril from a gigantic subterranean store of mines, which were liable, if not likely to explode. Peter Ford's solicitors argued that it did not necessarily follow that death arose out of or in course of employment because it occurred on the employers' premises. Notwithstanding that Fell's body was recovered in the mine, there was no evidence as to where he was working at the time of the explosion.

It was no fault of the respondents that the ammunition was stored so close to their property.

The judge concluded that the Air Ministry acted in a perfectly proper and indeed in many cases, a generous way, in connection with the terrible catastrophe.

Messrs Ford were entitled to be reimbursed the amount of the compensation, together with the costs as between the applicant and themselves by the Air Ministry.

The Day the Sun Disappeared, 27 Nov 1944

Payments made by P Ford & Sons Ltd to relations of deceased employees for week ending Dec. 13th 1944

Footnote: all these men were killed in Peter Ford's mines 1944

Name	Relationship	Children	Remarks	£	s	d
S Pickering jnr	Son	none	Lives at homes	1		
G Page	Wife	None		2		
F Bowring	Wife	7		3	15	
G Smith	Wife	None		2		
H Shepherd	Daughter	None	Daughter keeps house	2		
W Shepherd	Wife	None		2		
A Harris	Wife	None at home		2		
J Cooper	Wife	4		3		
A E Page	Wife	1		2	5	
T Hudson	Wife	6		3	10	
G L Cokayne	Mother in law	None at home	Mrs Gent keeps house	2		
W Ford	Wife	None at home	Wife in hospital. To be paid later & include last week	0		

The Day the Sun Disappeared, 27 Nov 1944

Name	Relationship	Children	Remarks	£	s	d
W Gent	Wife	None		2		
E Woolley	Wife	None		2		
H Carter	Wife	None at home		2		
E Barker	Wife	3		2	15	
O A Gilbert	Wife	None at home		2		
P Cooper	Wife	1		2	5	
P Page	Wife	None at home		2		
W Kidd	Daughter	None	Daughter keeps house	2		
E Fell	Wife	2		2	10	
B Fell	Sister	None	Sister keeps house	2		
G Priestley	Wife	None at home		2		
			£	49	0	0

....

For the small, sad parish of Hanbury, with its four hundred souls, the effects were to be felt for many more years. For the numerous widows and children left behind, it had been a devastating experience, a totally unexpected and terrifying event. Hanbury did not have the fatalistic attitude towards the disaster of a traditional coal mining community to fall back on.

Although no children were actually orphaned, the sentiment felt all over led to offers to adopt any orphaned children. A lady from Stoke on Trent and a gentleman in Sheffield and an orphans' home in Brighouse all offered to take in children.

Even five or six years after the explosion, men who had been gassed, were still in a sorry state – those men who had gone down the RAF dump and the Peter Ford mines, back and forwards, again and again, to try to rescue people – the people they managed to drag out, barely hanging on to life. The gas had affected their lungs and some just couldn't work again, could just about walk a few paces some of them. They were in pain and their lives had been ruined. The Fund Relief Trustees investigated each case and afforded assistance. They endeavoured to visit all the beneficiaries, even though they became scattered all over the country. In 1950 obstacles were being put in the path of the Trustees by the Air Ministry, who were not prepared to inform the Trustees of details of any payment made to claimants suffering from the effects of the Fauld Explosion, but would verify any statements made by applicants. This seemed to indicate duplicate and bogus claims.

....

Annual grants were awarded of £500-£600, peaking in 1951 to £838, and then falling slowly to £237. In 1959 the Fund was closed. I suppose, by this time, the National Health System was operating and there was social care.

....

CHAPTER 44

OLIVE ROSINA BOWRING

Fred Bowring's wife and family were obviously left distraught following Fred's death. He was gassed in Peter Ford's alabaster mine. He was a big guy and Charles Gibbs, his best friend, overcome with gas as he himself was, just could not move him. Fred had been just 39 when he died, leaving Olive alone to bring up their young family of seven children, the youngest being only a few months old, at their home in Wood End East, Hanbury.

Fred's body was brought up from the mine on the Wednesday, 29th November and a funeral was held some days later. Charles Gibbs, although Fred's best friend, did not attend. He did not attend any of the funerals as he was too distraught. He told people he had lost all of his friends and he didn't need a funeral to remember them. His whole life had just collapsed in on him that day. He wished he could turn the clock back, wished they had got out of the mine before the gas got to them but, no, that just wasn't going to happen. His wishes and prayers were not answered and Charles, from then on, was not the cheerful man he used to be, but somewhere between morose and dour. He never smiled again.

……..

The Bowring home was located between the Hardwick's at Top Farm and the Wooliscroft's at Hanbury Park Farm, fields that Fred had walked over daily to get to the mine. Fred's parents, Edward

The Day the Sun Disappeared, 27 Nov 1944

and Alice lived in the same house in Wood End. Edward Bowring, the father, had worked as a stone-breaker in the plaster mine and Fred's brother Tom, had also worked at Peter Ford's alabaster works above ground. Both of those were now out of work too, so there was no money coming in.

Olive was at her wit's end. They were trying to survive on hand-outs and waiting outside shops for any left-overs at the end of each day. The children were hungry, calling out for food and she had nothing much to give them. It all got too much for her. She wanted to mourn the husband she loved but couldn't do that with all the kids crying around her, constantly wanting her attention, and she began sinking into the depths of depression. She took to her bed, locking the bedroom door.

Her mother-in-law, Alice, was no better, and sometimes worse, carrying around a photo of her son, Fred, and crying constantly.

Eileen was the eldest of the brood, but she was just 11 years old. She had been home some time with peritonitis and was still not well. Baby Linda was just 7½ months old. Jean, Margaret and Kenneth were at school but Phyllis and Doreen hadn't started school yet.

Basically, Eileen had to become mother and daughter overnight as her mother had had a nervous breakdown.. She was in a deep depression, taking to her bed, not wanting to see anyone or do anything, and in no fit state to manage the home or look after the children. So Eileen found herself the sole person in charge of the children. She became mother and father to them – preparing what little she could find in the way of food, getting the children dressed, getting Jean, Margaret and Kenneth off to school, doing the washing and ironing plus looking after Phyllis and Doreen and little Linda - washing and changing nappies.

The poor little mites wanted attention and wanted to play. Doreen was saying, "Mum, have you got something to eat."

"I'm not your mum, Doreen, your mum's upstairs."

"But we haven't seen mum for ages and you are doing everything mum did, so you must be mum now."

Eileen was just too exhausted to argue, not being very well herself. The scraps that she could get together for food, just weren't enough and, as the days and weeks went by, those energetic children turned into sunken faces with black rings around their eyes. They had no energy and would just prop themselves up on the floor, uttering the occasional murmur, "I'm hungry".

Eileen would knock on her mother's door, "I have prepared something to eat. Are you coming down?"

Her mother just answered, "No dear, I can't eat anything. Just leave me be." Of course, Olive knew that, if she ate anything, it would take food out of the mouths of her children.

So her mother had taken to her bed, refusing any bit of food that could be scrounged. She was getting weaker and weaker.

Normally, if one of the children were ill, Olive would call the doctor, but there was no National Health Service in those days and doctors charged. Eileen knew her mother needed a doctor but had no money. There was no such thing in those days as counselling, or social workers - it was just 'stiff upper lip and get on with it'. Families had to take care of themselves. But neither Olive nor her mother had the stoic disposition to just get on with it. In one day their lives had changed forever and they could see no way forward.

The Day the Sun Disappeared, 27 Nov 1944

She had lost her beloved husband plus the stability of having three wages coming (including Tom's). It had just disappeared – up in a gigantic mushroom-like puff of smoke.

The Bowrings were a close family with cousins living in Hanbury too. Wilfred and Lesley Bowring were cousins. They lived in the Brickyard Cottages at Hanbury Woodend. Thomas was their father, the one who had been found buried in the mud of the field next to the Peter Ford's works and the same one of the RAF had managed to get a greatcoat for to cover him as all of his clothes had been ripped away. But at least he was alive.

Tom came over regularly. He tried to help as much as he could, but he was out of work too. He would bring in bits of cabbages and carrots from the farms but there was nothing much now to be had as it was dead of winter. He would go up to Olive's room and try to comfort her.

"You've got £1 a week coming in now for each of the children. I know that's not much but at least it's something. You need to fight this Olive, state your case. You need to go to court to try to get extra."

"I can't, Tom. You go for me." Olive replied, weakly.

So Tom had to apply to the court for extra money for the family. The court wanted to see Olive but Tom had to explain that Olive was too ill to attend. They sent someone round to check on the situation and Olive was awarded a further settlement.

The Hardwicks, the Mycocks (farmers at Barton-under-Needwood, old Mrs Bullock and the neighbours all helped out when then could.

The Day the Sun Disappeared, 27 Nov 1944

Olive began to get out of her depression, Eileen had kept the family, and her mum, going on watery soups and stale bread from the shops. Olive finally came downstairs, very weakened but ready to take over.

Eileen did go back to school, after Christmas, but left when she was 15, going to work at the Mycocks.

In January 1945 the first grants, of £4 to £8 were made to special cases, but this didn't go anywhere near the loss of three wages. Finally grants were coming in for children's clothing and in some cases, assistance with school fees. At Christmas the family got a further grant of £5 and in 1949 they started to receive a grant of £1.10s.0d for each child for the purchase of winter boots. However, if a widow had re-married, that was the end of the grants and children reaching the age of 16, no longer qualified for a grant. Eileen would now be 16, so any grant to her family would be stopped.

A couple of years later, Olive became ill with thyroid problems and spent six weeks in hospital. Again, the family was in deep hardship. This was before the days of the National Health Service and doctors' bills of £2.6s.0d and £5.2s.0d, which the family just couldn't meet. The Relief Fund Committee was able to alleviate this but still, it was decided that the children should be farmed out as there was no-one to look after them, most being at school. The family, that had been so close, was split up. Margaret and Jean went to the Hardwicks; Phyllis and Ken to Mr and Mrs Ford and Eileen went with Doreen and Linda to live with Tom and his wife.

....

In October 1958 the Fund totalled £580 and Christmas gifts of £316 were made. The balance of the Fund in May 1959 was £224 and the Trustees made a final distribution .of £5.14s.7d to each of the thirty-three remaining beneficiaries. So after fifteen years the Voluntary Committee and the Trustees wound up the Fund, their efforts over that period doing much to alleviate financial hardship.

CHAPTER 45

COURT OF ENQUIRY

The RAF top brass including Air Vice Marshall A. Lees (the president of the Court of Inquiry) and Group Captain G.C Allen, Group Captain, E J H Starling, Wing Commander E C Harding and Major J C Doherty – gathered at Fauld nine days after the explosion, on Tuesday, 5th December. They viewed the crater and went down the mine. The next day the inquiry members settled into their temporary courtroom at RAF Fauld and began taking evidence on oath at 9.30am.

They heard a total of 33 witnesses between the period 9.30am on December 6th and 10.45am on December 11th.

Wing Commander Kings was the first to be called. He told of the actions he took and orders he gave. The court was interested in why Kings had only twice gone underground to inspect the bomb stores. They also wanted to know why there was no system in place whereby it could be known exactly how many men were underground at a time. They also questioned the lack of emergency lamps, asking, "Was it not too much to ask for more lamps to be on hand at the mine head?" Kings was also questioned about security at the camp, as a reporter had managed to get onto the premises, especially as the explosion could have been due to saboteurs.

Squadron Leader Anness was called next. What he described was a total lack of senior officers on the day of the explosion, whether coincidental or mismanagement. Flying Officer Joseph Solomon was the officer in charge of the mine area, as directed by himself. but Solomon was on leave on 27 November. Solomon's deputy Pilot Officer Norman Rollo had only arrived at Fauld on November 13, had one day a week free, and November 27 was that day. Anness himself, however, had gone to Scropton.

John Bell, the station engineer, had two men in the mine each day, checking lamps – Mr Shipley and the Tutbury boy, Lewis Frow. "The quality of the lamps was poor and they often broke. They were all we could get. I did not hear any reports of electrical defects on the day."

Mr Buttle, clerk of works, stated, "In the five months I had been there, Fauld had had no roof falls, and the workings appeared to be in excellent condition."

The next two witnesses, Air Ministry policemen, were asked about 'smoking materials'. Chief Inspector Robinson told the court, "We checked people going into the mine for cigarettes and lighters." Then, when asked about access to the camp, he replied, "No unauthorised visitors were allowed through the main entrance- everyone had to show their passes, including the Italians."

Of course, the court knew that a reporter had got in, so Robinson's statement basically showed up the security as being very lapse. Robinson continued, "A constable was stationed at each mine entrance, however they did not keep a record of who went in or out of the mine."

Air Ministry Constabulary Sergeant Howard Langley gave a more detailed account, which basically undermined the account given by the chief inspector. Sergeant Langley actually said that only about one in ten were checked for 'smoking materials'. The danger of a worker lighting up among explosives was plain for the court to see.

The next four witnesses reassured the court about the mine's safety:

Horace Utting, a safetyman since 1940 at RAF Fauld and previously a worker in quarries locally for 18 years stated that he was in the incendiary area emptying watering holes. "I heard the rumbling, then the lights went out, but I managed to get outside." He added, "Tools used for tapping bombs to check they were intact, never caused sparks." Eric Bryant, the resident engineer since 1937 spoke of the 80ft barrier built in 1938 between the high explosive and the incendiary area. He added, "Probably it stopped a much bigger explosion."

George Whittaker and Ernest Parker, both safetymen were interviewed, but did not add anything else. They were both in similar jobs to Horace Utting.

Edgar Higgs, an AID viewer recalled, "I was examining bombs, replacing pistols, where necessary, and painting the lugs of the bombs to prevent corrosion."

The 14th witness was RAF armourer, LAC Ken McLeod. He and two others had joined up with Corporal Lionel Poynton and AC Patrick Sheridan, and had been perilously groping their way out in the pitch black, wondering if another explosion was imminent, which would possibly kill them this time. They were terrified and panicky.

However, standing in front of the high-ranking audience, with someone taking down every word for an official, typed record, obviously had an effect on how McLeod gave his statement. He stood to attention, straight-backed and said what he must have

The Day the Sun Disappeared, 27 Nov 1944

practiced over and over again. His account, therefore, was basically said in a rote fashion, eliminating all the emotion, fear, doubt and speed out of what had been a life-threatening situation at the time. He stated to the court, "I believe I was the closest to the source of the explosion. He told the court, "I was in the mine, putting steels bands around .5 ammunition boxes with two other airmen armourers. The work was taking place in the first right hand bay of F loop, when the first explosion took place at approximately 11 o'clock, followed by a second explosion. I was thrown up against the wall at the first explosion. I went to make my way out and was thrown to the ground by the second explosion. The second explosion had a greater effect than the first. There was a terrific rush of wind and dust. It is difficult to say from which direction it came, but it was from the general direction of the new area. Three of us decided to make our way out in the dark."

Aircraftman Patrick Sheridan was next. "I felt the explosion but could not ascertain the direction it came from." Sheridan did, however, give an insight into the slow, inefficient and dreary routine of an RAF maintenance unit. "As there was no work for the Italians to do, I decided to take the workless Italians outside for a break. That must have been 9.15am. I handed them over to LAC Deuchars. I had a pair of boots to hand in for repair, which I did, and returned to the mine at 10.30am. Sergeant Stanley Game told me to go back to the first gang of Italians. More stencils and a paint brush were required so I returned to the office. That's when I felt the first rumble, and a blast of air knocked me to the ground. I was one of the lucky ones as Sergeant Game, Deuchars and the gang of six Italians were killed or are missing.

The Day the Sun Disappeared, 27 Nov 1944

The next three witness had little to add. LAC Leonard Still, an office clerk in the mine, escaped with a man with a light, and Italians.

LAC Frank Rule stated, "I usually loaded and unloaded bombs in the mine. When the dump went up, one of the four men around me had a torch, so we made our way out.

RAF armourer LAC Michael Watson was painting boxes. He too met with a man with a light, and followed the main line to number two entrance.

As said before with Ken McLeod's statement, none of these statements indicated the terror, finding themselves in the pitch darkness and their utter relief at finding a man with a torch.

Air Vice Marshall Lees made a short statement, "On hearing these testimonies, I certainly have gathered and no doubt everyone here, will have come to the conclusion that, obviously there were not enough torches. Not everyone had a torch, and if this had been the case, with a torch issued to every person going underground, more people would have got out safely and in a quicker time. This has been a great failing on behalf of 21 MU."

One of the top brass added, "Listening to the witnesses, I also come to this conclusion but wish to add that, a torch, issued to each person, would have also served as a numbers count. There has been mention that there was no form of clocking-in, when entering the mine – which, may I say, appears to be an obvious and irresponsible failing on behalf of the 21 maintenance unit. The number of torches missing could have at least served to notify rescue unit of the number of personnel missing."

The next witness was LAC James Kenny, another armourer, the 19th witness. James Kenny gave the first evidence of possibly

The Day the Sun Disappeared, 27 Nov 1944

dangerous work underground that might have triggered a blast that could have made a second, greater, explosion.

"I worked in AID, preparing bombs for return to factories. On 11 November I had been working with LAC Fairbanks – who is missing, presumed dead. We were taking exploders from 500lb bombs in the AID compound. Those useless bombs would go back to the factory for breaking down. For this purpose we used a small cavern, near a triangle in the old HE area."

"Did the men receive any supervision while undertaking this work?" Lees asked.

"No, sir, we were not supervised, but the work was inspected at the end."

"No supervision, eh. Ok, carry on, LAC Kenny." Lees indicated, while writing notes for his own perusal and aide memoire.

Kenny continued, "Some of the high explosive bombs had exploder containers that proved difficult to remove. Sometimes you could spend two days working on removing the exploder, trying what we could. Mr Nicklin an AID viewer – unfortunately, also missing presumed dead – well, he visited us often. In this particular case, Mr Nicklin had tried himself to do the job, but it proved impossible. We eventually removed the container by using a special steel spanner provided for such work and white spirit to ease the RP cement."

"Hhmm, " Lees interrupted, "White spirit LAC Kenny? Surely in such dangerous work, white spirit would be against regulations - white spirit is extremely flammable."

"Yes sir," Kenny replied, "but, you see, the job had to be done and that was the only way of easing the cement."

The Day the Sun Disappeared, 27 Nov 1944

"It just occurred to me, LAC Kenny, should a fire break out, do you have fire-fighting equipment below ground."

"Regretfully, no sir. There was no fire-fighting equipment where we were working."

"Extraordinary," Lees said virtually under his breathe, and continued to enter something in his notes.

The next witness was called. This was Thomas Mylotte, the storeman. He had served at 21MU since 1939. He gave a detailed map of the mine, where the trucks and bombs were located. "I was working in the new area of the high explosive mine. On the morning of the explosion, I was on the microphone requesting trucks for loading 4,000lb bombs. Instead, four trucks arrived, but only one could take 4,000 pounders. Yes, I suppose this could have been that the person at the other end couldn't hear me properly, but it just caused a lot of delay, when we were pushed for time to get the bombs out. In the end I managed to get the correct trucks and loaded two 4,000lb bombs on the one suitable truck."

"So, what are you saying, Mr Mylotte. Would you say this was an example of high incompetence?"

Mylotte didn't answer, but hung his head.

"Well, it certainly seems to me to be so," Lees replied, and wrote another note down.

The next three witness had little to say:

William Deauville, a diesel local driver, had been taking seven trucks of small arms ammunition from number two entrance. "I was blown off my locomotive by what I can only describe as a

The Day the Sun Disappeared, 27 Nov 1944

rush of wind. I was knocked out and came to, several yards from the loco.

Next LAC Vernon Higgett and LAC Alec Frank Pooley, both armourers, were asked about two of the five dead RAF men, LAC Fairbanks and LAC Bailey.

The court, by now, had got the general gist of how things were managed, or not, at 21MU.

Senior fireman, William Jefferies stated, "I feel that standing orders and equipment were inadequate. My unit had been asking, in vain, for three more static water pools." Following a quizzical look from Lees, Jefferies went on to explain, "These are man-made ponds, common to RAF stations."

Jefferies carried on, and at this point the formal attitude of witness statements in the court, seemed to be broken. "I saw Squadron Leader Anness arrive and he asked me if the mine was on fire. I replied 'No, sir', to which he answered, 'Thank Christ'.

Flying Officer Joseph Solomon was the officer in charge of the mine area and on leave on November 27. Solomon told the court he had never seen or known of an exploder being removed from an HE bomb in the mine (in disagreement with the earlier claim by LAC Kenny)

Lees looked up, with an astonished look at this statement "As we have all heard in this courtroom, LAC Kenny, on oath, has told us otherwise, Flying Officer Solomon." Lees almost rose to his feet, but sat down again, pointing at Solomon. "As you know, Flying Officer Solomon, we are trying to get to the truth of the matter here. Your statement can mean one of three things – you only know of the proper practices and are not aware of any misdemeanours; in which case are you ignorant of some things

The Day the Sun Disappeared, 27 Nov 1944

going on, on your patch, or are you in fact lying to deny you know of wrong-doing that you did nothing about?

The courtroom broke into a muffled whispering at what some may have thought of as outlandish – an RAF officer actually lying!

"Silence in court," Lees shouted, banging on his desk

"Remember you are on oath, Flying Officer Solomon."

"I'm sorry, I can only reiterate that I have never seen or known of an exploder being removed from an HE bomb in the mine."

"So, that will be up to this inquiry to decide whether you are incompetent or lying. You are dismissed."

"Next witness"

Solomon slumped back to his seat. He was not a happy man.

The 26th witness was Jack Gorton of Ford's mine. He was the only witness who was not part of RAF Fauld.

"I recall a greater, second explosion a few seconds after the first, like many witnesses. The second blast even lifted up a wagon containing about four tons of gypsum. Then the electric light went out and we had to search in our equipment for tallow candles. I suppose I and my crew were about three-quarters of a mile from the fan opening between Ford's main line and the new area of the high explosive mine of RAF Fauld that was separated from us by a solid door of cement seven feet deep. I sent a man ahead but, when he didn't return, I went to find out what had happened to him. There was gas just beyond the suction fan, about a quarter of a mile further. I could taste it in the air, something like burnt sugar. It was there that I found a man lying unconscious, so I dragged him back. I went out again and found two dead men, but I couldn't' go on as the fumes were starting to affect me. I decided to send two men up the suction shaft for help and two RAF men came down and rescued me. By that time, I was in and out of consciousness."

"Thank you Mr Gorton, now I believe the next person to interview is Arthur Cox, an AID viewer."

One of the court interviewers questioned Cox about Fairbanks and Bailey. "Now, we all know that 21 MU was a gigantic enterprise - a never-ending operation of continuous coming and going of bombs and ammunition, all of which would entail a perfect stock-keeping system. Can you tell me how you feel Fairbanks and Bailey handled this system – their working methods?

The answer that Cox gave indicated that he felt the stock-taking was less than perfect.

"We have also heard about the problem extracting the exploder from a 4,000lb bomb. Can you throw any light on that incident?"

"Well, sir, the only 4,000lb bombs I know of were two unserviceable mark ones, each of which had been lying at that place for some 12 months. I am not aware that any work was being done on these bombs."

"So, you cannot enlighten us. Thank you Mr Cox. So, yet another case of what I can see as either blatant lying or you indeed were not aware, as you should have been, of work that was being carried out under your nose!"

An inexperienced officer, Acting Flight Lieutenant Brinley Williams was next. He gave the court an insight into the Italians working there. "The six dead Italians had reported from other maintenance units in September. We needed the extra help to replace RAF personnel requested to re-join their crews. The Italians had been coming in batches since that date but they hardly had the training, or the language, even, to do much, so they were given the simplest of jobs. They were happy to do menial tasks as they were paid more than in the prisoner of war camps."

The 29th witness was Charles Goddard, an electrician. His testimony was quite enlightening, after questioning, as to other dangerous practices that had seemingly become accepted at 21 MU.

The interviewer stated, "We have heard, from Mr Lylotte, the storeman, who said in an earlier statement that he had never seen anyone stand on a cluster of bombs to replace a lamp. Do you agree with that statement?"

"Well, sir, there were a few things that shouldn't have been done. For example, we would normally use step ladders to reach a light that needed changing, but if the steps weren't tall enough, an electrician would indeed sometimes climb on a stack of bombs to get to the light."

"So, another example – this time from Mr Lylotte, of things happening under the noses of those who should be on top of things, or such actions being ignored even – another falsehood perhaps on the part of Mr Lylotte – I dare not say in this case, a 'lie'!"

There was a spate of coughing in the court on hearing this pun on M Lylotte's name and Lees had to bang on his desk again to bring order to the courtroom.

Coming close to the end of the list of witnesses, Corporal Lionel Poynton was called, an armourer at 21 MU since July 1944.

Lees stated to the court that Corporal Poynton had not been placed near the end of the witnesses on purpose but that he had been the only RAF man out of 10 injured men who could attend. He had been suffering from shock, and the American military hospital at Sudbury had only just discharged him.

Corporal Poynton's statement in fact gave damning evidence.

"I was doing checks underground in the new area and had taken Sergeant Game with me on the inspection. Sergeant Game had never been in the mine and wanted to inspect the workings. LAC Fairbanks and LAC Bailey were working on 1,000lb bombs, which I believe were unit returns, having been jettisoned.

This work consisted of removing nose and tail blocks, where possible and removing the exploder container complete, or when it was not possible, removing the CE from the exploder pocket and collecting it in an ammunition box."

Here Poynton was asked to explain what the CE was.

He explained, "A bomb usually consists of a thin outer case containing a large quantity of relatively stable high explosive, usually TNT/RDX, which is quite difficult to detonate. Running through the middle of this filling is a steel exploder tube, which contains a materials known as Composition Explosive or CE, which acts as an intermediate between the detonator attached to the fuse cap, that is to say, the composition explosive containing the pellet in an exploder container, sir."

Poynton continued, "While I was there, I saw a bomb with the transit plug in the tail removed, set up horizontally on some form of batten, about a foot from the floor. LAC Bailey was chiselling out the CE from the exploder pocket. He was using a brass chisel and a hammer."

"Please explain the significance of using a brass chisel, Corporal."

The Day the Sun Disappeared, 27 Nov 1944

"Yes sir, brass striking steel could make a spark that could set off a bomb. The use of a brass chisel would be against regulations."

"And what was this hammer made of, Corporal?"

"I'm sorry, sir. I do not remember whether the hammer was made of steel or brass but I think it was while LAC Bailey was doing this job that we were joined by Mr Saunders of the AID.

The examiner interrupted again, "I understand that Mr Saunders was killed so, do you agree that the area you were in was at the centre of the explosion?"

"I believe so, yes sir."

"Please continue, Poynton."

"I was taken aback that this type of work was being done in the HE mine, rather than in the exploder bay and I took it upon myself to warn LAC Fairbanks and LAC Bailey to take care as this was a dangerous job. I then made my way to the other gang of prisoners, who I had seen stencilling boxes. That's when I got hit in the back by the blast, then hit again by the second blast. I never saw Sergeant Game again. He was killed along with everyone else in the blast area."

"So, damning evidence, surely." The examiner stated, looking at the jury.

"I wonder if Group Captain Storrar actually knew that the use of brass instruments was against regulations?" Looking at his notes, the examiner addressed the court. "From my records, I see that Group Captain Storrar had only undertaken a one-week X-course, at 31 MU, RAF Llanberis, in September 1944. That surely was extremely inadequate and Group Captain Storrar would have had to rely on his men, because he lacked training to make his own checks. I reiterate that, from the witness statements there seems to be a lack of adequate checks from the AID examiners plus, owing to the vast turnover of RAF staff and inadequate training, adequate checks were not carried out by the RAF either. This, to me, seems a disaster waiting to happen."

The last three witnesses, senior men, added little. Ernest Larkham, a senior examiner in the AID last visited the high explosive mine on the Friday before the explosion, which tallied with his claim that he visited that mine area about four or five times a week. Pilot Officer Norman Rollo, who had completed an explosives course at RAF Llanberis only weeks before, said, "I would go down the mine once in the morning and once in the afternoon. However, on November 27, I was not on duty. Although I was aware that AID inspections were going on, I had no detailed knowledge of these inspections, nor did I see any inspection work except on bombs outside the mine in C8 shed."

The examiner commented, "So, from what Pilot Officer Rollo, Corporal Poynton and others, have indicated, I get the general impression that there was no real interaction between the RAF and the Aeronautical Inspection Directorate, known in short as the AID. In fact this meant that the RAF did not know what the AID inspectors were doing, and may have indicated that men like LAC Fairbanks and LAC Bailey were allowed to break the rules - I surmise this was either on purpose or innocently."

The court decided that they wished to re-interview four men, Pollard, Anness, Bell and Salt. All four had had responsibility underground.

The examiner stated to the court, "Mr Saunders of the AID had the dump's paperwork, but this has disappeared underground as well as the unfortunate Mr Saunders himself. Maintenance Units were supposed to keep another record of its stores above ground but, for some reason, Fauld had stopped this practice."

The examiner called Pollard and read out the evidence of McLeod, Kenny and Poynton to him. Most of Pollard's replies were no more than 'yes' or 'no' and he continued to say that he knew nothing of handling of bombs in the mine that went against regulations.

The examiner asked Salt, "Have you ever seen an exploder pocket being removed in the mine?"

Salt answered, "Yes, on one occasion only, about a month ago. I saw an airman – I don't know who it was but it may have been LAC Bailey – removing an exploder pocket from a 4,000lb bomb in G loop on Ford's level."

"What action did you take?"

"I asked him if he knew such work must not be carried out in the mine. He said that he was working for the AID, but I noticed he stopped doing what he was doing after I had spoken to him and, as far as I know, no further work was done on this bomb."

"Did you report the matter to anyone else in authority?"

"No, sir. I just assumed the guilty airman would explain the stoppage of work to the AID viewer or examiner he was working under.

"So, you 'assumed', Mr Salt. I do not like this word – some say it basically means 'making an ass out of you and me. In my profession people should never 'assume' that something will be done….. So, individuals, such as yourself, Mr Salt, appeared to be too willing to leave responsibility to someone else. The time to tell off a wrong-doer, so that he would not dare break the rules again, had slipped by and the perpetrator would continue to believe he was 'getting away with it'. In fact Mr Salt, we do not know if the action of November 27 was an isolated incident. LAC Bailey could have been carrying out the same routine, in G loop, using a brass instrument at other times – it was merely this one incident that blew everything up!"

There were murmurings in the court again, but a glaring look around the court from Lees, soon returned silence again to the courtroom.

Anness was asked about his records of incoming and outgoing bombs and ammunitions.

"Records were discontinued above ground as Mr Salt had accurate records."

Outcome

During this inquiry several other possibilities as to the cause were considered and rejected by the court.

For example, the court found no evidence that any aircraft or bomb fell in the area of the mine on November 27th nor that any enemy action was involved."

The court also examined the possibility of sabotage but found no evidence in support of this".

They pointedly added: "Any stories or rumours concerning the above two points can therefore only be considered as without foundation."

That seems to dispose, once and for all, of the sabotage theory.

Members of the court also found no evidence of a roof fall nor of spontaneous ignition. Other possible reasons and the court's ruling were:

Electrical short – "Unlikely"'

Defective plant – "No evidence"

Gas explosion in the mine – "Highly improbable"

On the possibility that there was 'mishandling or unduly rough handling of any stores present in the mine – "No evidence.

The final possibility: Incorrect practice – "The most probable cause".

Having heard all of the witnesses, the examiners adjourned to decide on what should be recorded as the outcome of the Inquiry. They in fact returned a verdict of 'Accidental Death'. However, they added riders to the effect that sabotage or blasting at the mine was not responsible for the explosion and added a list of criticisms of safety procedures.

1. Regulations and standing orders were adequate, but were not being fully observed.
2. Local relaxations in safety procedures may have led to familiarity, breeding contempt
3. Urgency a keynote, manpower of poorer quality and quantity – more work expected of a unit than that for which it was designed.
4. Brass chisel used instead of copper
5. Short cuts with safety were part of daily life.
6. Make-do-and-mend mentality
7. Kings had only gone down the mine twice.
8. Roll-call taken, so no clocking in or out system.

9. Only 1 lamp at hand at the mine head – these could have represented the number down the mine if there was a lamp for each person down there.
10. No security, as a reporter got access to the premises.

Without any reflection on the ability of the commanding officer and, although the court realises that it is not always possible to fill established posts appropriately, it feels that the posting of a non-X commanding officer to such a maintenance unit may be a handicap to the officer for the first two or three months of his appointment (a time scale that applied to Storrar at Fauld on the day the dump went up). The court recommends that this be borne in mind when filling such appointments in future and that an officer be given a full X course before taking up his appointment.

They concluded that neither the Chief Inspection Officer (AID) [Pollard], nor the acting chief Equipment Officer [Anness] can be entirely absolved from all responsibility as they do not appear to have been sufficiently aware of the work undertaken in the mine area nor to have adequate records or control of such work.

All 32 witnesses were sworn to secrecy. In truth, the court had written its conclusions, acted on them, and stamped the findings as confidential weeks before. These findings would not be released until 1974, the statutory 30 year period imposed by defence regulations.

It was eventually revealed that the explosion was thought to have been caused by a method used to chip out composition explosive from a 1,000lb bomb. When it exploded, it triggered a chain reaction, detonating others down the line. It was officially revealed that the explosion was caused by bombs being taken out of store, primed for use and replaced unused, with the detonators still installed.

Frighteningly, the inquiry revealed that the explosion could have been ten times greater, possibly wiping Burton-on-Trent off the face of the earth, had it spread to the main area where more bombs were stored.

The court's findings went to the Air Officer in Chief, Maintenance Command for his confirmation and the records show that he agreed with the findings.

He agreed that the regulations were not observed and that there was negligence on the part of the A.I.D supervisory staff present in the mine.

Fauld was visited by the then Air Minister on Tuesday, July 31st 1945, some eight months after the explosion and, following this visit, it was recommended that the site could be repaired and used again and this was subsequently notified to the U.S. War Department, who later had a unit at Fauld.

....

Air Marshal Donald forwarded the court of inquiry's report to the Air Ministry, arguing that he was 'not convinced' that an MU commander needed the X-qualification. Storrar had 17 X-qualified officers under him, and maintenance units generally barely had enough trained staff. "I have a very high opinion of the present commanding officer Group Captain R C Storrar, and I submit most strongly that these recommendations should not be allowed to result in his posting away from 21 MU."

Air Marshal Donald would defend Storrar's posting as he had agreed to it himself. However, his letter to the Air Ministry seemed to be contradictory as how did the two pieces of information tally if, as he said, Storrar had 17 X-qualified officers

The Day the Sun Disappeared, 27 Nov 1944

under him to rely on but then stating that qualified men were in short supply!

Storrar did indeed stay in place and so did Donald, though as late as June 23, 1945 Donald was having to defend his command, in writing:

"I am fully satisfied that there is no further evidence of the chipping out of CE from exploder containers and that the act performed at Fauld on November 27, as evidenced by the 30th witness (Poynton) was an isolated incident."

Yes, this public inquiry was carried out but it was shrouded in secrecy and the Air Ministry enforced a statutory 30-year-period on the findings. This meant the case was closed, nothing else could be reported and the 'secret' explosion in Staffordshire was to remain secret. The findings were not to be released until 1974. A Ministry of Defence spokesman said, "The inquiry presumably conducted its business to the satisfaction of the government. This is now a closed affair and all the papers are with the Public Records Office."

Remarkably, the man in command of RAF Fauld, Ronald Storrar, was awarded an OBE in 1945 for his work after the explosion. He stayed in the same branch of the air force and retired with the rank of air vice marshal.

....

The RAF did not want outsiders to tell them how to run their war effort as this could impede supply of arms to the air force, which would mean they could no longer continue to protect the UK. So, if it was deemed that RAF Fauld had suffered an 'Act of God', everyone could carry on as before. If something more general, such as procedure or equipment at fault, every ammunition and bomb store had to know. In this case, as other RAF bomb stores had not had an explosion, this could suggest an extraordinary event was to blame – it was decided accordingly that, although regrettable, the event could be safely written off.

The most punishment handed out to RAF Fauld men was a letter of 'grave displeasure'. Officers lived to draw a pension – more than the bereaved of Fauld and neighbouring towns got. They did not take the responsibility and hid behind the need for secrecy.

Improvements were made, however, although there were still shortcomings. An inspection on July 31 1945 showed 20 sets of two-hour self-contained breathing apparatus had been provided, although no training had been provided in use of the equipment.

Below ground there was a reasonable supply of soda hand extinguishers and buckets although one bucket was almost empty and another being used for mixing cement. Still, it was given the go-ahead to join the Cold War against the Soviet Union.

It also says here that the Air Minister says he is glad to have had the opportunity to pay tribute to the invaluable and heroic work carried out by the Mines Rescue Organisation, In all, 15 Mines Rescue Brigades, totalling 100 men. Unfortunately one of the rescuers lost his life."

Aircraftman Malcolm Kidd

A person who should have been called as a witness was young aircraftman Malcolm Kidd. He attended at the inquiry, but was not called. As the inquiry had heard, an experienced armourer told the hearing he had seen a civilian worker trying to dismantle a bomb

The Day the Sun Disappeared, 27 Nov 1944

using a brass chisel. However, Malcom Kidd had a different story, which didn't come to light. The inquiry had decided that they had heard all the witness statement they required in order to come to a conclusion, so Malcolm Kidd wasn't called.

Kidd's story was, on that morning he was sent to deal with two 1,000lb bombs, which had been recovered from a crashed RAF bomber. The routine was simple. Ordered by a sergeant, Malcolm Kidd stencilled each bomb with "For Dumping in Deep Water". They were then to be jettisoned at sea. But, soon afterwards, a civilian munitions worker intervened.

There were RAF and civilians working together at Fauld. The RAF were fully trained and did things by the book, but the civilians were a law until themselves. While Kidd was at the restroom, a civilian said, "I will get some Stillsons (a large wrench), take the noses off those crash bombs, and we can send them out again" It was a 'make-do-and-mend' mentality. Kidd is convinced that the civilian caused the explosion by trying to unscrew the nose-pistol on one of the 1,000lb bombs. To this day, Mr Kidd regrets not intervening. "But I was very young and very junior. My father had been in the Guards and I was taught to carry out orders and not to question anything. I was just an ordinary aircraftman. I wasn't my job to say, 'Don't do that.'" It wasn't until fifty years later that he was able to put the record straight. On the 60th anniversary a letter from him was printed in the Derby Evening Telegraph telling his true story.

The Day the Sun Disappeared, 27 Nov 1944

Another explanation

In a newspaper, I came across this letter from a Mr W Young, of 4 Harbin Road, Walton on Trent. I was bemused by this report, especially as he states below that 'brass is non-magnetic and will not produce sparks.' My query is, if the RAF thought that brass instruments caused sparks, and should never be used, as they were against all regulations, why indeed were bomb disposal units issued with them? However, apart from that, Mr Young states that, over time, the bomb will form tiny crystals of nitro acid and will detonate at the slightest disturbance. These bombs were being re-fused and re-armed at an exceedingly rapid turn-around, therefore, I do not see the bombs being at the site for enough time to allow for the 'sweating out' of the nitro-glycerine.

Anyway, this is Mr Young's report. You can make up your own minds.

"Over the weeks, I have followed the story of the tragic event of the Fauld explosion. Also marvelled at some of the explanations that have been put forward.

No matter how wide one's explanations, or experience is, and my own is quite considerable, having worked in the explosives and weapon departments of the Royal Ordnance for a number of years, one can only make a good educated guess. The truth is we shall never know.

Checking through the known facts, I found that one important issue had been overlooked, which could have led undoubtedly to this tragedy, or even been its cause. I refer to a condition known as Exudation or sweating.

High-explosives that are manufactured from nitro-glycerine or nitro-cellulose are subject to a little known phenomenon, which is only likely to appear after long storage of the explosive.

What happens as far as we know, there is a slow breakdown of the mixed chemical structure, which leads to the sweating out of the nitro-glycerine. This forms greasy marks around the weapon's plug and fuse housings where, given time, tiny crystals of nitro acid will grow. These crystals are highly sensitive, and will detonate at the slightest disturbance.

The filling of British bombs GP or SP was all most exclusively Trinitrotoluene (TNT). Most bombs were tailed fused with a mechanical mechanism known as a pistol, which worked on a set-back principle.

TNT cannot be induced to detonate by spark or flame. It must be detonated.

Most bomb disposal units were issued with a set of brass tools, the reason being, that brass is non-magnetic and will not produce sparks.

I am sorry that I must pour cold water on the latest explanation for the Fauld incident. In my opinion, it should never have happened. I put it down to lack of understanding of the situation and pure ignorance."

I found a further theory, in the Derby Evening Telephone, which stated:

"Work was constantly being performed inside the mine to restore so-called 'Dirty bombs'. These were bombs which had been returned to Fauld from various operational bases as being unfit for use for various reasons, i.e. past their use by date or having been left exposed to the elements. These batches of bombs on return were usually coated with mud.

A part of the operation of reconditioning required drilling the bomb casing and possibly heat generated by the use of a drill ignited the explosive material within the bomb, causing it to detonate and be the forerunner of the major explosion."

The Day the Sun Disappeared, 27 Nov 1944

CHAPTER 46

A BIT OF LIGHT RELIEF

(From PC Mackay's report)

I think you've had enough of disaster for the time being, so here's a spot of light relief. A man took his lorry into a garage for repair. Whilst he was there the explosion occurred, but the man had no knowledge of this, being some miles away He was doing a minor job to his lorry whilst awaiting the repair, when suddenly his lorry began to move slowly backwards and forwards repeatedly.

The man thought a prank was being played on him by the garage employees and, being of humorous disposition, decided to retaliate. He seized a swab of oily waste and crept to the back of the lorry, intending to throw the swab at the jokers, but to his utter amazement, no-one was there and his vehicle was still moving backwards and forwards. At that moment, the garage foreman dashed out of his office shouting, "What the b….. hell's going on here?"

Apparently his office furniture was dancing about his office.

Eventually, they heard the news and realised what had caused the strange actions in the garage.

Another very amusing story – and it is quite true and concerns two farm labourers. One was sitting on a split rail fence of a field, watching another labourer mangle-cutting. Suddenly both were amazed to see the field move and the mangle tops shake violently. The one cutting the mangles cautiously peered at his pal, thinking he had imagined what he saw, only to see his pal sitting on the ground, having fallen off the fence. The fallen man climbed back on the fence, saying nothing. The man engaged cutting mangles continued with his work, also silent. After some minutes of silence, one said to the other, "You don't look very well, Jim," whereupon the other replied, "And you b...... don't either. Let's get out of here."

It is often said that animals have highly developed instincts.

Not including the account already told of the horse that stopped in its tracks just before a great boulder of alabaster fell from the sky, onto the very spot where they would have been had the horse continued. But here are three other stories which appear to support this belief.

Ten minutes before the explosion occurred, an old farm labourer was engaged cutting, or as it is called 'laying a hedge', near the scene of the explosion. Suddenly to his amazement, the cows in the field began to frantically race across the field and continued to do so for several minutes. The farm labourer was so astonished that he shouted, "What be the matter with them cows. They bain't gadding at this time of the year."

Mr Goodwin, the farmer, of Upper Castle Hayes Farm, had a spaniel dog, which never strayed from the buildings unless with his master. After the explosion, this dog was found at the RAF station, some distance away, unhurt. How and why it went there will never be known. It was the only living creature that survived from that farm.

The Day the Sun Disappeared, 27 Nov 1944

My last story concerns two cats lying in front of a fire at a farmhouse four miles away.

A few minutes before the explosion, both jumped up from their comfortable position and stalked out of the house, to the astonishment of those who saw them.

These three stories are quite true. I leave you to judge whether or not there is any truth in the old belief that animals have instincts beyond our own.

The Day the Sun Disappeared, 27 Nov 1944

CHAPTER 47

MEMORIES

(Taken from Mark Rowe's After the Dump Went Up: The Untold Story)

Anyone who was there can tell you what they were doing the day the dump went up. It was stamped on people's memories, as surely as the assassination of President John Kennedy or the death of Diana, Princess of Wales.

Margaret White, née Woolley, just 8 years old, was sitting at her desk at school, in Sudbury, the day the dump went up.

"The teacher was talking to us and all at once the ground sort of heaved up. The next thing we knew the windows were shattering and falling in.

The teacher ordered us all to get under or desks, as we had been taught to do in a bombing raid. We were all cramped down on the floor when the door opened and someone told us all to go outside."

Barnard Cripwell, from Hanbury was in a classroom at Uttoxeter Grammar School. "The classroom doors blew open and windows rattled. We found out that damage in Uttoxeter was slight, but townspeople could guess where the explosion came from – and many Uttoxeter men worked in the dump and thereabouts. The teacher didn't tell us a thing so we were all quiet and scared.

At dinner time, I went into the town. Everyone was talking about it.

The Day the Sun Disappeared, 27 Nov 1944

I rang a neighbour, because my family did not have a telephone, and was told that everyone in Hanbury was safe. My mother had sheltered under a table. My father was working with a horse in a field near the New Inn pub on the outskirts of Burton on Trent. He told me that, as the shockwave of the explosion passed across the ground, the horse fell to its knees."

Shirley Husselbee wrote: "I remember the explosion quite vividly. I was living at The Noah's Ark Farm, Uttoxeter. It was a Monday and I had been ill over the weekend, so my moth kept me away from school that day. I was sitting at a table in the parlour, listening to the schools' programme on the wireless when suddenly everything in the room shook and I was standing in the middle, watching the windows shaking. I remember shouting 'They can't blame this on me'. My mother rushed downstairs wondering what all the fuss was about. A little later someone called to say there had been an explosion at the Dump. Sadly one child in my class lost a father and uncle, their surname was Cartwright."

Frank Cartwright from Uttoxeter. He was the Transport Manager. He was 41 and left a widow. His body was never found.

Reginald Cartwright, Frank's brother, was the head clerk there. He died. He was 46 and left a widow and three daughters.

Walter Wesson was a Leading Aircraftman at RAF Lichfield, in Fradley. He was 31 at the time. And just halfway through his four years of service in the air force. RAF Fradley trained Australians on Wellingtons, as at Church Broughton, Lichfield's satellite. Walter stated, "I was working at a petrol bowser outside the motor transport department, looking at the carburettor, and the carburettor just went to the ground, either that or the ground came up to meet it. It was a terrible feeling, but we had to carry on with our work just the same."

Bill Kelleher, an Australian, had been serving with the RAF, at Lichfield, from April that year, after seeing combat with Lancaster bombers. He said, "We didn't know where the obviously enormous explosion had been initiated. However, it was followed by a seemingly gale force wind. Later we found that the small building we were in had been moved four inches away from the blast."

Leslie Smith – can remember Eric a German prisoner, saying that was a big noise. I had a runaway horse to stop. The German was laughing, but the gaffer wasn't as all the milk was spilt. Eric was a good influence on me. He taught me how to repair most things. He was a carpenter before the war. I never forgot him.

....

The following is a map of Uttoxeter. The numbers 1-4 refer to the addresses of contributors to this book, telling their stories, in the pages following the map.

The Day the Sun Disappeared, 27 Nov 1944

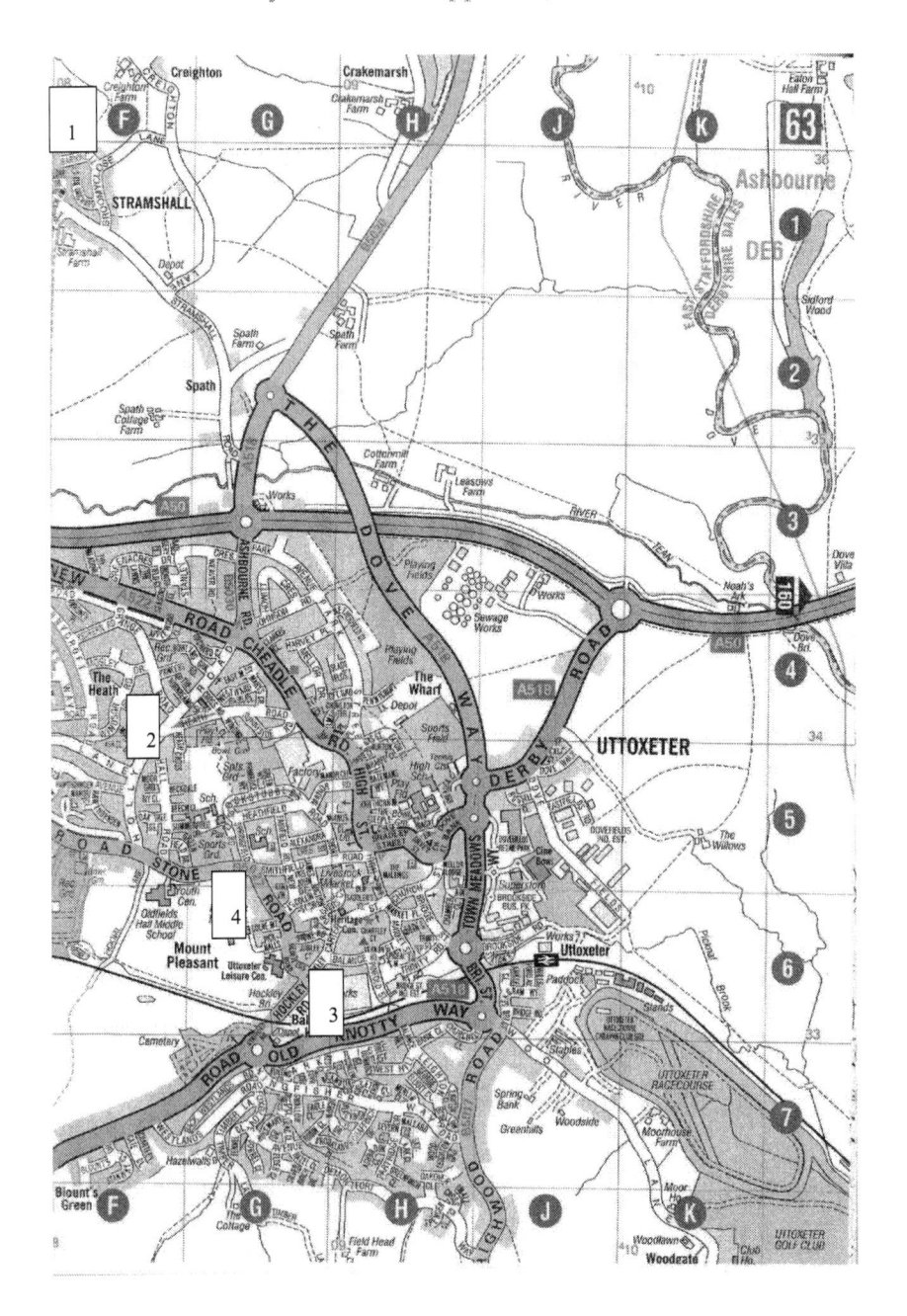

The Day the Sun Disappeared, 27 Nov 1944

Lynn Noreen McNamara a niece of Bill Philips wrote. We lived in Broomyclose Lane (No. 1 on map) for 17 years. It looked over to EatonWoods. Ms Birch, next door, who lived there since it was built, said that cracks appeared when the dump went up. My uncle, Bill Philips was caught in the explosion. Also our house in Stramshall, Uttoxeter, was in line with it and it caused a crack in the building.

David Denny – my mother Noreen Smith often told us a story of how the windows of Bradley Street School (No 2 on the map) rattled when it blew up. Jean Eckersley confirmed this. She was at Bradley Street School Uttoxeter, and felt the explosion. The windows had paper crosses to stop them shattering. Bradley Street School was opposite the bus station, now a car park for Alleyne's (from Elizabeth Goodwin).

Jean Eckersley. I can confirm that I was in Bradley Street School and we felt the explosion. The windows had paper crosses to stop them shattering. I'm sure there have been radio programmes on BBC radio 4 about it. Bradley Street School was opposite the bus station – now a carpark for Alleyne's.

David Denny also wrote, saying his mother Noreen Smith, often told them a story of how the windows of Bradley Street School rattled when the dump blew up.

Stewart Allen wrote: I was 4 years old. The explosion blew open the frontdoor of my grandmother's house at 31 Balance Street, Uttoxeter (No 3 on the map) – opposite the Police Station.

Edward Lewis wrote: My grandfather, William Lewis, lived at 16 The Picknalls, Uttoxeter (No. 4 on the map). He told me he was walking down the hallway towards the open front door when the blast from the explosion blew him down the passageway. Also, my mother, Ida Lewis, lived at Mill Cottage, Cubley, Derbyshire and two of her friends, who were neighbours at the farm next door, were working on the farm by the Dump and were killed in the explosion. These were Stephen and John West.

....

Richmond Leason wrote saying that he can remember his grandad showing him one of his bedrooms, where the plaster had come off the wall and all the windows were cracked. His grandfather lived in the Marchington area all his life. He used to travel to various parts of Staffordshire/Derbyshire as a Wesleyan Lay Preacher. He lived with the family at Brook House Farm, about a mile from Marchington on the Uttoxeter Road. It lies in a pretty direct line to the plaster pits, where the explosion was.

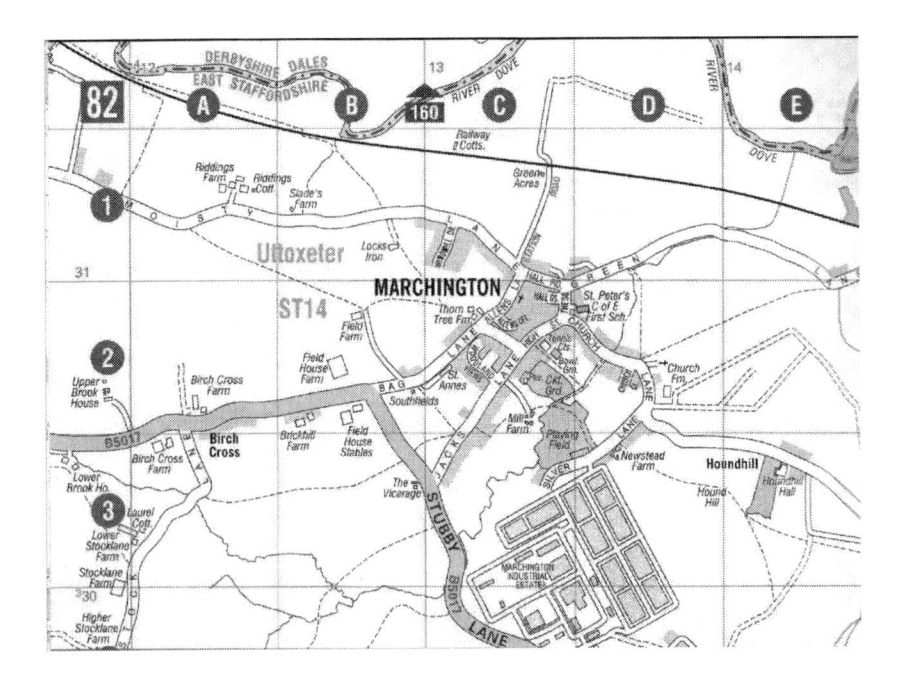

The Day the Sun Disappeared, 27 Nov 1944

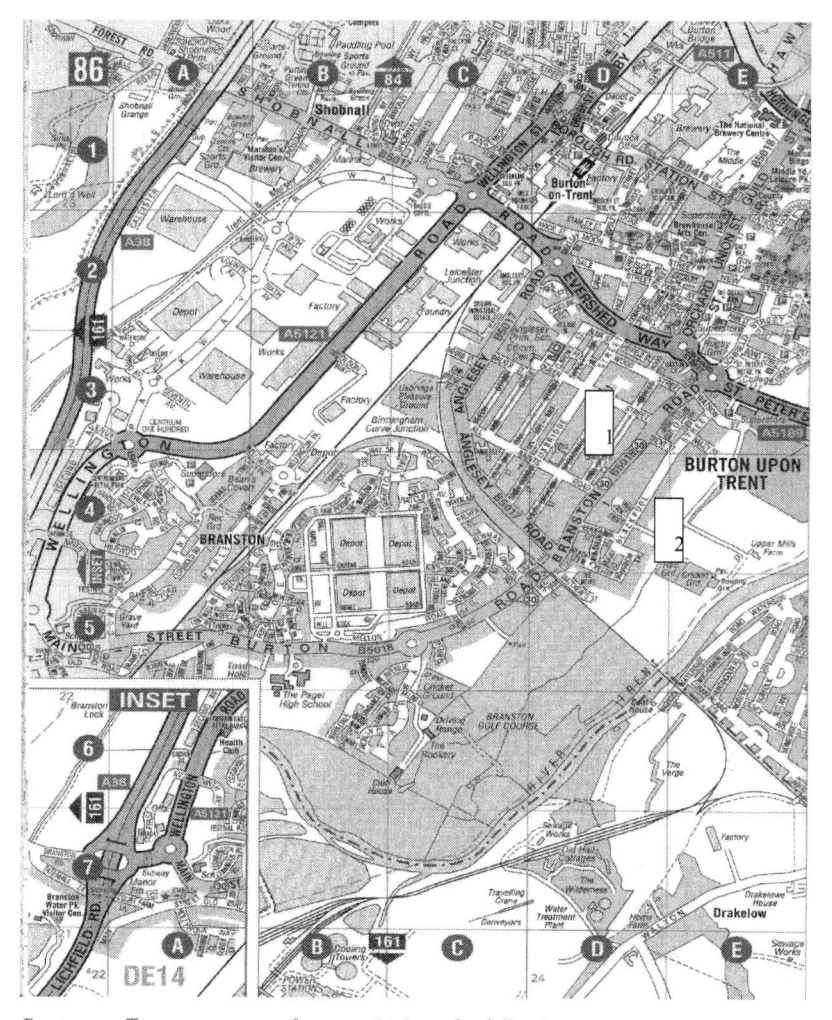

Burton-on-Trent map - see references 1+2 on the following pages

The Day the Sun Disappeared, 27 Nov 1944

Ian Arkesden: I mentioned your post to my old man this afternoon. He can remember sitting in the classroom at the Uxbridge School (No 1 on above map) and his table lifted off the floor a few inches, and came down with a thud. A few panes of glass cracked in the classroom. When he got home, there was a big crack in the entry at his house in Queen Street, plus he was looking at the spire on the church in Moor Street and said it was leaning badly.

Diana Pointon-Griffiths wrote: My mum, at the time, was asleep. She was on nights at the Munitions factory in Branston Road, called Chesters (No 2 on the map). She said the wardrobe blew over onto the bed, but she was unhurt. She had also heard the Lord Haw Haw propaganda, saying the Germans had bombed Burton and the streets were running with beer. Diana's dad heard it too, and he was serving in Italy.

Margaret Rose Bates wrote: "I was at Uxbridge Street School (No 1 on above map) at the time and I can remember the classroom floor started to move and we were told to get under the desks. As we did so, the desks moved forward. When I got home, my mum was in a state as my dad (Mr Murfin) was out delivering in that area. He used to deliver petrol to the farms. He was later getting home that day and, when he did get back, he was really shook up as he had just delivered to a farm, when he felt the earth move and, when he looked back, the farm he had just been to, had disappeared!"

There were American soldiers around, and one or two soldiers had girlfriends in the village. I am aware of a lady who had a child out of wedlock, and her daughter never knew her dad. (I believe that she's still alive too). The American disappeared.

The Day the Sun Disappeared, 27 Nov 1944

In Tutbury, three miles away, Vic Price rushed outside to see fully-grown trees raining down like matchsticks and neighbours racing for cover. "I had been working on a lathe in my garage. The shock wave was like some terrible nightmare, which sheared the lathe from its bolts."

Jane Bentley wrote: I was 4 years old and remember it very clearly. We Lived on Thorney Lanes, a fair distance away (No. 1 on the map below). Mum heard the noise, grabbed me and ran out onto the road. A neighbour joined us. Mum said, "Look at Jane's ribbon, covered in dust." My dad was down the mine. He was unhurt but it blew his bike to bits. It was very late when he finally came home. I don't remember much but, yes, I presume my dad had to walk home. I know all of them went back down to get any injured out. My other memory was school friends who lost their dads. Very sad.

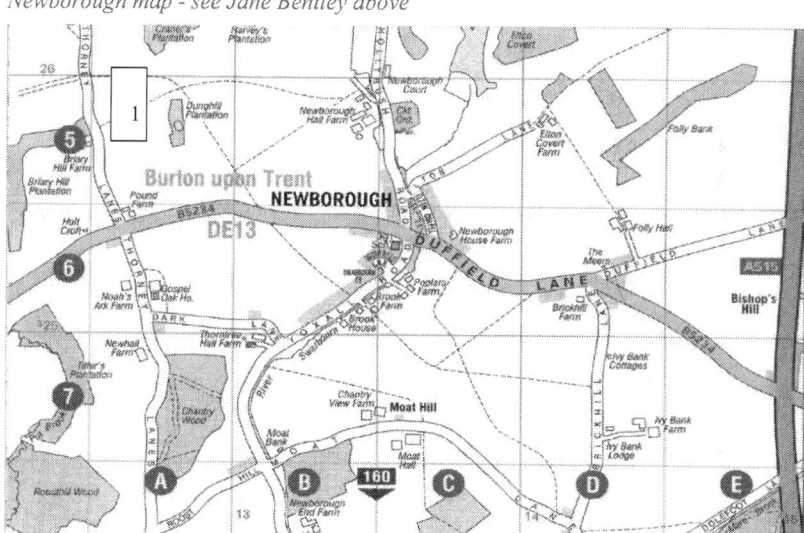

Newborough map - see Jane Bentley above

The Day the Sun Disappeared, 27 Nov 1944

Sarah Crockett My Dad was Reginald John Barker. Everyone called him John. He was born and lived at the Bagot Arms in Abbots Bromley, south of Uttoxeter and west of Fauld. His grandparents owned and lived in the pub. Dad and his parents lived there too.

Dad was almost four years old on the day of the explosion in Fauld where his Uncle Harry worked. At the time of the explosion dad was in the kitchen at the Bagot Arms, cupboard doors burst open, pots and pans flew into the air and items smashed on the floor. Dad's Mum, May, initially thought that Dad had caused all the mess, but luckily for him she discovered the explosion was to blame. No-one heard from his Uncle Harry that day and they were all worried, but thankfully he returned home on his bicycle the following day. He had been helping out at the crater.

Dad passed away in March 2020. This was one of his stories he liked to tell.

The Day the Sun Disappeared, 27 Nov 1944

Sarah Lindsey-Smith – I grew up surrounded by families of people who had died. The children in the school on that day are family friends, but some of the key people listed in many of the books on this subject have died, even only recently. Long term Hanbury residents still feel the effects of that day. My great uncle was one of the first on the scene and part of the rescue, but he kept the full story to himself. It was a very real event and may be history to many, but part of the lives of many too.

Excerpts from the BBC The One Show – by John Sergeant:

Alistair Jones, Shropshire
My parents had evacuated from Shirley, Croydon, to get away from the flying bombs, to my uncle and aunt's in Tutbury Road, near Burton on Trent. I was there when the explosion went off. Although we were about three miles away, the house seemed to go up in the air and rock. We were told not to talk about it at the time so I have waited all this time for news of what happened.

Anne Hordley from Wales, posted 25 October 2007

My father was flying out of Ashbourne in a Whitley at the time of the Fauld Explosion and saw it occur. He has his flying log for details of the weather and height they were flying at. They flew back round the event, wondering if some secret weapon had been detonated. He remembers a column of brown smoke and debris, which mushroomed out at the top. They were able to see buildings burning on the ground, but could not make out what they had witnessed. They returned the next day and were amazed to see half the hillside gone.

The Day the Sun Disappeared, 27 Nov 1944

Charles Mitchell – Post Office Newspaper, May 18, 1977

I was in an RAF bomber, flying over the Fauld ammunition dump when it exploded. I was the wireless operator and air-gunner in a six-man crew returning from East Anglia to our base at Ashbourne, on a training flight in November 1944. Flying with me were: bomb-aimer, Ken Haugham; tail-gunner, Jock Burgess; pilot, Paddy Roberts; navigator, Peter Fitzgerald; and flight-engineer, Tom Mundy.

From the twin-engine Whitley aircraft I had a bird's eye view of the biggest explosion in the country at the RAF underground bomb store, in a maze of caves and tunnels on the site of a gypsum mine and plaster works.

We were on the approach run-in at about 7,000 feet, when I saw the Fauld mine disintegrate directly below.

It was one hell of a something, which obliterated everything, but surprisingly we felt no shock waves.

It seemed rather like looking into a blue arc-lamp when the explosion occurred. The whole area was covered in smoke and dust clouds.

We were probably the start of rumours that a German bomber had scored a lucky direct hit as a survivor is said to have heard a plane overhead before the blast. However, there were no German aircraft in the vicinity. The Whitley – nicknamed the Flying Coffin – strongly resembles the German Dornier 17 – known as the Flying Pencil – and any eye-witness would think we were the enemy.

The Day the Sun Disappeared, 27 Nov 1944

Jayne Earp wrote: I was only 4 years old when my grandfather died, so don't know much about him. He was Joseph Clifford Salt, known as Cliff. He worked at Fauld and received the George Medal for his rescue effort.

My late mum (Carole Anne Wilkinson), despite only being 3 or 4 could remember going to Buckingham palace with her mum and dad to collect the medal. He went on to run a newsagents in Castle Donnington.

My grandmother, Elsie Annie Salt (known as 'Pop') – Cliff's wife had worked at the Burton depot until 1942. She had been in the offices, I believe, something to do with Army issue of clothing/uniforms.

My grandfather never said much about it. It had obviously been very traumatic and he said he'd seen awful things. He did, however, tell my mum that one man had been blasted into a thin crevice. My grandmother said he was never quite the same again. It had obviously affected him greatly.

After the blast he went on courses in mines rescue and undertook a great deal of training in safety etc.

My mum passed away last year (2022), so I now have my grandfather's medal and treasure it with great pride.

The Day the Sun Disappeared, 27 Nov 1944

JEAN FISHER

Reported in StaffordshireLive on 27 September 2017

Reporter Jenny Moody –

When 4,000 tonnes of high explosives detonated in the UK's biggest ever non-nuclear blast Jean Fisher adopted the British wartime motto of "keep calm and carry on" - by reaching for a cup of tea.

Jean was an innocent 19-year-old at the time and working in the office at RAF Fauld near Hanbury, with the Second World War still raging after more than five years of terrible conflict.

Here, for the first time since the tragic events of 78 years ago, she shares memories of the fateful day, when at least 70 people perished, with news reporter Jenny Moody.

The explosion at RAF Fauld could be heard six miles away in Burton and left many lives devastated - but the day had started for Jean Fisher like any other.

She was just 19 years old and had been called up, like many women, to do their bit for the nation in the Second World War in the battle against Hitler. She was living in Burton at the time and had started her working life selling wholesale tobacco before she received the letter asking her if she would prefer farming or office work.

As her family was protective, she opted for office work and her first job was at BTR, in Horninglow Road. But this led to occupational dermatitis as the rubber irritated her skin and she was eventually sent to Fauld on October 12, 1944, as a temporary civil servant.

The Day the Sun Disappeared, 27 Nov 1944

"In all the confusion we didn't know what happened. I just remember the office moving, it was terrible. A lady in the office asked if we should have a cup of tea and we just sat there because it was chaos. All we could see was this huge cloud of smoke and panic as the fire service, ambulance and RAF were there.

"We continued working. We were told we could go home if we wanted to but we would have to walk to Tutbury, which was quite a walk as they could not spare the transport, so we stayed until the end of the day.

Jean Fisher was just 19 when she was working at RAF Fauld and the explosives detonated

"I then got the bus, the yellow peril as we called it, as it was a terrifying ride, back to Victoria Crescent, near Farringtons. I lived in Grange Street near St Paul's Church and I used to walk there and back every day.

"As I was walking home I could see this little face at the window and I knew who it was instantly. It was my mum making sure that

The Day the Sun Disappeared, 27 Nov 1944

I was safe, she had been in the hairdressers in Burton when she found out.

"I was very innocent and I don't think I realised how dangerous it was. If our building had been the other side I wouldn't be here, we were the right side of the fence if you like.

"One of my friend's fathers was working in the mines and he was talking to a mate. His friend was fine but they couldn't find a thing of her father.

"I used to go on walks around there at lunchtime but we weren't allowed to go there for two weeks. It was a shock seeing it all but there was no panic in us and we just carried on."

Despite the devastating explosion, Miss Fisher, who now resides at Oakland Village, in Swadlincote, was back at work the next day and continued to work there until April 21, 1947, when she was made redundant. She had only been working there for six weeks when the explosives went off.

Miss Fisher said: "What could you do? The next day I went back to work and worked as normal. Everyone in the office turned up. We just kept waiting for the work to come in. It was very different in those days, it was the way we were brought up.

"We just went on as if it was normal as it didn't really affect our offices. People knew about the blast in Burton, as they felt it. We did see the men in the mines but we did not mix with them socially. I worked there for two years but we knew it was going to end as they were not needing the equipment after the war. We used to sit there some days, just with one piece of paper, for hours.

The Day the Sun Disappeared, 27 Nov 1944

"We did have a very nice looking Air Force officer who, if we were lucky, come round to check on us but we had to be careful to make sure we were working and we didn't know when they were coming."

After finishing at Fauld, Miss Fisher found herself out of work for two months before landing a job at Marks and Spencer, in Burton, where she worked for 39 years. She worked her way up to retail staff manager and is still fondly remembered by the people she worked with today.

CHAPTER 48

CORONER'S ENQUIRY

An inquest by coroner, John Auden, and a jury of eight, was arranged on February 5th, 1945 at the Tutbury Institute. The hall in which the inquest was held was crowded with survivors of the explosion and relatives of the dead and missing.

The first item was that tributes were made to the Staffordshire police, rescue workers and other services for their efforts.

The Coroner and the jury paid special tribute to three people:

I, PC A.T. Mackay had been acting as Coroner's Officer throughout the investigation;

Mrs Mary Elizabeth Cooper, who, although she lost her husband in the explosion, voluntarily took over the job of superintending the temporary mortuary established in the battered village near the dump;

Mr Joseph Foster, works manager of the mine, who, after a miraculous escape from inside the devastated works, went on with rescue work ceaselessly, and has continued with it for the past 72 days 'never showing any sign of nerves'.

Following these tributes there was a round of applause – an unusual incident at an inquest.

……

The Day the Sun Disappeared, 27 Nov 1944

The Coroner sat with a jury and, among others present were Mr W Brown, H.M. Inspector of Mines, Mr H B O Mitchell, H.M.Inspector of Factories, Mr W Widdas, H.M. Inspector Mines (watching brief), Mr A E C Goodall, Transport and General Workers' Union, Mr C Leslie Hale, for the union and relatives, also representing the Ashby Rescue Station; Mr H V Argyle, representing the plaster mine owners; Mr P G A Lowe, barrister for the Secretary of State for Air; Mr R S Murt, County Surveyor and Superintendent H G Heath, Staffordshire Police.

Also the court was attended by many relatives of the victims.

The foreman of the jury was Major Parson.

Mr Auden opened the court by saying, "I have had instructions to treat the explosion as a civil accident. Inquests relating to enemy action are beyond the remit of a coroner, however I still believe there are questions to be asked relating to this case as enemy action, I believe, does not have any bearing on this case.

What he did not say was that, as the explosion was to be treated as a civil accident, this in turn meant that the RAF could not be tried for any misdoings or errors in this inquiry! The RAF did not want outsiders to tell them how to run their war effort!

"I call as my first witness, Group Captain Storrar."

It was ascertained that Group Captain Ronald Storrar, commander of RAF Fauld had actually been on leave that day. Captain Storrar was reticent in his answers.

Group Captain Storrar was asked if he knew of any evidence of sabotage.

Storrar replied: "All I am authorised to say in answer to your question is 'negative'."

"Do you have any evidence that the Italian prisoners of war or the IRA played a part in the explosion?"

Storrar replied: "Again, all I am authorised to say in answer to your question is 'negative'.

"Do you have any evidence that the neighbouring Peter Ford's alabaster mine was to blame?"

Storrar replied: "All I am authorised to say in answer to your question is 'negative'."

"Do you mean to indicate that you know nothing or that you have been authorised not to say anything?"

Storrar replied, "All I can say is the official investigation is not yet completed but, so far as my information goes, I am authorised to say that the answer to all of those questions is 'negative'."

The investigator then stated to the Court, "I have information that you were a witness at a secret court of inquiry at RAF Fauld between December 6 and 11, 1944.

Storrar replied: "I am not at liberty to divulge any information relating to that court of inquiry.

This certainly seemed to smack of a closed door as far as the RAF were concerned. The investigator then gave up questioning Storrar and he was allowed to return to his seat. Any outside investigations were frowned on and they would carry out their own investigations.

So, Storrar was adding nothing to the investigation. He did not give anything away or even indicate that he had information to divulge. However, he was allowed to stay throughout the proceedings and ask questions of witnesses, so, how seriously were the inquiry members seeking to uncover wrong-doing by one of their own?

What he didn't say was that he had been a witness at a secret court of inquiry at RAF Fauld between December 6 and 11, 1944. All 32 witnesses had been sworn to secrecy. The RAF did not want outsiders to tell them how to run their war effort. And the government was going to let the RAF get on with it.

After hearing the recollections of a number of witnesses at the inquest, the jury returned a verdict of 'Accidental Death'. The jury found that the victims died accidentally as the result of an explosion, the causes of which are at present unknown. They found that from the evidence, it did not appear that the explosion was due to sabotage or to operations in the adjoining plaster mine. The jury was satisfied that every effort had been made to recover the bodies of the missing persons and death could be presumed.

Of the 19 people officially listed as missing, they said that they were satisfied that every effort had been made to find them and that death could now be presumed."

Mr J Auden stated that the total death toll was 70, including 19 persons whose bodies may never be recovered. Of the 51 bodies that have been recovered (one unidentified); 14 were killed at the dump, 31 at the plaster mine and six on farm premises nearby. Out of the 19 persons who were missing, these are now presumed dead. Three RAF personnel at the dump, nine civilian employees, two at the plaster mine and five on the farm. Six of the dead were Italian co-operators.

"There is a sea of mud studded with tree trunks and boulders stretching for more than half a mile over an area that was formerly offices and green fields. Under this it is known that there are at least 13 bodies, but it is impossible to ascertain their exact location."

It was stated that any trace of the site of Upper Castle Hayes Farm had been obliterated and local inhabitants had difficulty in pointing to where it stood. From this area, six bodies were recovered and five persons were still missing. Members of the RAF and others killed at the dump numbered 14; their bodies had been found, but on this site there were missing three RAF men and nine civilians. From the plaster mine, 31 bodies had been recovered and two were still missing.

The court session lasted nearly three hours. The jury retired for about half an hour and found that the victims named by the coroner died accidentally as the result of the explosion, the causes of which were at present unknown.

The jury added that, "It does not appear that the causes were due to sabotage or to mining operations. With regard to the missing, the jury are satisfied from the evidence given, that every effort has been made to recover the bodies and that death can be presumed.

The jury commend the following for meritorious services – Mrs Mary Elizabeth Cooper, PC A.T Mackay, and Mr J Foster, and express sincere sympathy with the relatives of the deceased."

....

The Coroner, Mr J L Auden, following the Court of Inquiry decided to put matters straight as to the number of rumours of sabotage being bandied around, blaming the Italians working at the Dump, was up in arms.

He wrote a letter to the Derby Daily Telegraph, tendering an apology 'on behalf of the general public' to the Italians for the rumours. His letter was printed on 7 February 1945.

The Day the Sun Disappeared, 27 Nov 1944

"I have heard, or even been informed by letters, many of which are anonymous, that the explosion was caused by:

1. *The IRA*
2. *Sabotage, possibly by the Italian collaborators*
3. *That the effects of blasting at the neighbouring mine had spread underground*
4. *A 'technical mistake' by the RAF*

*Although the RAF investigation has not yet completed, I have been given permission to say by what had **not** caused the explosion.*

The question of sabotage has completely been wiped out. The Italians did not ask to be sent to the dump. They only did their duty there.

Following the explosion, their lives have become somewhat unpleasant in the district owing to what I can only call hot-house gossip. They were no more to blame than the IRA.

I think also that there is sufficient evidence that the mine was not the cause of the explosion. It was an RAF 'private accident'.

Group Captain Ronald Charles Storrar, Officer commanding the dump, also said that, although the official investigation has not been completed, he was in a position to say that the cause did not arise from sabotage or from the mine.

I have listened throughout the afternoon of the Inquest to a succession of witnesses – service people, civilians and experts, some of whom had miraculous escapes from death – the jury returned a verdict of 'Accidental death' as a result of the explosion at the RAF dump, the causes of which are at present unknown in respect of the 52 bodies recovered from the area.".

CHAPTER 49

CLEAR UP

Air Marshal Donald wrote to the Air Ministry on December 23 that three shifts of 30 men were clearing 300 or 400 tons of explosive a day from the mine.

Civilians and Americans had done their best with spades and diggers, remaking the roads. The bodies of those that had been found had now been buried, one funeral after another.

A giant US Army mechanical excavator broke down in the narrow lane leading to the plaster works on 29th November and impeded track vehicles and bulldozers getting to the site. However, it was moved later in the afternoon and the convoy headed on to help the Civil Defence team, including that of the Derby Rescue Team from the Rowditch depot, who are still digging for bodies.

An appeal had been launched across the whole of the UK, for funds to help the bereaved.

RAF Fauld's satellites such as Bagots Wood, and nearby RAF airfields took recovered munitions. RAF Church Broughton, for instance, was storing Fauld small arms ammunition in the open from January 1945.

Within weeks, the RAF authorities could look ahead to using Fauld again, above ground, if not below yet. Air Marshal Donald continued in his letter to the Air Ministry: "It is clearly most desirable to keep Fauld as an ammunition depot, whatever use may be made ultimately of the mine, since the civilian labour is

The Day the Sun Disappeared, 27 Nov 1944

available, the transportation facilities (sidings, cranes etc.) are also available and the geographical position is convenient from the supply aspect."

Ken McCloud (LAC), who was among the last to escape from the mine on 27 November, was there making sure the bombs were safe before transportation.

He went to see if his tunic was still hanging up on the nail where he had left it when he escaped from the mine. It was there but the gas had turned the blue colour of the cloth to green. His tan-coloured wallet, left in the pocket, had turned black. He then saw the bicycle lamp of one of his pals was hanging in a knapsack close by. Memories of being in that pitch black tunnel, grappling his way through, crawling on hands and knees, just using his hands to guide him, all came flooding back to him. He doubted if those memories would ever fade. "If only I had had that with me, we could have got out that much sooner," he said to himself.

By late March 1945, the RAF had recovered all high explosive bombs from the mine, except those buried under big rock falls. Clearance of these falls began on April 4, 1945 but the workers could not keep up the predicted rate of 300-400 tons a day as Air Marshal Donald reported. By September 20, 1945 32,000 tons of 'stores' had been recovered, or roughly less than 100 tons a shift, with teams, including Ken, working through the night. It is believed the last explosives lost when the dump went up, came to the surface in October 1945.

The search for bodies was officially abandoned on 10 February 1945. There were still 19 persons missing, presumably dead, but no hope of finding them, or what parts of them remained, under what had become a wasteland. A moon-like scene of dust and dirt with no sign of life. Not even a blade of grass had found its way through, over what had been lush pastureland, and no birds were heard to sing over the desolate landscape.

Meanwhile, the urgency was to find and remove bombs from the 'old' area of the dump, where there were still approximately 15,000 tons of high explosives remaining in the untouched area and another 4,000 tons in the damaged area. The fear was that these bombs could still explode and cause an explosion even greater than the first. The 'new' area, that had been completely wrecked, was totally inaccessible. 3,670 tons of bombs had exploded in this area, but there could have up to 8,000 tons of bombs stored there, leaving a possible 5,000 tons of bombs, or thereabouts, unfound.

It was at first thought that the 'old' area could have been cleared but this was proving extremely difficult and deemed highly dangerous, as the damage was found to be more extensive with sensitive explosive mixed up with debris, serious roof fall and the alabaster pillars were partly supported by stacks of explosives.

However, the parts that could be reconnoitred were cleared of the bombs and these were transferred to RAF Tatenhill, six miles away. Crews of men were allocated to perform this clearance – 30 men (one day shifts of civilian volunteers and two night shifts of airmen). They were clearing around 3-400 tons a day.

On September 1, 1945, Dr Rotter reported to Maintenance Command that one cavern was still piled to the roof with mud, "which has entered from above and has, on several occasions broken through again and forced workers back." However, Dr Rotter went on to say he discounted the danger of unexploded bombs. "The principal risks to be encountered are those normal to quarrying in unsound rock and to the mud. Given the crater above ground, and the 150 acres of farmland ruined and another 250 acres damaged, underground seemed remarkably intact!"

About 1000 acres of land were affected. In my interview with Graham Shaw and his uncle Joe Cooper in February 2023, Graham said, "All the land was levelled, most of it anyway, all it could be used for was grazing. That's all they could do, couldn't plough it because of the restrictions, that I think are still in place."

Graham continued, "When I was a young lad, there were massive lumps of alabaster sticking out of the ground, but they've disappeared, or sunk. It's wet out there, with pools that won't drain." Joe Cooper replied, "Oh the holes aren't bomb craters, they are the mines giving away, so that would be big enough for the alabaster to drop back down into. Gypsum would fill up the mine runs when they were finished. They always held water. As a rule they'd finish up as a little pond. Years ago, there were a lot of these little ponds. Snipe birds used to nest up there. Loads of them. They'd found this spot suitable for them and moved in. amongst the bulrushes. But once the ground had settled, after about 2-3 months, Gypsum would go and fill them in. If they filled them in too quickly, it would sink again.

Nothing worked as there is no top-soil anymore. Trees have grown up, sending their roots deep down, and there is grass of sorts, but the pools are still there, covered with green slime."

It was a year to the day after the explosion, 27 November 1945, when the last of the bombs from the 'old' sector were finally removed. Dr Godfrey Rotter, a 66-year-old retiree was called on by the Air Ministry to supervise the work. Dr Rotter had been director of explosive research at the Woolwich Arsenal. He, together with Eric Bryant, who had been the resident engineer,

The Day the Sun Disappeared, 27 Nov 1944

who had advised on the original conversion of the mine into a bomb store, undertook the life-threatening job of getting the remaining bombs out of the 'old' sector of the mine that had sustained damage. They knew any false move could be the end of them. It took personal courage day after day. They started on 7 April and, with a team of civilians, along with Horace Utting (Dick Utting's brother), scrambling on top of overlying dangerous explosives and crawling under a roof, which was liable to collapse at any moment, for the next five months.

The team of civilians included Mr Maxted and Mr Fox, who led a small party engaged in the precarious work of recovering damaged explosives. Great care was necessary, as it was not known, whether the safety devices of certain of the damaged stores were still intact.

Mr Parker and Mr Utting worked fearlessly, shoring up a bad roof to prevent falls. They had to be careful not to dislodge the roof, which might have fallen on more explosives.

Labourers, quarrymen and others commended for their conduct during the clearance were: Arthur Frederick Merrick, Thomas Mylotte, George Edward Whittaker, Charles Herbert Fletcher, David Hickson, William Henry Green, Joseph William Ford, Horace John Edwards, Thomas Eccleston, Albert Henry Croft, George Henry Clower, Edward Malcolm Andrews and Thomas Wainwright.

All worked on, through the worst of conditions, regardless of their own safety. Some 22,000 tons of explosive stores were removed.

On 11 September 1945, four months after the war in Europe had ended, the clearance was almost complete, with the exception of one cavern which was thought to contain only semi-armour-piercing bombs not exceeding 70 tons. In all, 23,000 tons were removed (4,000 from the damaged area).

George Medals were presented to Mr E Bryant, resident engineer, No 21 MU, RAF and Mr G Rotter, scientific adviser to the Air Ministry.

On 3rd October 1945 it was reviewed that Derby itself was in peril as a result of the bomb dump explosion. The dump was in two sections in an alabaster mine, but only the smaller part exploded. In the other portion were 20,000 tons of bombs and shells, some covered with debris, caused by extensive roof falls. Explosives of a highly sensitive character were mixed with the rubble and clearance work carried with it the risk of an upheaval of far greater magnitude than the first.

The configuration of the ground gave certain protection to neighbouring towns and villages in the event of an explosion, but the blast destroyed one of these natural barriers on the Derby side.

As it was, the effects of the explosion were more noticeable in the Tutbury and Derby direction than in any other.

The official announcement of awards for clearance work stated, "A further explosion might well have caused damaged to the town of Derby, and would most certainly have damaged towns and villages in the neighbourhood, since a natural protecting traverse had disappeared in the explosion on November 27th.

. . . .

The Day the Sun Disappeared, 27 Nov 1944

Reported in the **Burton Chronical on 21 August 1947**:

Last week, at about 12.30pm on Tuesday, 11 August 1947, almost three years on from the explosion, while moving earth with a bulldozer, workmen from the prison, uncovered a tractor and something resembling a body. The body was identified at Friday's inquest, held at the Dog and Partridge Hotel, as that of Stephen West, of Hanbury, a tractor driver employed at Upper Castle Hayes Farm. The coroner, Mr J L Auden, who was on holiday at the time, has been informed of the discovery and is returning to open an inquest on Friday. He would ask the Home Secretary to remove his name from the list of unrecovered bodies. The discovery was made about 200 yards from the edge of the main crater.

Joseph James West of Mill Farm, Cubley, Stephen West's brother, said he last saw his brother alive at 9pm on the day before the explosion. He identified the body from certain articles of clothing. His brother was in the habit of wearing the tops of a pair of Wellington boots as leggings. He also identified two tobacco pipes, a tobacco pouch, a belt from a waterproof coat and a leather belt as belonging to his brother. He told the inquest that, after the explosion, he went to the farm to look for his two brothers, but the farm had disappeared.

Classius Peyman, of the Swan Inn, Draycott-in-the-Clay, said he was employed by the Air Ministry Works Directorate as a general foreman, in charge of restoration of land known as Hanbury Fields, devastated by the 1944 explosion.

At 12.45pm on August 12th, from information received, he went to see a body, which had been unearthed. They had been reclaiming with a bulldozer, pumping water from small craters and filling up. It was in this way that the body was unearthed.

The Day the Sun Disappeared, 27 Nov 1944

Mr Auden stated that he intended to send a letter to the Governor of Stafford Prison commending the work of long-term prisoners who are engaged on reclamation work at the site. Following his letter, the four prisoners who discovered the body each had their sentences remitted by 21 days.

The remains of Stephen West (aged 37) were buried near his father in the St Andrews Churchyard, Cubley, Derbyshire, on August 15th.

A rumour circulating in Hanbury village, that unexploded bombs had also been uncovered by bulldozers at the same spot, was not denied or confirmed by the RAF authorities at 21 Maintenance Unit Fauld, which is in charge of the entire area.

....

A report in the **Burton Daily Mail dated 30 November 1948** stated:

"Almost back to normal after four years."

For some time after the explosion it was thought that the land could never be reclaimed, but the seemingly impossible had almost been achieved.

For three years after the explosion prisoners from Stafford Gaol had been clearing the site and had moved many thousands of tons of earth.

A tribute was paid to those prisoners in London on 29th November 1948, by Mr Chuter Ede, the Home Secretary. Mr Ede was addressing the Howard League for Penal Reform, and stated that, since the work of reclamation had started a small band of prisoners had levelled the site, drained it, seeded and planted it.

The Day the Sun Disappeared, 27 Nov 1944

He added that, although they worked in the open, not one prisoner had tried to escape."

Report in The Sentinel - The way We Were: Your letters, Saturday, January 2, 2010

Fauld tragedy killed our pals - *from Joan Burgess (nee Redfern), Manchester.*

After reading the article in The Way We Were about the Staffordshire explosion at Fauld, I've decided to write in to say that I remember it very well.

I was 16-years-old at the time and my family lived at Mill Cottage, Cubley.

We knew the West family, at Mill Farm.

I remember the tremor as being like an earthquake and there was a large, black cloud as we looked towards Sudbury.

John and Stephen West both worked at Castle Hayes Farm. John, the younger brother, had been recently married and lived at Hatton. His body was found on the day of the explosion and buried at Hatton.

Stephen West's body was not found until 1947, when he was brought to Cubley to be laid to rest with his family.

Jack Redfern, our cousin, was also killed in the Fauld explosion. Ryan Kirk Locker also wrote that Jack Redfern was his great, great uncle.

.....

Although unidentified, the funeral took place of who was presumed to be Jack Redfern. The vicar, in a short address, spoke of the sadness of unidentification on earth but said he was definitely sure that the man would be identified in heaven.

The Day the Sun Disappeared, 27 Nov 1944

CHAPTER 50

MEMORIAL

The Fauld Explosion

AT 11 MINUTES PAST 11 ON THE MORNING OF NOVEMBER 27TH, 1944, THE MIDLANDS WAS SHAKEN BY THE BIGGEST EXPLOSION THIS COUNTRY HAS EVER KNOWN.

4,000 TONS OF BOMBS STORED 90 ft. DOWN IN THE OLD GYPSUM MINES IN THE AREA, BLEW UP, BLASTING OPEN A CRATER 400ft DEEP AND 3/4 MILE LONG. BUILDINGS MANY MILES AWAY WERE DAMAGED. THIS PUB HAD TO BE REBUILT AND ONE FARM, WITH ALL ITS BUILDINGS, WAGONS, HORSES, CATTLE AND 6 PEOPLE COMPLETELY DISAPPEARED.

YOU ... ND THE STORY OF THE ...

The earliest memorial was a cross, placed deep into the crater, soon after the explosion. The cross was made of stones of white gypsum found scattered around the crater. Local people, RAF and prisoners alike had moved these stones into position, so heartfelt was their sorrow.

The Day the Sun Disappeared, 27 Nov 1944

Staring down into the vast and awe-inspiring crater, was to experience a highly personal sense of loss. People gazed down into a war grave like none other: a grave which the many victims who were never found still share with an unknown quantity of unexploded bombs.

A witness at the scene, a veteran of the First World War, spoke to the person standing next to him, "I was in the last war and I've seen some sights but nothing like this. We used to think that the 'Jack Johnson' shells were pretty bad but they were like kid's toys compared to this." The person he was speaking to replied, "I am a veteran of the Great War and was at Passchendaele and the Somme. I've seen the horror and desolation of the battlefields with towns and countryside blasted by bombs and high explosives, but I've never seen such destruction as the like of this, all in one blow."

On 25 April 1945, the Second World War in Europe had less than two weeks to come to an end. On that day, six Nazi mayors were made to view Belsen, the Nazi concentration camp, to face the inhuman truth of the war the Nazis had created. That evening, the band of RAF Cranwell led a procession from Hanbury parish church, St. Werbergh's, to the edge of the 25 yard-wide crater. The memorial was attended by a huge gathering. There was a chill in this spring evening that was recreated in the chill felt down the spines of those remembering that day, just five months earlier. Some would be remembering the fields that they use to work in, cross over and play in – fields that were no longer there, just barren desolation.

The Day the Sun Disappeared, 27 Nov 1944

St Werbergh's Church, Hanbury

Group Captain Allen was there along with Group Captain Storrar and Wing Commander Kings, along with other RAF officers in their blue uniforms, surrounded by civilians from Hanbury, Tutbury and Burton, in muted dark colours, along with a brass band that played the Last Post followed by the national anthem. People were remembering the dead and missing that had been vaporised by a cauldron-like crater. Staffordshire no longer had to fear enemy air attack, but the grim battle to make ends meet would carry on. It was the military's way of honouring the dead but they weren't open to questions by the valiant few who dared approach them.

....

A memorial ceremony was held, on behalf of the explosion victims, at a temporary Memorial Hall opened at Hanbury, on Saturday, 23 July 1949. It was beautiful weather for the opening of the hall.

The Day the Sun Disappeared, 27 Nov 1944

A service before the opening ceremony was conducted by the present Vicar of Hanbury, Rev R R Osborn.

Mr Ford, who had been the director of Messrs Peter Ford & Sons, performed the opening ceremony.

The hall, provided by the National Council of Social Services for use until materials were available for the erection of a permanent hall, stands on an acre of land given by Major Leigh Newton and is intended as a memorial to villagers killed in both World Wars, as well as to those who died in the explosion.

A Roll of Honour, inscribed with all the names, had been placed in the hall and was unveiled by the Rev. J Crook, who had been the vicar of Hanbury at the time of the explosion, but who had since transferred to Morton, Newport, Salop.

Rev Crook gave a speech, "I recall the morning of November 27, 1944, at ten minutes past eleven." There he paused, with his head bowed, then he resumed – his voice emitting an emotion felt by everyone there. "These names will always stand in my memory."

He then went on to give a moving vote of thanks to various people, including Mr Rowland Ford and Mr Leslie Shotton (Chairman of the Parish Council).

Gordon (then aged 15) and Marie Goodwin (then aged 12) were present. Their parents Mr and Mrs W Goodwin, were killed when their home, Upper Castle Hayes Farm, was destroyed in the Fauld explosion. Gordon presented a buttonhole to Mr Rowland Ford, and Marie presented a bouquet to Mrs Ford.

The Day the Sun Disappeared, 27 Nov 1944

HANBURY MEMORIAL HALL, commemorating the victims of the two world wars, and of the Fauld explosion, and replacing the hall destroyed in the latter catastrophe in 1944, was opened on Saturday by Mr. Rowland Ford, who is seen accepting the key from Mr. G. Eds. Also in the picture are Mr. R. Marler, the Rev. R. R. Osborn (Vicar of Hanbury), the Rev. J. B. Gooding, the Rev. J. Crook, Mrs. Gordon Cox, Mrs. R. Ford, Wing Commander A. L. Cornford (C.O., Fauld R.A.F.), Miss M. Goodwin and Mr. G. Goodwin.

No-ones know what anguish they must have gone through, following the tragic loss of their parents, in such catastrophic circumstances, when they were still just young children. What were they thinking at this ceremony, while still in their formative years, to be reminded of the hurt they had both suffered? They looked nervous and Gordon hung his head. Both had been placed on a platform to be looked at by everyone present, insecure and not sure what they should be doing. This reminded me of the young Princes Will and Harry at Princess Diana's funeral. It may have been five years on but it would have brought back those horrible memories, of when they first heard the news.

……………….

On the fifth anniversary, 27 November 1949 a memorial window was unveiled at St Werburgh's Church, Hanbury. It was decided to use what is perhaps the church's greatest treasure, some 14th century stained glass, which for years had been in the vestry

The Day the Sun Disappeared, 27 Nov 1944

window. In the centre is depicted the Holy Trinity. You can see the lower part of a figure of the Almighty wearing a purple robe with an ornamental border. The left hand supports a cross on which hangs our Lord. From his pierced hand drops of blood are falling onto the robe. At the foot is an orb and at the top of the panel are the letters 'IHC'. In the left hand window is the figure of John the Baptist and above a fragment of a monogram

Peter Ford and his wife and Joseph Foster with his wife, Maud, were at this unveiling, among others.

The memorial window reads:

"The ancient glass was placed in this window in memory of those parishioners who died in active service during the Second World War 1939-45 and all those who lost their lives in the Hanbury Explosion November 27th 1944."

On the right hand side of this window is a framed plaque – a Roll of Honour - listing the names of all those who lost their lives.

These died in the Fauld Explosion [Munitions] at 11.11am on the 27th November 1944.

The first eighteen people named have no known grave and the crater is their resting place

BAILEY John Thomas, Leading Aircraftman 1503421, Royal Air Force Volunteer Reserve killed 27th November 1944 aged 23. Son of Thomas Ernest and Phylis Mildred of Wednesbury, Staffordshire. Commemorated on the Runnymede Memorial, Surrey

BRASSINGTON James of 55, Monk Street, Tutbury aged 60. He was the son of Henry and Mary A, who in 1901 were residing in Balance Street, Uttoxeter, Staffordshire. In 1911 he was residing with his in-laws, James and Ann Treadwell and his wife Annie at 27, Church Street, Tutbury and his occupation was a general labourer. His father in law worked in the plaster mine in Fauld. His grandson, Stewart was four years old.

CAMPBELL Fred, of Harehill, Boylestone, Derbyshire killed at Fauld aged 59. Husband of Edith, nee Watkins whom he married in 1908. He was the son of Isaac and Emma, who in 1901 were residing at 17, Sidney Street, Cheadle, Staffordshire, Fred was working on a mine railway. In 1911 he and his wife (no children) were residing at Osgathorpe, near Loughborough, Derbyshire and was working in a lime stone quarry as a loader. He is native of Cheadle Staffordshire

CARTWRIGHT Frank, of Redcroft, Ashbourne Road, Uttoxeter, Staffordshire. Killed at the Plaster Pits, Hanbury, Staffordshire, aged 41. Husband of Florence May. He was the son of John Richard and Lettice Constance Gertrude of 84, New Road, Uttoxeter, Staffordshire. His brother Reginald was also killed in the same explosion

FAIRBANKS Henry Charles, Leading Aircraftman 1434417, Royal Air Force Volunteer Reserve killed 27th November 1944 age 39. Son of Rosa Fairbanks and husband of Doreen Mary Fairbanks of Battersea, London. Commemorated on the Runnymede Memorial, Surrey

FROW Lewis Dudley, of 24 Castle Street, Tutbury aged 15. He was the son of Joseph Edward (born 1901) and Kate, nee Riggall (Born 1895) who in 1911 were all residing at Benniworth, Lincolnshire. Lewis was born in the registration district of Horncastle, Lincolnshire.

HOGG Charles Edmund aged 57. Son of Thomas and Dorothy of 2 Queens Street, Benfieldside, Durham. Born in the registration district of South Shields, Co Durham

MAHON Gerald Augusta of Newborough, Burton on Trent, Staffordshire died at Fauld aged 47. Son of Martin and Clara nee Moss who in 1901 were residing at Sowley Cottage, Marchington Woodlands. His father was self-employed farmer and is native of

Ireland. In 1911 were all residing at Bank Top, Draycott in the Clay, Staffordshire

MELLOR Albert William, of Park Cottage, Hollington Lane, Stramshall, Staffordshire, aged 55. Husband of Florence, nee Banks whom he married in 1930. He is the son of Samuel Albert and Theresa who in 1901 were residing at Park Cottage, Stramshall, Staffordshire 1901 Census shows her name as Theresa, but on the 8th March 1886, Samuel married a Miriam Fisher in St Michaels Church, Stramshall. His father died 3rd December 1923 aged 63 and his mother (Miriam) died 26th October 1932 aged 67 and are buried together at St Michaels churchyard, Stramshall. His wife Florence died 8th September 1964 aged 63 and is buried in the same place. His father joined the army as Driver T4/084129 187 Coy, Army Service Corps at the age of 37years and 11 months. He enlisted on the 26th March 1915 and joined his unit at Woolwich on the 1st April 1915. He served in France (Le-Treport) with the Expeditionary Force from the 4th September 1915 to 8th April 1916. He was sent back to England on the next day, 9th and was admitted to hospital the same day until 9th May 1916 and then he was discharged from the army. He suffered from Myalgia, which is severe muscle pain. It is not caused by strain or overuse but from an infectious disease like, influenza. His problem started in civil life and not caused by war service

MILES Russell John of Upper Castle Hayes, Hanbury, aged 16

NICKLIN Frederick, of 16, Monk Street, Tutbury, Staffordshire, aged 46. Husband of Ada Helen, nee Whitehead. . He was the son of William and Betsy, nee Press. In 1911 they were all residing at 15, Monk Street, Tutbury

The Day the Sun Disappeared, 27 Nov 1944

REDFERN John William, of Glass House, Gorsby Hill, Marchington Woodlands, Staffordshire, aged 32

ROCK Frederick George of Church Cottage, Hanbury, killed at Moat farm, featherbed Lane, Hanbury aged 40. Husband of Florence, nee Knight. [The death ref surname as Roch] He was the son of Frederick and Mary Ann who in 1911 were all residing in Castle Bromwich, Birmingham. He was born in Uttoxeter and is knows as George

SAUNDERS Tom, of Green Lane, Tutbury, Staffordshire, who is believed to have been killed at Hanbury aged 54. Husband of Emily

SHIPLEY Alfred Arthur, of 62, Milton Street, Burton on Trent, who is believed to have been killed at Hanbury aged 47. Husband of Elizabeth Rutherford Shipley He was the son Mary Ellen formerly Geary, nee Marriott who in 1911 was widow and residing at 31, Haydock Street, Roe Lee, Blackburn, Lancashire occupation, cotton weaver. He was born in the registration district of Burton upon Trent and his father was called Ernest

SMITH Elizabeth Miss, of Upper Castle Hayes Farm, Hanbury aged 39. She may be the daughter of George and Elizabeth who in 1901 were residing at Hanbury Woodend, Hanbury and in 1911 just gave Hanbury, most likely the same address

STANLEY Bert Henry, of Hanbury Wood End, Hanbury aged 34. Husband of Agnes. He was the son of Hugh Henry and Amy who were all residing in 1911 at Hanbury Wood End, Hanbury In 1911 his parents gave his name as Bertie

WAGSTAFFE Robert, of New Road, Draycott in the Clay accidentally killed in the Fauld Explosion at Upper Castle Hayes Farm, Hanbury aged 68, husband of Ann Jeffrey, nee Goodall.

The Day the Sun Disappeared, 27 Nov 1944

Commemorated on his wife's memorial in All Saints churchyard, Denstone, Staffordshire. He was the son of Robert and Martha residing in 1881 at Bank End, Norbury, Derbyshire and 1891 at Roston Common, Norbury, Derbyshire In 1901 he was residing with his wife at Shaw Lane, Marston Montgomery, Derbyshire and, in 1911, he was living with his wife and family at Hales Green Farm, Yeavely near Ashbourne, Derbyshire

The Day the Sun Disappeared, 27 Nov 1944

Grave to the 18 missing.

My parents always wanted a memorial at the crater, so several years ago I wrote to the then Prime Minister, Margaret Thatcher, The Burton-on-Trent Member of Parliament, Ivan Lawrence, The Ministry of defence, The War Graves Commission, The British Legion, but the replies were always no, it was not possible. Each had their own reason. I destroyed those letters and the replies some years ago, so I am not able to enclose them.

After the crater was fenced off, Hanbury Parish Council was able to get a memorial there, although I am pleased after 46yrs the memorial was erected, I have always been disappointed with it. Donations were asked for and given by families, Hanbury Parish Council, Tutbury Parish Council, Duchy of Lancaster, and several Businesses. The money which was given was not used for the memorial, the stone was donated from Italy. Half of my donation was given on behalf of my deceased parents, because that is what they always wanted. I am sure a nice stone from this country would have been more appropriate, and the money given used for that purpose.

I am also disappointed Hanbury Parish Council decided to stop the service at the crater after the 60th anniversary which was November 2004, even though the Reverend T Fox was still willing to conduct the service there. After the service was stopped Ken still went across to take flowers, he is not able to go now.

On VE day 8th May 1945, I went to a dance at the R A F station at Fauld, it was there I met Ken, now my Husband, little did I know then that he had been trapped in the mine and was one of the last four to get out alive. He knew where my Brother would be, right at the heart of the explosion. He never told me about it until years after, also he never told me about being a witness at the Court of Enquiry. He did not speak about it much, he says now it is still as clear as all those years ago.

This was written by me, Joyce McLeod in 2011, before donating this folder Tutbury Museum.

OTHERS KILLED:

APPLETON Henry John, of 10, Watson Street, Penkhull, Stoke on Trent, Staffordshire died at Peter Ford and Sons Works, Ltd at Tutbury aged 62 and brother of Emily Elizabeth and Edith May who were spinsters at the time of the accident. He was the son of Thomas and Amelia Sophia Pleszskowski. In 1881 his parents and siblings were residing at Victoria Street, Basford, Staffordshire and his father was High Bailiff of Hanley Court. In 1891, they were residing at 14, Howard Place, Hanley, Staffordshire, father still employed in the same occupation. In 1901 they were all residing at Queens Road, Penkhull, Staffordshire, his father in the same occupation. In 1911 his mother, now a widow and some of his siblings were residing at 43, James Street, Stoke on Trent, Henry was now known as John. Both of his parents were born in London

BARKER Joseph Edward of Bridge Cottage, Marchington, Staffordshire died at Fauld Royal Air Force Maintenance Depot, age 42. Husband of Lilian nee Trowell

BEARD James, of 2, Tamworth Road, Ashby de la Zouch, Leicestershire died at Hanbury aged 51. Husband of Edith Emily nee Marston of Ashby de la Zouch

BELL Joseph of 32, Burton Street, Tutbury, Staffordshire aged 39. He was a single man, the son of Eli and Minnie and in 1911 were residing at 53, Burton Road, Tutbury. His father was an Alabaster Dresser in a plaster mine at Fauld. His body was recovered on Tuesday 28th November. He has two brothers serving abroad and a brother, who has been missing for two years. His funeral was on Thursday, 21st December.

BOWRING Frederick Charles of Wood End East, Hanbury, aged 39. Husband of Olive Rosina. He was the son of Edward and Alice and in 1911 were all residing at Hanbury Wood End, Hanbury. His father was a stone breaker in the plaster mine at Fauld

CARTER Harold, of Black Brook, Hanbury, aged 47. Husband of Rose. He was the son of George and Emma of who in 1901 and 1911 were all residing in Stubby Lane, Draycott in the Clay, Staffordshire. His father was working in the plaster mine at Fauld Harold was born in Oxfordshire

CARTWRIGHT Reginald, of Ashdene New Road, Uttoxeter. Killed at Peter Ford and Sons Works, at Fauld aged 46 husband of Ethel. He was the son of John Richard and Lettice Constance Gertrude of 84, New Road, Uttoxeter, Staffordshire. His brother, Frank was also killed in the same explosion

CHAWNER Sydney, of Villa Cottage, Blackbrook, Hanbury, killed at Moat Farm, Hanbury aged 50. Husband of Violet. He was the son of William and Ann and in 1911 were all residing on a farm at Anslow Gate, Anslow, which is short distance from Hanbury, Staffordshire. His father was a self-employed farmer

COCKAYNE George Lawrence aged 49 husband of Violet May nee Gent. of 11, Church Street, Tutbury, Staffordshire. Commemorated on his wife's memorial in St Marys churchyard, Tutbury, Staffordshire. His effects went to Private Geoffrey Thomas Cockayne. He was the son of George Thomas and Hannah and in 1911 was residing with his parents at 36, Bridge Street, Tutbury. His occupation then was as assistant glass blower in Tutbury. He joined the army for 72 days as Private 2356, North Staffordshire Regiment and gave his father George Thomas as his next of kin who was residing at Fauld and occupation as apprentice blacksmith. He joined 1st September 1914 and was discharged on the 7th November 1914, reason, not likely to become an efficient soldier. He is buried at St Mary's Priory Church, Tutbury

The Day the Sun Disappeared, 27 Nov 1944

COOPER Joseph, of 1, Council Houses, Hanbury aged 48. Husband of Mary Elizabeth. In 1901 he was a visitor aged 4yrs at the home of Mary Jackson, widow, head of the house and a farmer, also John and Eliza Shelley in Tutbury. 1911 shows him on the farm of William and Sarah Shelley at Castle Hayes, Hanbury

COOPER Percy, of Rough Croft, Hanbury aged 40. Husband of Clarice Mary. He may be the son of William and Annie who were all residing in 1911 in the Main Street, Hilton Derbyshire

DANIELS Ernest William Gustave, of Tall Chimneys, West Drive, Mickleover, Derbyshire aged 35. Husband of Jean. He was the son of Harold and Amy Irene and in 1911 was living with his parents at 6, Langdale Avenue, Levenshulme, Lancashire. He is native of Lancashire

FELL Benjamin, of Hoar Cross, Burton on Trent, Staffordshire aged 46. He was the son of William and Elizabeth, they were all residing in Hoar Cross, Staffordshire in 1911 and brother of Edgar who was also killed in the explosion, and the father of Thomas Bradley, labourer and Edith

FELL Edgar, of Newborough Village, Staffordshire aged 39. Husband of Charlotte Sylvia. He was the son of William and Elizabeth, they were all residing in Hoar Cross, Staffordshire in 1911 and brother of Benjamin who was also killed in the explosion

FORD William, of Purse Cottages, Fauld aged 57. Husband of Nellie. He may be the son of John and Jane of 31, Leighton Road, Uttoxeter. Staffordshire He was born in Ellastone, Staffordshire

GENT William, accidentally killed aged 43 of 8. Monk Street, Tutbury, Staffordshire. Husband of Fanny. Commemorated on his wife's memorial in St Marys churchyard, Tutbury Staffordshire.

The Day the Sun Disappeared, 27 Nov 1944

He was the son of Sydney Charles and Mary Emma of 18, Monk Street, Tutbury, Staffordshire. He is buried at St Mary's Priory Church, Tutbury

GILBERT Alma Omar, of Rushley Lea Marchington, Staffordshire, killed at the Plaster Pits Hanbury aged 61. He was the son of George Omar and Mary Ann, nee Whitehouse and in 1901 were all residing in March Cross, Marchington, Staffordshire. He was the husband of Mary Susannah nee Walker whom he married in 1910. In 1911 he was residing with his wife at Rushley Lea Cottages, Marchington, Staffordshire, occupation, Bricklayer his father was also a bricklayer

GOODWIN Mary Walley, nee Smith of Upper Castle Hayes Farm, Hanbury aged 41. Wife of William who also died the same day. She was the daughter of John Joseph and Mary Walley Smith who in 1911 were all residing in The Cottage, Boylestone, Derbyshire. Her father was self-employed farmer

GOODWIN William Maurice of Upper Castle Hayes Farm, Hanbury aged 45. Husband of Mary, nee Smith who also died the same day, brother of Sidney Burton and Wilfred John, farmers he was the son of William and Sarah Emma nee Burton whom he married at Leigh, Staffordshire 10th April 1888 aged 25. His father was called James and her father was called Thomas. In 1911 William, Sarah and family were all residing at Pool Green Farm, Tattenhill, Staffordshire

HARRIS Arthur, of Hanbury Wood End, Hanbury aged 56. Husband of Hilda Martha Richardson Harris. he was the son of Alfred and Mary Ann and in 1911 they were residing in Marchington Woodlands, Staffordshire, occupation Labourer on an estate with his father.

The Day the Sun Disappeared, 27 Nov 1944

HARRISON Frederick William of 8, Wyggeston Street, Burton on Trent aged 40. Husband of Leah

HILL Harry John, of Purse Villa, Fauld died at Fauld Plaster Works. aged 53 His wife Sarah Louise also died the same day. They had a son Leading Aircraftman William Charles, Royal Air Force. He was the son of Charles and Eliza and in 1901 and 1911 they were all residing in Pipe Hay Lane Draycott in the Clay, near Hanbury. His father worked as an alabaster mine labourer at Fauld. Harry was working as a railway clerk for the North Staffs railway

HILL Sarah Louise, killed with husband aged 54

HUDSON Thomas of Newborough House Cottage, Newborough, Burton upon Trent, Staffordshire, died at Fauld R.A.F Maintenance Depot, aged 38. Husband of Nellie. He was the son of Thomas and Beatrice Elizabeth of Marchington, Staffordshire

KIDD William of Stubby Lane, Draycott in the Clay, Derbyshire aged 67. He was the son of George and Ann who in 1881 were residing Newborough, Abbots Bromley, Staffordshire. 1891 William was working as a servant to William Foster, farmer at Gorsty Hill, Hares Cross, Staffordshire. In 1911 he was residing with his wife Sarah Ann, and children at Stubby Lane, Draycott in the Clay, and gave his occupation as a loader in the Plaster Mine. He was born at a place called Flour Cross, Staffordshire

PAGE Ernald Alfred of Stubby Lane, Draycott in the Clay, Derbyshire, died at Fauld R.A.F. Maintenance Depot, aged 36. Husband of Ida. He was the son of Alfred and Sarah who in 1911 were all residing in Duffield Lane, Newborough, Staffordshire. His father was working in the Gypsum mine at Fauld. George and Philip were his uncles, his father brother to George and Philip

The Day the Sun Disappeared, 27 Nov 1944

PAGE George Edward, of the Folly Hall Cottages, aged 58. Husband of Alice. He was the son of David and Sarah Ann, nee Stokes who in 1891 were all residing at Bank Top, Draycott in the Clay. His father worked in the Alabaster Mine. His brother Philip was also killed in the explosion. In 1901 he was a farm labourer for William Turner of Stubby Lane, Draycott in the Clay. In 1911 he was living with his wife and son at Duffield Lane Newborough, Staffordshire, occupation, Gypsum Miner

PAGE Philip, of Hanbury Wood End, Hanbury, aged 59 Husband of Emma. He was the son of David and Sarah Ann and brother of George who was also killed in the explosion In 1911 he was living with his parents at Parsons Brake, Hanbury. His siblings had fled the nest

PATTERSON Ambrose killed aged 47. He was the son of George Robart and Isabel of 10, Fontaine Road, Durham Sunderland. Born in the registration district of Sunderland in 1911 his occupation was Apprentice ships joiner and butchers errand boy. He is buried at St Mary's Priory Church, Tutbury, although with no known headstone.

PICKERING Samuel of 44, Monk Street, Tutbury, Staffordshire accidentally killed aged 36, husband of Elizabeth. Buried in St Marys Churchyard, Tutbury, Staffordshire He was the son of Samuel and Nellie of 14, Monk Street, Tutbury

POWELL George Henry, of 7, Church Street, Tutbury, aged 57. Husband of Alice Mabel. He may be the son of Alfred and Hannah Maria of Cote Fields, Church Broughton, Derbyshire. He is buried at St Mary's Priory Church, Tutbury, although with no known headstone. He was a brother-in-law of George Powell, of Church Street, Tutbury.

The Day the Sun Disappeared, 27 Nov 1944

PRIESTLEY George, of 13, Park Lane, Tutbury, Staffordshire, accidentally killed aged 63. Husband of Esther Elizabeth. Buried in St Marys Churchyard, Tutbury, Staffordshire. He was the son of William and Maria of Corn Mill Lane and in 1891 his father was working in the plaster mine. In 1911 he was residing with his wife and family at 11, Corn Mill Lane, Tutbury and gave his occupation as plaster labourer. He was a native of Sutton Bonnington, Nottinghamshire. He is buried at St Mary's Priory Church, Tutbury

SHEPHERD Henry, of 15, Burton Street, Tutbury aged 73. He was the husband of Eliza and father to William Henry who was killed in the Fauld Explosion the same day. Henry was the son of William and Emily (Shephard) who, in 1881, were residing in the Leopard Inn, Tutbury. 1901, his mother was a widow and Henry was not listed. His brother Ernest was a loader at the Gypsum Mine and his brother in law, Eli Bell was a blower at Gypsum Mine. They were all residing at 24 Burton Street, Tutbury. Henry had worked away from home for a brewery, as a carter, and had lodging at 40 Agard Street, Derby. In 1911 he was residing at 15, Burton Street, Tutbury and gave his occupation as a Alabaster Filler in a Plaster Mine. He is buried at St Mary's Priory Church, Tutbury, although with no known headstone.

SHEPHERD William Henry, of 15, Cornmill Lane, Tutbury, accidentally killed aged 39. Husband of Elizabeth. Buried in St Marys churchyard, Tutbury, Staffordshire he was the son of Henry and Eliza and in 1911 were residing at 15, Burton Street, Tutbury His father worked and was killed in the Plaster Mine Explosion at Fauld.

The Day the Sun Disappeared, 27 Nov 1944

SKELLETT John of 19, Small Holding, Knowles Hill, Rolleston on Dove, Staffordshire, killed at Fauld Mines aged 47. He had multiple injuries. Husband of Gertrude Annie, nee Campion. He was the son of John and Mary Elizabeth who in 1911 were all residing at 94, Branstone Road, Burton on Trent, Staffordshire

SLATER Frederick William of New Road, Draycott in the Clay, Derbyshire aged 37. Husband of Alice Mary. He was the son Frederick William and Emma of Pipe Hayes Lane, Draycott in the Clay. His father worked in the plaster mine at Fauld

SMITH George, of 16, Park Lane, Tutbury aged 74. Husband of Eliza. 1901 he and his family were at Hanbury Woodend, Hanbury and his occupation was a coachman. In 1911 He was residing with his wife and daughter, Nellie (could be Elizabeth aged 15) at Hanbury. He was working in the Alabaster Mine at Fauld, and gave his occupation as a cement worker. He is buried at St Mary's Priory Church, Tutbury

WEST John William of 1, Council Houses, Hanbury died at The Castle Hayes, Hanbury aged 23

WEST Stephen, of Cubley Mill, Cubley, Derbyshire, who lost his life in the Staffordshire Explosion aged 37. Buried in St Andrews Churchyard, Cubley, Derbyshire. He was the son of Stephen and Emma of Cubley. His father was a self-employed farmer

WOOLLEY Edman of 3, Cornmill Lane, Tutbury, aged 59. Husband of Mary Jane nee Priestley. He was the son of Tom and Emma who in 1901 were all residing at 23, Corn Mill Lane, Tutbury and in 1911 were all residing at 15, Corn Mill Lane, Tutbury, Staffordshire. Edman was working as a fitters-labourer at the Plaster and Cement Mills at Fauld.as shown in the 1901 and 1911 census. He was a former clever half-back footballer. He is buried at St Mary's Priory Church, Tutbury

WORTHINGTON Norman, of Coton Farm, Hanbury aged 17, son of Mabel

DEUCHARAS William, Leading Aircraftmen 1341152 killed 27 November 1944 aged 38. Son of John and Christina Deucharas of Crieff and is buried at Crieff cemetery, Perthshire [CWGC have his surname as Deuchars]

DUROSE Alan Sydney, Corporal 540880, Royal Air Force Volunteer Reserve killed 27th November 1944. Husband of Margaret E nee Barber of Burton on Trent, Staffordshire and is buried at Burton on Trent Cemetery

GAME Stanley Gordon, Sergeant 1257881, Number 21, Maintenance Centre, Royal Air Force Volunteer Reserve, killed 27th November 1944 aged 37. Son of William and Minnie Game of Colchester, husband of J K DE of Colchester and is buried in Colchester Cemetery, Essex

CROOK Lilian Emma Mrs [died subsequently] died 4th December 1944 aged 68, of The Vicarage, Hanbury, wife of the Reverend James Crook.

FORD Nellie, Mrs, [died subsequently] She may be the Nellie Ford from Purse Cottages. She died 6th May 1947 and lived at Owens Bank, Tutbury, (widow) aged 56.

The six Italians who died were:

LANZONI Aldo, Private, aged 31
NOVELLO Rocco, Private, aged 27
Di PAOLO Emilia Di, Private, aged 29

The Day the Sun Disappeared, 27 Nov 1944

RUGGIERI Salvatore, Private, aged 28
SCUTO Luigi, Corporal, aged 21
TROVATO Salvatore, private, aged 29

A new Memorial Hall was opened on 24 November 1962. This hall replaced the one destroyed on the explosion.

On the fortieth anniversary in November 1984, the RAF provided floodlights around the St Werburgh's Church, Hanbury, and joined the service in tribute to the victims. A choir from St Mary's Church, Tutbury joined the Hanbury choir and music was provided by the Royal Air Force Midlands Band.

On Sunday, 25 November 1990, 46 years after the explosion, a permanent memorial stone was erected at the crater. A plaque on the stone lists all the names of those who lost their lives in the Fauld explosion. Over five hundred people attended the Fauld Explosion Memorial Dedication Service held at the site. This stone, made of Italian diorite, was a gift from the Italian Air Force, transported by the RAF. Many of the relatives of those who were killed, attended, including Maurice Goodwin's 91-year-old brother. Also present was the niece of one of the Italians who perished, including some of those who had taken part in the rescue operations. Hanbury Parish Council laid a dozen red rose at the memorial.

The Day the Sun Disappeared, 27 Nov 1944

The Day the Sun Disappeared, 27 Nov 1944

A 50th anniversary was held, in 1994. John Cooper was amongst the many, standing at the edge of the huge crater. John was the son of Mary Cooper, who had set up the temporary morgue and whose father, Joseph was the first body she received. His thoughts were playing through the events of that day and the mighty blast that killed his father, exactly 60 years before. A dedication was made, "The hurt lasts for decades. A look is sufficient to recall the event and its subsequent effect on those of us who lived through it."

The Day the Sun Disappeared, 27 Nov 1944

John Hardwick, from Top Farm, was there too. He tried to say something, paused, then apologised at being lost for words, finding it hard to describe what he had seen that day.

At last he said, "This beautiful morning gave way to rain. Then the sky started to come down. We are talking about a sky full of soil. I made my way through Hanbury, but the scene was unrecognisable. Not a chimney pot remained. A neighbour's house was no more than a heap of bricks. The village hall had been blasted into the next field, 'with piano keys all over the place. The crater looked like a wide ice-cream cornet. It was a moonscape, with trees upended, nothing living or growing."

A service was held.

The Day the Sun Disappeared, 27 Nov 1944

The Day the Sun Disappeared, 27 Nov 1944

Order of Service

Bidding — We are met together in the presence of our Heavenly Father, to commemorate all those who lost their lives in the Fauld Explosion on 27th November 1944, and to pledge ourselves anew to the service of God and the cause of Peace.

Hymn

Praise my soul, the King of Heaven
To His feet Thy tribute bring.
Ransomed, healed, restored, forgiven,
Evermore His Praises sing.
Alleluia! Alleluia!
Praise the everlasting King.

Praise Him for His grace and favour to our Fathers in distress.
Praise Him still the same as ever, Slow to chide and swift to bless. Alleluia! Alleluia!
Glorious in his faithfulness.

Father like He tends and spares us,
Well our feeble frame He knows,
In His Hands He gently bears us Rescues us from all our foes.
Alleluia! Alleluia!
Widely yet His Mercy flows.

Angels in the height adore Him,
Ye behold Him face to face.
Saints triumphant bow before Him Gathered in from every race.
Alleluia! Alleluia!
Praise with us the God of Grace.

Lesson; Psalm 67.

Prayer — O God, pour your blessing we pray, on those who seek to make and keep peace on earth, and on those who promote love and concord. Grant your healing and sustaining strength to those who still suffer in body, mind or spirit as a result of war, conflict or strife.

All say — O God whose love we cannot measure, and whose blessings we cannot number together. We praise you that in our weakness, you are oustrength, in our darkness, light, and in our sorrow you are our comfort and peace. Amen.

Lesson; Ephesians 4/ 1-7/

Act of Remembrance: Let us remember before God, and commend to his sure keeping those who died in the Fauld Explosion and whose memory we treasure.

The Day the Sun Disappeared, 27 Nov 1944

READING OF THE ROLL

They shall grow not old as we that are left grow old,
Age shall not weary them nor the years condemn.
At the going down of the sun and in the morning
We will remember them.

All   We will remember them.

SILENCE -   Last Post and Reveille

Prayer   Almighty and Eternal God, from whose love in Quist we cannot be parted either by death or life, hear our prayer for those whom we remember this day. Fulfil in them the purpose of your love and bring us with them to our eternal home.   Amen.

All Lord's Prayer

Hymn   The Lords my shepherd I'll not want
He makes me down to lie
In pastures green He leadeth me
the quiet waters by.

My soul He doth restore again,
and me to walk doth make
Within the paths of righteousness,
E'en for His own namesake.

Yea, though I walk in death's dark vale,
Yet will I fear no ill;
For Thou are with me, and Thy rod
and staff me comfort still.

My table Thou hast furnished
in presence of my foes,
My head Thou dost with oil anoint,
And my cup overflows.

Goodness and mercy all my life
Shall surely follow me,
And in God's house for evermore
My dwelling place shall be.

The Day the Sun Disappeared, 27 Nov 1944

Address: Mr John Hardwick

Hymn
Offertory

Abide with me, fast falls the eventide,
The darkness deepens: Lord, with me abide;
When other helpers fail, and comforts flee,
Help of the helpless, O abide with me.

Swift to its close ebbs out life's little day,
Earth's joys grow dim, its glories pass away.
Change and decay in all around I see;
O Thou, who changest not abide with me.

I need Thy presence every passing hour;
What but Thy grace can foil the temper's power.
Who like Thyself my guide and stay can be?
Through cloud and sunshine, Lord. abide with me.

I fear no foe with Thee at hand to bless.
Ills have no weight and tears no bitterness.
Where is death's sting? Where, grave Thy victory?
I triumph still, if Thou abide with me.

Hold Thou Thy cross before my closing eyes.
Shine through the gloom, and point me to the skies.
Heaven's morning breaks, and earth's vain shadows flee.
In life. in dealh. O Lord, abide with me.

BLESSING.

At the crater approximately 11.10am
Act of Remembrance as used in the Order of Service in Church at 10.00

The Day the Sun Disappeared, 27 Nov 1944

At the National Memorial Arboretum in Alrewas, Staffordshire is a memorial stone and plaque. These photos were supplied by an ex RAF friend, John Cooper (no relation to the John Cooper, son of Mary Cooper).

In Memory of the 70 people who lost their lives in the underground explosion at **Fauld Munitions Store**, near Burton upon Trent, 27th November 1944

The Day the Sun Disappeared, 27 Nov 1944

> On 27th November 1944 the biggest explosion this country has ever seen took place at Fauld, near Burton upon Trent.
>
> 4000 tons of bombs stored 90ft down in old Gypsum mines blew up, leaving a crater 400ft deep and almost 3/4 mile long.
>
> The tremor was felt over 50 miles away, the noise heard in London and local terrain was damaged by over a million tons of falling debris.
>
> Seventy people lost their lives.

In November 1999, a dozen people gathered at The Cock Inn car park to cross the muddy fields. They gathered at the memorial stone at the crater's edge. Hymns were sung, but with just so few people there, their voices could not penetrate down to the crater.

Time had changed the crater, trees had grown, hiding the black, churned up soil and somehow making the crater softer. Birds were even singing as the area seemed to have become a wildlife sanctuary, undisturbed by the footfall of people.

The vicar of Hanbury, the Rev. Cordon Whitty said that the area had now become a place of beauty, but not a place to pass lightly. "I regard our dead and missing as victims of a war against evil. God is for them as He is for all the victims of war, the mentally distressed and refugees. He then read out the names of the missing and killed from the memorial plate. When he came to the names of the six Italian prisoners of war, who perished, it was a poignant reminder that the disaster didn't just happen in a small corner of Staffordshire, but its effect was worldwide.

A memorial had been held, every year up to 2004, on 27 November, at the crater at 11am with a church service on the nearest Sunday to 27 November, which was attended by representatives from the RAF.

Ida Roberts (née Harrison), stated in her later roll as a parish councillor, "Not many people are left in Hanbury who had relatives who died in the explosion. It is sixty years now and we felt it was time to hold the last one."

CHAPTER 51

AWARDS TO HEROES

The full story of the feverish effort of RAF men, NFS personnel and civilians to rescue victims of the bomb dump disaster with the announcement of awards for gallantry to 14 of the rescuers and commendations for ten others.

The men were faced with a bewildering situation, with poisonous fumes percolating through the labyrinth of underground passages, a danger of roof falls and a possibility of a further explosion of the remaining bombs.

In these conditions, men worked until many of them collapsed and had to be carried out.

The rewards are:

OBE -,Mr John Robertson, chairman of the Leicestershire and South Derbyshire Mine Owners' Association of The Limes, Nailstone, Nuneaton.

MBE (Military Division) – Flight Lieut. Harold John Shuttleworth

MBE (Civil Division) – Mr George L Brown, manager of the North Midland Coal Owners' Rescue Organisation of Yorke Street, Mansfield, Woodhouse.

Mr John B Drinnan, agent to the Moira Colliery Co, of The Hall, Donisthorpe.

George Medal – Mr Joseph Clifford Salt, a foreman employed at the dump, of 219 Goodman Street, Burton –Acting Wing Commander Donald Leslie Kings.

Flight Lieut. John P Lewis, RAF

Dr Godfrey Rotter, of Dogmaels, Pembrokeshire

Mr Eric Bryant

…..

BEM (Military Division) – Corporal Sidney B Rock

Corporal James S Peters

BEM (Civil Division) – Company Officer Richard C Elliott, NFAS of 96 Malvern Street, Stapenhll

Leading Fireman George Roden, NFS, of 17 Union Street, Burton

Mr James Appleby, formerly a leading fireman in the NFS, of 25 North Street, Winshill

Mr Jack Perry, superintendent of Ashby-de-la-Zouch Rescue Team

Mr Harold Coker, foreman at the dump of 22 Alma Road, Doveridge.

Commended for Brave Conduct:

Mrs Maude Evelyn Degg, welfare assistant at the dump, of 26 Park Lane, Tutbury.

Plus nine mine rescue team leaders:

Mr F F Bates, of 122 York Street, Mansfield Woodhouse

The Day the Sun Disappeared, 27 Nov 1944

Mr H J Hall, of Coalville Road, Davenstone, Leicestershire

Mr A Hazell, of Moira Road, Donisthorpe

Mr J Hinds, of Wilncote, near Tamworth

Mr A Hunt, of 194 Whitehill Road, Ellistown, Leicester

Mr H Insley, of 19 New Road, Newhall

Mr D G Roberts, of 2 Manners Road, Ilkeston

Mr J K Tivey, of Tamworth Road, Ashby

Mr John Webb, of Avenue Road, Ashby.

Police Constable Mackay was specially commended by the Chief Constable in General Orders.

In a letter to Mr Auden from the County Treasurer, dated 9 February 1945, the County Treasurer made remunerations to Mr Auden for costs.

1. Police: a total sum of £21.13s.10d (including £8.17s.4d for travelling expenses.
2. Hire of room for Inquests - £1.10s.0d including use of chairs and benches
3. Mrs Mary Elizabeth Cooper, an inclusive payment of £5.5s.0d.
4. Joseph Foster – an inclusive payment of £5.5s.0d.
5. Special remuneration to Coroner: a special payment of £125 to be inclusive of remuneration and out-of-pocket expenses.

The County Treasurer requested information as to the total expenses in connection with the Inquests on the Fauld explosion, including the allowances mentioned, which he would pay by cheque, with a separate cheque for the amount of Mr Auden's personal remuneration.

(The following letter is courtesy of Graham Shaw.)

The Day the Sun Disappeared, 27 Nov 1944

All Communications to be addressed to G. J. GERMAN, ESTATE OFFICES, ASHBY-DE-LA-ZOUCH

The Leicestershire and South Derbyshire Collieries Rescue and Fire Station.

Telephone No. 36, Ashby-de-la-Zouch
Railway Station, Ashby-de-la-Zouch, L.M.S. Railway
Secretary and Manager:
G. J. GERMAN.
Chief Officer & Superintendent:
~~XX. WADSWRIGHT.~~
J. Perry.

ASHBY-DE-LA-ZOUCH.

LEICESTERSHIRE.

June 8th 1945.

Dear Sir,
              Explosion at the R.A.F. Storage Depot at Fauld.
              November 27th 1945.

      I have pleasure in enclosing letter received from the Under-Secretary of State with reference to the gallantry shown by the Rescue Teams on the occasion of the explosion at Fauld on the 27th November 1944.

      The Members of the Committee of the Leicestershire & South Derbyshire Collieries Rescue and Fire Station wish me to convey to you their appreciation of your excellent services in highly dangerous conditions.

      I give below extracts from letters received from F/Lt. J.P. Lewin, G.M., and Mr Hugh Ferguson of the British Plaster Board Ltd., of which Messrs Ford's Works were a section:-

Extract of letter from F/Lt. J.P. Lewin, G.M.

      "I would, however, like to add my humble and sincere admiration for the very gallant work which the members of the Rescue Teams did at this unit - work which demands cool courage, and often the Supreme sacrifice. I know only too well the hazards of those engaged in the coal mining industry, and can personally appreciate the grand spirit which exists in the Volunteer Rescue Squads.
      The Battle of Europe is ended, there remains only Japan between us and final Victory - after that we shall be faced with the toughest battle of all - the 'Battle for the Peace'. Coal is one of our greatest industrial assets - fight in the future as you have in the past six years, and the 'battle for Peace' will be a sure victory".

Extract of letter received from Mr Hugh Ferguson.

      " I take this opportunity on my own behalf and on behalf of The British Plaster Board Ltd, of thanking all who rendered such heroic service on the occasion of the explosion at Fauld."

Yours faithfully,

The Day the Sun Disappeared, 27 Nov 1944

AIR MINISTRY, LONDON.

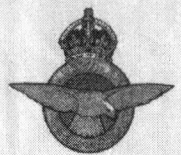

Sir,
                                                                                         1st May, 1945.

I am commanded by the AIR COUNCIL to say that it gives them much pleasure to put on permanent record their high appreciation of the gallantry shown by the TEAMS of your COLLIERIES RESCUE ORGANISATION on the occasion of the explosion which occurred at the R.A.F. storage depot at FAULD on the 27th November, 1944.

The explosion was unprecedented in character and magnitude and gave rise at once to highly dangerous conditions throughout the passages and recesses of the storage mine. It was essential to penetrate and explore the mine with least possible delay, partly in the belief that the lives of workers cut off by the explosion could still be saved, & partly in order to control the dangerous physical conditions & guard against the risk of further explosion.

Rescue teams were brought to the depot with admirable promptitude. The mine was systematically and continuously explored for some twenty-four hours, with further intermittent work during the days following.

Each Team Leader was awarded a Commendation by His Majesty the King, partly for leadership & partly in token of the gallantry of the individual members of the team under the leader's direction.

Subjoined are two lists: one, of the Active Teams, i.e. of the men who entered the mine and went into the danger area with full rescue and breathing apparatus; the other, of the Stand-by Teams, i.e. of the men who responded to the call and stood by, ready to take the full risks if required in support of their comrades.

The Air Council desire to pay their tribute of honour and respect to these men, and in particular to the memory of JAMES BEARD who sacrificed his life in the operations.

                                                                                         I am, Sir,

John Robertson, Esq. O.B.E.J.P.   Your obedient Servant,
Chairman, Leicestershire & South Derbyshire
Collieries Rescue & Fire Station,
Ashby-de-la-Zouch, Leicestershire   Permanent Under-Secretary of State

Active Teams.

LEADERS —
Herbert James Hall
Arthur Hazell
Albert Hunt

MEMBERS —
John Thomas Adcock
Job Arnold
James Beard
William Percy Betts
Clifford Bradford
George Henry Broadhurst
Eric Burton
Wilfred Corner
Harry Crowder
Frank Alonzo Garland
Wilfred Hart
Roland Hill
Percy Hogg
Walter Harold Haughton
George Edward Jeori

Harold Insley
James Kendrick Tovey
John Webb

John Thomas Kenny
Joseph Francis Lee
Kenneth James Mousley
Frank Poxon
Samuel William Preston
William Slater
Leonard George Snape
Frederick Thomas Starkey
Joseph Storer
Arthur Augustin Tompkin
Timothy Toon
Willis Want
John Cyril Whetton
Stanley John Wright

Stand-by Teams.

Frank Beaumont
Stanley Billings
Harold J. Boulstridge
Cecil Albert Boulton
Alwyn Brown
Harold Brown
Samuel Brown
Bertie Chipman
Jack Clamp
Frank Corker
John Cowley
Francis Dennis
William Oxley
George Gamble
Leonard Gilliver
Howard Leslie Goucher
Charles Donald Harvey
Sherrard Jervaise Joyce

Charles William Lane
Harold Lunn
William Malpass
William Millington
Harry Milson
George Lawrence Moore
James Moore
Alfred Parker
Hubert Noel Poole
Frederick W. W. Ralfern
James William Rice
George Smith
Jim Smith
Albert William Walton
Frank Harry Webb
Frederick R. Whetton
Thomas Mathew Wilson
Bernard Wykes

Written out on the 10th May 1945 by E. C. Oliver, A.R.C.A., London.

The Day the Sun Disappeared, 27 Nov 1944

CHAPTER 52

30 YEARS ON – OPENING OF CLOSED DOCUMENTS

(By Tom Layton)

> This land is private property belonging to the Ministry of Defence. The land contains unexploded bombs and in the event of an explosion, injury or death could be caused to persons on the land.
> In the interests of safety therefore, members of the public are warned not to enter the land in any circumstances.

Findings into the inquiry into the 1944 Fauld bombs explosion at the end of the 30-year period of secrecy imposed by the defence regulations showed that it was virtually certain that the cause of

The Day the Sun Disappeared, 27 Nov 1944

the explosion was the method used to chip out composition explosive from a 1,000lb bomb.

The official findings, were released by the Public Record office in Chancery Lane, London.

The bomb was one of a row which were presumably exploded by sympathetic detonation or by fragments, when the one on which work was taking place, exploded.

The findings also show that this 'dangerous operation' should not have been carried out in the mine itself, and there is criticism of the supervisory staff.

The lifting of the 30-year 'secrecy ban' also discloses another fact – that the explosion could have been ten times greater, possibly even wiping Burton off the map, had it spread to the main area where many bombs were stored.

The most important of the 30 witnesses whose evidence was heard by the Court of Inquiry was an RAF Corporal, now living in Bretby Lane, Burton. He is Mr L W Poynton, whose story follows.

It was his evidence concerning the method of 'chipping out; explosive from defective bombs, which had been sent to Fauld, which was really decisive.

Corporal Poynton was the last man to get out of the 'New Area' of the mine, alive, and his story, which he gave at the Court of Inquiry, can now be told for the first time.

They found no evidence to support the possibility of sabotage and, similarly, there was no evidence of bombing in the vicinity, which could have caused the explosion. Also ruled out by the Inquiry, was 'gross negligence'.

The Day the Sun Disappeared, 27 Nov 1944

But the inquiry did come to the conclusion that regulations were 'not fully observed' and that there was some negligence on the part of supervisory officers.

The cause of the initial explosion was 'in all probability' the work of chipping out the composition explosive. The primary charge exploder from a 1000lb medium case using a brass chisel.

The court stated in their findings, "It is known that composition explosive will explode easily if struck between brass and steel surfaces.

This bomb was one of a row of 1000lb medium case bombs, which were presumably exploded by sympathetic detonation or by fragments. Subsequently, the whole (or the great part) of the content of the 'new area' exploded.

The Court find that Current Regulations and Standing Orders were adequate, but in the case of extracts from Air Publication 2608A, as published on Form 1005 (General Rules for Danger Areas and Danger Buildings). They were not fully observed."

The court added that "There are obviously mitigating circumstances during wartime when urgency is a keynote, manpower is of poorer quality and quantity, and more work is expected of a unit that for which it was designed.

Some relaxation can be made with safety, and there must have been a tendency to extend relaxation locally owing to 'familiarity breeding contempt'.

It appears from the evidence of Witness No. 30 (Corporal L W Poynton) that an airman was permitted to perform a dangerous operation in the mine. This indicates negligence on the part of the A.I.D (Ammunition, Inspectorate Department) supervising staff present in the mine, due either to lack of knowledge, lack of a proper sense of responsibility, or lack of proper direction from senior authority."

The court found that '"neither the Chief Inspection Officer (A.I.D) nor the Acting Chief Equipment Officer, can be entirely absolved from all responsibility as they do not appear to have been sufficiently aware of the work undertaken in the mine area, nor to have adequate records or control of such work."

In the final paragraph, the court stated that standards of sensitivity of various explosives in the mine were not available.

The Day the Sun Disappeared, 27 Nov 1944

CHAPTER 53

PROBE CALL ON HIDDEN BODIES

60 years after the explosion, in 2004, a news report by Kim Bruscoe, in the Daily Mail, stated that victims of the explosion are convinced that two bodies still lie in the fields near the crater and are requesting the Government to excavate the area. This followed a TV documentary suggesting that human remains were recovered in 1947.

This TV documentation indicated that a farmer, John Bowley, had discovered two bodies while ploughing his fields between 1948 and 1952. These were found between Hare Holes Farm, Hare Holes Rough and Lower Castle Farm. At the time, the Official Secrets Act was still in place for anything relating to the explosion, and Mr Bowley claimed that he was instructed, under threat of 25 years' imprisonment, should his findings come to light. He, therefore, had to bury the bodies without anyone knowing. He buried the two bodies, wrapped in a sack, in one of the minor craters in the area.

As the Official Secrets Act had now expired, John Cooper, the son of Mary Cooper, who had set up the temporary morgue at the time, and whose father died at the explosion, decided that it was about time this information came to light. He had been discussing this report with a few people, one of whom was Mrs Joyce McLeod, the wife of Ken McLeod, in Tutbury. "I know my brother, Lewis, wouldn't be one of the bodies as, unfortunately, he was right at the centre of the explosion, but surely two bodies couldn't have been covered up like this? We need to find out who they could possibly be."

"Yes," John answered, "there are still bodies missing and, whoever they might have been should have had a church burial".

"You're right. The only thing I can think of doing is to contact my MP, Janet Dean, and see what she can do to get the site re-examined."

"There might not be any truth in it but, just in case, I think we should try to get this resolved." John commented.

They set about gathering evidence in the hope that the Under Secretary of State would fund the excavation, retrieve the bodies and give them a proper funeral, stating "They want putting to bed properly. For those involved it can never be forgotten."

Joyce McLeod actually wrote to her MP, passing as much information as they had to her and the MP duly wrote to the Ministry of Defence,

They did receive a letter back but the outcome of that was, "As far as they are concerned it's a closed book. A body was found in 1947 and that was dealt with in the correct manner. The Ministry said they do not see any reason that, if two bodies were found later, they would have been dealt with any differently,"

The Day the Sun Disappeared, 27 Nov 1944

Ivor Caplin MP

MINISTRY OF DEFENCE
OLD WAR OFFICE BUILDING
WHITEHALL LONDON SW1A 2EU

PARLIAMENTARY UNDER-SECRETARY OF STATE FOR DEFENCE
AND MINISTER FOR VETERANS

Janet Dean MP
House of Commons
London
SW1A 0AA

D/US of S/IC 3059/04/C

27th July 2004

Dear Janet,

Thank you for your further letter of 16 June (reference: JD/rigencor mcleod mod2) to Miss Taylor at the MOD Ministerial Correspondence Unit enclosing further information from your constituent, Mrs Joyce McLeod of 133 Tutbury Road, Burton Upon Trent, concerning the tragic events at RAF Fauld in November 1944. I am replying as this matter falls within my area of responsibility.

You will recall that Mrs McLeod was concerned at the suggestion made in a BBC documentary that human remains were recovered in 1947 but were then disposed of secretly and improperly. We have now reviewed all the material you so kindly sent to us, including the tape of the BBC documentary, and we have also recalled and consulted all the available historical documentation from The National Archive. The allegation made in the programme by Mr John Bowley was vague and in part contradictory in that it separately alleged that the human remains were thrown over a fence into a crater in a wood, or were disposed of in a pond. You will appreciate that this makes it extremely difficult to undertake any sort of physical search of the area, as the descriptions are not only at variance but are too vague to permit identification of a particular site in the area. Mr Bowley is now in his eighties and resident in Australia and is apparently not in the best of health, which adds to the difficulty.

In addition, however, there is strong evidence available which contradicts the suggestion that officials at the time would have behaved in such a manner. The BBC interview stated that an official arrived at the site where the bodies were allegedly ploughed up, instructed Mr Bowley to dispose of the bodies improperly, and told him that the matter was then closed, before reading him "The Riot Act". The implication being that he was being frightened into silence on the grounds of national security.

However, contemporary press cuttings show quite clearly that a single body was discovered in the course of work being undertaken to restore the area in August 1947, at exactly the time that it is alleged the "cover up" incident took place. The press cuttings show that a public inquest was held at Tutbury, which concluded that the body was that of a local man killed in the Fauld explosion. The coroner issued an order for

The Day the Sun Disappeared, 27 Nov 1944

the body to be buried, and we have no reason to doubt that that was done. It is therefore difficult to see why bodies supposedly found at almost exactly the same time should be treated in the manner suggested in the programme, and why officials should have acted in the manner alleged in one case and yet not in the other. A more likely explanation must be that a body was indeed recovered at the time, and that the due process of the law was followed, with the remains being properly treated and decently buried, but that local legend or the vagaries of human memory have since created a distorted recollection of events. I am very sorry that Mrs McLeod should, understandably enough, have been distressed by the programme, but I hope this letter will reassure her that there appears to be little to substantiate the allegation and much to suggest that it is simply mistaken.

Various other allegations have been made concerning the events at Fauld, perhaps inevitably so given their magnitude and the quite proper degree of secrecy imposed during the War. These include suggestions that the Court of Inquiry was a "cover up" and that the Germans had used aircraft or a radio directed V2 rocket to cause the explosion, or that some sort of "special", possibly nuclear, weapon was involved. We are satisfied that these explanations are untrue and in many cases technically impossible, and that the Court of Inquiry, which is now available in the National Archive, was honestly conducted and established the most likely cause of the disaster, i.e. poor munitions handling practices caused by a shortage of skilled labour combined with the pressure the unit was under at the time.

As you may be aware the large crater caused by the explosion is still fenced off in the interests of public safety. It is the responsibility of RAF Stafford to conduct an annual inspection of the fenceline and warning signs at the site, and this was done on 21 June this year, when all was found to be in order. Periodic visual surface inspections of the crater itself are also undertaken by No 5131 (Bomb Disposal) squadron to ensure that no unexploded munitions have been exposed by weather or other natural action, though so far as we are aware none has ever been found. The next such inspection is scheduled for August 2004. We have also taken steps to have an environmental assessment made of the site as a precaution, though again there is no reason to suppose that there is any real concern in this regard.

I therefore hope that this letter has served to reassure you and Mrs McLeod, though very sadly it appears now to be very unlikely that her brother's mortal remains will ever be recovered.

The Day the Sun Disappeared, 27 Nov 1944

CHAPTER 54

70 Year Memorial

Photo donated by John Pye

The crater's tranquillity today is at odds with its destructive creation.

The Day the Sun Disappeared, 27 Nov 1944

Near the crater's edge is a memorial where the names of those who lost their lives are carved.

It was here that a memorial service was held every year until a decade ago when, as numbers dwindled, the act of remembrance was dropped.

Parish council chairman Trevor Ball said: "The outdoor services began when the memorial was erected 30 years ago but ten years ago there were only three of us, including the vicar. There was one lady who lost her brother but she admitted that it was getting beyond her. It's hard to get down through the fields to the crater.

"Even in the middle of the summer it can be hard work for some people let alone on November 27, even though we got a grant to put the kissing gates in 10 or so year ago so that people who wanted to see the crater had an easier path."

But as the 70th anniversary approached there was a growing feeling that the tragedy should receive more attention this time and the parish council canvassed opinions from those with a connection to the explosion at the site, officially known in the war as RAF Fauld.

As a result, a service will be held on the morning of the anniversary but this time at the site of a new memorial at British Gypsum at Fauld, a much more accessible site.

Trevor says: "There was much more interest in that than a service by the crater and the parish council are supporting it.

"There has been a big response. We believe the RAF at Stafford and the Ministry of Defence will be among the people attending."

Invitations have been sent to all those known to have a connection with the tragedy but Trevor says that if anyone has been missed they would be welcome, although the service at British Gypsum is not open to the public at large.

He says: "I think it will be a fitting way to mark the anniversary."

Today, the memorial service at British Gypsum at Fauld at 11am will be preceded by a gathering for tea and biscuits at The Cock Inn in Hanbury, which will be open from 9am. People will move to British Gypsum from about 10.15am to 10.30am. The service will conducted by Hanbury's vicar, the Rev Les Rees. He will also be conducting services at St Werburgh's Church, Hanbury, at 7.30pm, and then again as part of the Sunday service on November 30 at 10.30am, where wreaths will be placed and the names of those who died read out

The Day the Sun Disappeared, 27 Nov 1944

CHAPTER 55

DANGER, UNEXPLODED BOMBS

Photo supplied by John Pye

The Day the Sun Disappeared, 27 Nov 1944

There are signs warning ramblers or passers-by not to go into the area - which covers a 12-acre patch of countryside - because of unexploded bombs.

A full search of military installations at Fauld buried in the explosion was never carried out because it was considered too dangerous.

This has led to speculation that unexploded ammunition is still buried at the former munitions depot at Fauld.

A Freedom of Information request previously submitted by the Burton Mail showed that while the site is secured, and inspected annually, there is every possibility that some of the thousands of tonnes of munitions did not detonate during the explosion, and remains on site.

The information revealed by the Ministry of Defence stated: "The crater has not been fully cleared of ordnance, as it would be too dangerous to do so. As there is no public access and a security fence, it is not high risk

People have been warned not to go anywhere near. Some of the tunnels have been blocked up, even cemented up. Those bodies never found are in a stone sarcophagus, never to be retrieved.

Today however, the Fauld explosion, which changed the landscape forever, remains virtually unknown to the nation at large. It seems to have been almost airbrushed from history and become a mere footnote. It seems to be a disaster the nation forgot.

People like Jason Kirkham and Ian Siddals are not only risking their testosterone-filled lives by going down into the tunnels, taking photos, something even the military have decided is too risky, but they are risking the lives of the whole community surrounding these tunnels. Should one of these very old bombs be disturbed, the whole place could go up again, bringing down buildings in Hanbury, Tutbury, and even further afield, killing masses of people, something that the inhabitants are all too aware of but keeping it under wraps to any newcomers planning to move into the area. Of course, this second disaster wouldn't be on their consciences as they would be dead, their corpses scattered in tiny fragments. The signs saying 'Strictly no admittance' must **never** be ignored.

My message is to say that this disaster, although it should never have happened, should never be forgotten. I trust lessons have been learnt and such a catastrophe will never happen again.

These photos are out there, on the Internet.

The Day the Sun Disappeared, 27 Nov 1944

The Day the Sun Disappeared, 27 Nov 1944

The Day the Sun Disappeared, 27 Nov 1944

The Day the Sun Disappeared, 27 Nov 1944

The Day the Sun Disappeared, 27 Nov 1944

JOHN PYE

The Day the Sun Disappeared, 27 Nov 1944

I met John Pye, an ex-police detective, at a history talk in Hanley, Stoke-on-Trent, run by a good friend, Mervyn Edwards. I told John I was interested in writing a book about the Fauld explosion and he kindly supplied me with the above report he produced for the Sentinel – The Way We Were. – transcript follows.

The Way We Were: Your Memories – Saturday October 3, 2009

By John Pye, of Newcastle, looks back at the devastating day when the earth exploded and dozens of innocent lives were lost.

At 11 minutes past 11 on the morning of Monday, November 27, 1944, windows and doors rattled throughout North Staffordshire, chimney pots crashed to the ground in Burton-on-Trent and a seismograph 1,400 miles away in Casablanca darted its nib across the paper recording an apparent earthquake with an epicentre pinpointed on an area known as Fauld, near to Tutbury, in Staffordshire, just 30 minutes from Stoke-on-Trent.

The gigantic blast, which caused the apparent earthquake, could be heard as far away as Weston Super Mare and even London, 140 miles away.

Those Londoners who may have heard it were probably only very temporarily interested. Explosions to them were an everyday occurrence.

There was, of course, a war on and the German V1 doodlebug bombs that had rained down upon the city had now almost paled against the huge V2 missiles, which had by then become the current and most terrifying threat.

The Day the Sun Disappeared, 27 Nov 1944

They couldn't possibly have realised that the distant blast they had heard was from an explosion of such magnitude that it made a V2 rocket seem almost insignificant.

At the scene of the explosion, huge pieces of rock and earth rained down onto the landscape, some weighing up to one ton, as an enormous black mushroom cloud ascended to several thousand feet, hanging over the area for some time.

A steady rain of ash and particles then continued over the next hour, covering the surrounding countryside.

When the smoke subsided, a massive crater was revealed, measuring 380 feet deep and more than a quarter of a mile in diameter.

Upper Castle Hayes Farm had disappeared from the face of the earth in an instant, taking with it the farmer, his wife, sister-in-law and three other farm workers – not a single trace of any of these people was ever found.

The cause of the annihilation of the peaceful Staffordshire landscape was a devastating underground explosion within a secret RAF bomb store, where up to 20,000 tons of munitions were stored for use in the ongoing fight against Germany.

The landscape above had been ripped open, killing many people both employed underground in the store and above, who worked the farms and at the nearby plaster factory.

It was the mining of the gypsum rich ground beneath Fauld which had firstly presented some of the extensive old mine workings as a useful place to store the valuable munitions away from prying German eyes.

The Day the Sun Disappeared, 27 Nov 1944

Gypsum is the main ingredient of plaster and the staff at the old plaster factory of Peter Ford's were busy with their daily routine when the tragedy occurred, milling, all 42 of them.

The entire plaster factory had also vanished in an instant, along with most of the surface buildings of the RAF base codenamed "21 MU".

The nearby pub, The Cock Inn, was completely wrecked, most of its roof, along with some of the top half of the building was missing, and very few of the houses and buildings in the nearby village of Hanbury survived without serious damage.

A terrible scene met the rescue teams that eventually arrived; the whole area was smothered in a soft blanket of vaporised debris, which had floated down as 'fall out' covering the surface with a four-inch carpet.

As teams of firemen and other volunteers from Stafford, Burton and Lichfield, made their way on foot across the landscape, looking for bodies and any possible survivors, an eerie silence was created by the thick insulating "fall out" under their feet.

Hundreds of dead cattle and animal parts littered the fields. Trees had been blown down flat.

One team came across a cow standing motionless, twice its normal size, apparently inflated by the blast.

The party shot the animal to put it out of its misery, but it failed to fall down. It was obviously already dead, but the position of its legs were keeping it upright.

To make matters even worse, the explosion had ripped open the side of a local reservoir, spilling its entire contents of six million gallons of water down onto the scene, turning it into a sea of liquid mud, and causing even further devastation and death.

At 3pm (four hours after the blast) another rescue team entered a farmhouse and found an elderly couple still in shock, sitting at the table, gazing blankly across at each other, with the remains of their meal still in front of them, and roof debris strewn all around.

Twenty-six workers were killed at the bomb store, most of whom were, of course, RAF personnel, but the number, sadly, also included six Italian prisoners of war.

The exact death toll has always remained uncertain as many people died over a period of time following the explosion, either from injuries or from the effects of gas created by the blast.

Estimates for the final toll vary from 75-90, including Penkhull resident Henry Appleton, of Watson Street, who was a 62-year-old official at the plaster works and was killed instantly.

Attempts were made to uncover the cause of the explosion and, as years passed by, various espionage theories were suggested, along with one that claimed the destruction had been an intentional and precise attack by a German V2 rocket, although many experts discounted this theory, due to the accuracy and range available to the V2.

An official explanation issued in 1974, announced that the explosion was caused by bombs being taken out of store – primed for use and then often replaced if they were not required with the detonators still installed.

An eye witness also testified that he had seen workers using a metal chisel instead of wooden mallets in defiance of the strict regulations in force.

The Day the Sun Disappeared, 27 Nov 1944

This official explanation, be it correct or not, was not so thrilling as the espionage and V2 theories.

Of the 20,000 tons of munitions stores, it was estimated the actual explosion was created by a chain reaction of 4,000 tons of bombs detonating.

There remain, to this day, a considerable amount of unexploded munitions deeply buried beneath the crater site, as it was decided that it would be uneconomical and too dangerous to attempt removal.

In 1990, a memorial was erected at the site, using a piece of fine white granite supplied by the commandant of an Italian air base.

This memorial marks the crater site, which is fenced off for public safety, but still clearly visible from a distance.

The crater is immense and can be seen via satellite from space.

By today's standards, this terrible catastrophe would have held the public spellbound with front page news reports over many weeks.

However, during the troubled times of those days, when death, disaster and everyday heroism were a regular occurrence, the story would only hold the front pages for two days.

The Fauld bomb store explosion was, at the time, the biggest ever man-made explosion the world had seen and remained so until the first nuclear bomb test in July 1945.

The blast still remains high on the list of 'biggest ever non-nuclear explosions' and hopefully will always rate as the largest on British soil.

The Day the Sun Disappeared, 27 Nov 1944

The explosion left a crater 300 yards wide by 35 yards deep, the size of six football pitches. Picture from John Pye

....

John Pye also introduced me to Graham Shaw (also ex-police) the grandson of Mary Cooper, who set up and ran the temporary morgue. Graham, in turn, supplied me with newspaper cuttings, photos and maps that his family had collected of the event.

While writing this book, I have just learnt that John Pye has won the prestigious Arnold Bennett book prize for 2022 for his book, 'Where the Silent Screams are Loudest', which is a brilliant, exciting police story, one of the best I have ever read, particularly as the story is set close to me, so well worth a read.

The Day the Sun Disappeared, 27 Nov 1944

MARK ROWE

Bygones: Book coincides with 70th anniversary of giant explosion at RAF Fauld, near Burton

By Derby Telegraph Posted: October 06, 2014

By JANE GODDARD

AFTER decades, author Mark Rowe has finally brought to an end his years of research into the tragic Second World War ammunition dump explosion at RAF Fauld, which claimed 70 lives.

The publication of the third and final edition of his book, The Day The Dump Went Up – the 1944 Fauld Explosion, has been timed to coincide with the 70th anniversary of the accident, on November 27, 1944.

Mark, 46, of Burton, first became interested in the story of the explosion when, as a student, he interviewed dozens of people in Burton and district who recalled "the day the dump went up".

Seventy people were killed or listed as missing after the Monday morning blast at the bomb store at RAF Fauld, between Tutbury and Hanbury.

The explosion, said to be the largest the country had ever experienced, was felt around the Midlands and a mushroom-like cloud of debris was seen as far away as the foothills of the Derbyshire Dales, some 20 miles distant.

The Day the Sun Disappeared, 27 Nov 1944

During his painstaking research, Mark has uncovered what he claims is evidence of major shortcomings in the rescue effort in the immediate aftermath of the disaster.

He said: "I remember writing an essay about the explosion as English homework while I was at The Paulet School.

"The first edition of my book came out in 1999 and I assumed that would be the end of it. But I found more material and put together a booklet, After the Dump Went Up.

"Then, yet more material came to light and I wrote another book, The Trees Were Burning. I brought it all together in a book in 2006 which sold out, and people have continued to ask about it."

Most of the research for this final edition dates from 2012 and includes police and other archive material from Staffordshire Record Office, in Stafford.

Mark says that a sharper and more bitter tone has come into his work, whether because he has got older or because of his findings.

These include that Burton's chief of police, Superintendent HG "Snowball" Heath, admitting in a written report to superiors after the explosion, that despite the noise and a mushroom-like cloud seen for miles around, he went outdoors to investigate, only to go inside again, not realising what had happened. Burton police were only alerted to the disaster by a phone call from Tutbury colleagues minutes later.

Uttoxeter police, like their Burton counterparts, made for the scene by car. However, in their rush to reach RAF Fauld they drove past Ford's plaster works, which had suffered a mudslide from a burst reservoir above, and which saw the largest single loss of life on the day.

The Day the Sun Disappeared, 27 Nov 1944

A mine rescuer from Ashby, Jim Beard, died underground because of a mishap with his oxygen tank as his party searched in vain for trapped men.

According to Mark, his death was completely unnecessary and the search should never have happened.

Mark said: "It should have been plain from the experience of the airmen who did escape from underground after the dump went up, and from the rescuers' need to use oxygen, that there was no prospect of finding survivors and their mission was pointless.

"The failings in the response and rescue following the accident were mirrored in the slack routines that caused the disaster, which were hushed up and only in 1974 made public under the then 30-year rule for disclosure of official documents."

While airmen got out alive from the mine after about 4,000 tons of explosive blew up, and the actual camp above ground was barely touched, workers above ground at the neighbouring Ford's plaster works had to flee for their lives, as did gypsum miners underground, some of whom were killed by poisonous gas from the connecting RAF Fauld tunnels.

Mark said: "Despite some heroic work by airmen and American soldiers from the then US Army camp at Sudbury who drove to the scene, witnesses from the day speak of official confusion.

"Many of the civilians caught up in the disaster, the dead and survivors alike, came from Hanbury. The village, always quite remote compared with Burton, then had to endure media intrusion and flights overhead by nosey air force pilots taking a look at the 250-yard crater and the devastated fields."

The RAF banned flights over the area but, Mark says, a sense of grievance lingered in the village.

Other documents at Stafford include the Hanbury School log book and records kept by the vicar, the Rev James Crook, whose wife died days after the explosion and whose death is counted among the 70 victims.

Crook resigned from the parish only months after, in June 1945. Mark says: "Despite a visit to the district by the Bishop of Lichfield, James Crook wrote that he felt 'unequal to the task of rebuilding the parish'."

Mark says there is a question mark over the support given to the vicar by his Church of England superiors, just as Hanbury in general was left to get on with it.

Many roofs in the village were damaged as debris from the explosion crater rained down, hurled three-quarters of a mile.

The Cock Inn, on the side of the village nearest the crater, was partly destroyed by this debris. The pub was pulled down and replaced after the war.

The village school, now apartments, was so cold in the winter after the explosion that the schoolmistress recorded a temperature inside of 34 degrees Fahrenheit – barely above freezing.

She wrote: "It has previously been 40 and 41 but never as bad as this. All children's desks were drawn as near as possible to the fire and coats were worn."

As a church school, the vicar had the final say; he allowed it to close until it turned warmer.

Mark says: "Some old people might say, and do say, that in the war there was no such thing as counselling, as if to query why people after trauma today might have counselling.

The Day the Sun Disappeared, 27 Nov 1944

"Times were different in the 1939-45 war, but that doesn't make a lack of counselling right. Fauld was, and still is, a forgotten and unappreciated disaster outside the immediate area.

"People suffered mentally and physically and were bereaved and, while there was a charity fund that did not bring the dead back who had nothing to do with RAF Fauld and were going innocently about their business when their lives were violently cut short.

"Monuments were slow in coming, though they do stand now at the crater's edge and at the National Memorial Arboretum.

"Remarkably, the man in command of RAF Fauld, Ronald Storrar, sat on the RAF court of inquiry into his own accident. He was awarded an OBE in 1945 for his work after the explosion.

"He stayed in the same branch of the air force and retired with the rank of air vice marshal."

The Day The Dump Went Up, published in paperback and priced £12, has 90 pictures, including some of Fauld above ground today which have been taken by David Ward.

It's on sale at the Magic Attic and Swadlincote tourist information in Sharpe's Pottery, Spalding Books in Barton and at Waterstone's in Burton.

Proceeds go to the Magic Attic, where Mark is a trustee. The book is dedicated to Donald McCutcheon (1929-2003), a teacher of Mark's at Paulet, who helped him with his interviews and Mark's father Peter, who died in May.

Mark says: "While I am glad to publish my fullest account yet of Fauld, I do feel sad because so many of the people I spoke to and who were helpful to me are dead, including my father, Peter, who was in New Street when the dump went up, and whose uncle,

The Day the Sun Disappeared, 27 Nov 1944

Percy Cooper, was among the two dozen who died in the Ford's mudslide."

People interested in finding out more about the explosion can visit Tutbury Museum but it is only open in the summer as it is run by volunteers.

There are also numerous graves in the area. Despite a suggestion at the time that the dead might have to be buried in a mass grave, gravestones of civilians killed are scattered around local churches, notably St. Werbergh's, in Hanbury, which also has a plaque inside.

Hanbury Methodist chapel (now a private house) and Tutbury graveyards also contain the graves of victims.

The six Italian "co-operators" who died underground have military tombstones and are buried on the Elms Road side of Stapenhill cemetery.

Arguably the most telling memorial, though silent, is the crater itself. Mark found evidence from the 1960s and 1970s of proposals for the crater to be filled in with power station or general waste.

Instead, the 100-foot deep crater, which was bare as late as 1970, is now filled by trees and is a haven for bird and animal wildlife. Paths around it are popular with dog walkers and ramblers.

Mark says: "It is remarkable how within a relatively few years nature has hidden man's destruction.

"The first-time visitor would hardly know the crater was unnatural. Winter is the best time of year to visit, to feel the bleakness."

The Day the Sun Disappeared, 27 Nov 1944

Acknowledgements

Graham Shaw – grandson of Mary Cooper

Joe Cooper – son of Mary Cooper

Mark Rowe

John Pye

Robert Minchin – curator of the Tutbury Museum

WW2 People's War – Life in Burton on Trent by cornwallcsv – Peter Birtles, Article ID A6024331

The Great Fauld Explosion – Trevor Jones

Burton Daily Mail

Burton Observer and South Derbyshire Weekly Mail,

Daily Mail, November 28th, 1994

Derby Evening Telegraph

London Daily Mail

Staffordshire Advertiser

Disasters Underground by N J McCamley

The Day the Sun Disappeared, 27 Nov 1944

Sergeant Mackay and his wife, Olive, in 1951

Index

Allen, Bill, Flight Sergeant
293
Allan, Fred
126
Allen, G.C, Group Captain
333,396
Allen Philip
125
Allen, Stewart, 164,366
Anness, SL
50,56,173,207,214,334-5.341,347,349,351
Appleby James
187,192-3,428
Ashmore, Len
162,165,167-8
Auden John, Coroner
80.135.251.156-7,315,317-8,379-40,382-3,391-2,429
Bailey, John, LAC
59,208,217,220,341,343,346-9,401
Beard, Charles
285
Beard James
188-9,190-1,194-5,254,280-1,286,407,459
Bell, Eli
93,315,413
Bell John
52,175,335,347
Bell, Joseph
91,315,407
Bell, Richard
253
Bishop of Lichfield – Dr E S Woods
3,303-5,307,312,460
Bowring, Edmund
329
Bowring, Fred
2278.230-4,237-8,253,321,325,328,407
Bowring, Lesley, 331
Bowring, Olive
253,328
Bowring, Tom
115,148,305
Bowring, Wilfred
331
Brassington James AID
93,221,275,401
Bryant Eric
336,388-9,428
Buttle, Mr L D
193,335
Campbell, Fredk
221,401
Cartwright Frank
111,123,363,402
Cartwright Reginald
123,363,408
Cockayne George Lawrence
92-3.109,115,253,408
Coker Harold
181,185-6,428
Cooper, Brian
126
Cooper Joe
7,26,35,99,115,136,148,240-1,388

The Day the Sun Disappeared, 27 Nov 1944

Cooper John
89,125,211,241,418,424,436
Cooper Joseph
14,187,228,232-4,239,244-5,254,321,325
409
Cooper, Margaret
144
Cooper Mary
7,85,131-2,134-6,144,240,257,261,379,
383,418,423,429,436,488
Cooper Percy
116,254,326,409,462
Crook James, Rev
125,133-4,259,320,322,398,415,460
Crook, Mrs Lilian
126,415
Deauville Mrs
229
Deauville, Tony
129
Deauville, William
340
Drinnan John B
187-8,191,428
Donald, F M, Sir Graham
49-50,62,85,198,352-3,385-6
Durose, Corp A
187,313,415
Eccleston Thomas
389
Ede George
105-6,150,153
Ede, Nora
105

Ede, Chuter
392

Elliott, Charles – CO
175-6,181-2,184,238,428
Fletcher Charles Herbert
389
Ford Fred
25,35,148,228
Ford Nellie Mrs
81,104-6,109,118,152,242,415
Ford William
27,243,254,325,409
Foster Joseph
104-5,111,113,117-89,121-
2,124,135,247-8,250,252-3,
292-3,305,379,383,401,429
Frow, Lewis
93,209,213,217,219,221-4,335,402
Frow-McLeod,Joyce
222,224,436-7
Gent, William
93,110,116,119,264,326,409
Gibbard LAC
214
Gibbs, Charles
105,228-9,230,232,235-6,,245-
7,240,243,328
Gibbs Ernest
121
Goodwin Gordon
35,38-9,90,397
Goodwin Marie
35,38,90,397
Goodwin Mary
90,314,397,409
Goodwin Maurice
16,25,28,30,35,40,90,148,154-
5,261,292,314,359,397,409,415
Gorton Jack

91,228-9,232,235-6,239,247,304,341-2
Gretton, John, MP
286,302,304,317,319,322
Gregson, Roy
259-60
Green William Henry
388
Harding, E.C. WC
333
Hardwick, Bert
19,228,236,246,304
Hardwick John
25-6,29,31,35,149,418,422
Harrison Clara
242
Harrison Dorothy
98-9,242
Harrison Fred
8,106-7,255,410
Harrison Ida
87,144,148,242,425
Harrison Bernard
30,144,146-7
Harrison Peter
87,125
Harrison Sandy
111
Superintendent H G Heath
4-5,82,136,251,379,457
Heathcote Jim
25,27,38,97-9,104,106,115,117,120,148-9,242
Hickson David
388
Higgett Vernon, LAC
340
Hill Harry
27-8,105,109,118,151,242,253,255,410
Hill Kathleen and Ronald
151,152
Hill Sarah
105,-7,109,118,151,255,410
Hudson, Thomas
138,253,324,410
Hunt John
130-1,133
Hurstfield, Alf
112,117
Jefferies Wm, S.Fireman
55-6,340
Kelly, John PC Sergeant
80-1,83,94-5
Kenny, James LAC
54-5,337-40,347
Keys Doddy
121
Kings W C
50,53,56-8,62,176,180-1,183,201,333,349,396,427
Langley, Howard, RAF, Police Sergeant
52,334
Lanzoni Aldo
220,414
Lees, A,Air Vice Marshall
337-41,343,348
Lewis, FL John P
181,427
Lindsay, Fred
110,123
Lovatt, William
110,117,119,264
Mackay, PC Albert Thomas

4,78-9,92,106,120,136,215,218,240-1,246,249,255-6,258,278,282-3,304,358,378,382,428,464
Mackay Barbara
4,11,17,22,24,74,309
Mackay Connie
4,12,17-19,33,74-5
Mackay Constance, Olive
13,22,26,31,41,300-1,317,319,321-2
McLeod, Ken LAC
53,212,217-8,224,335,337,346,436
McLeod, Joyce – see Frow
Merrick Arthur Frederick
388
Miles,Russell
42,92,154,401
Morris Herbert
232,234
Moseley Wm
110,121
Mylotte Thomas
61,176,179,183,339,388
Nicklin, Fred AID
55,93,209,221,338,402
Novello Rocco,
220,253,414
Page Alf
70,235,239,247,324
Page Ernald
410
Page George
70,252,324,411
Page, John
73
Page, Philip
253,325,411
Paolo Emilia Di,
220,414
Parker Alfred
188
Parker Ernest
335,388
Perry Jack, Supt
187-91,194,427
Peter Corporal
236,246-7,427
Peters, James
427
Pittaway John
18,21,283,296,308
Pollard James
51,57,346-7,350
Pooley A.F.LAC
340
Poynton Corp Lionel
53,39-60,207,211,335,343-7,352,432-3
Priestley, George
93,325,412
Priestley Percy
230-2,239,253
Radcliffe James
112,117
Redfern John
110-1,119,121,150,246,392,403
Robertson John
187,188,191,426
Rock, Corporal Sidney B
236,246-7,427
Rock, Edward John
262
Rock, Fredk George
130-2,136,258,262,403
Rollo, Norman, Pilot Officer
57,173,334,346

Rotter Dr Godfrey
386-7,389,427

Rowe Fred
239
Ruggeri Salvatore,
54,220
Rule, Frank LAC
56,337
Saunders, Tom (AID)
60,62,208-9,345-6,403
Scuto Luigi,
220,415
Shelley, Sarah and William
127-8,144,408
Shepherd George
228-9,239
Shepherd Harry
91,93,232-5,237-8,252,324,412
Shepherd, William
92,93,234,412
Sheridan, Patrick LAC
53-4,335-6
Simpson – Warder
183
Simpson Jesse
236
Skellet, Constable
52
Skellett J
413
Slater, Frederick William
188-90,220,252,413
Smith Elizabeth
35,37,42,90,403
Smith Gary
271

Smith George
92-3,232,234-5,312,324,413

Smith John
163
Smith Nancy
271
Snape Leonard G
188,190
Solomon Joseph
57,173,334,340-1
Still – Airman
182
Storrar, GC
57-8,61-2,173,207-8,345,360-2,379-80,383,396,460
Treadwell James
232,239,400
Trovato, Salvatore
54,220,253,415
Utting Dick
25-7,99,115-6,148-9
Utting Horace
29,335,388
Wagstaffe Robert
30,36,40,42,92,154-5,403
Wainwright Thomas
388
Walker G J
117,122,150-2,230
Watson Michael LAC
337
Watson William
106,214,230-7,239,243,247
Webb John
188-90,194,428
Wetherill, Ena,

2
Wetherill, Harry
106,111
West John
25,28,42,70,90,1545,253,366,,392,413
West Stephen
25,28,42,90,154,366,390,391-2,413
Whetton Cyril John
199-201
Whittaker George Edward
3448,401
Wright Jack
245-7
Zucca Mr and Mrs
39,153-5

The Day the Sun Disappeared, 27 Nov 1944

Other historical novels by the author:

Series:

Footsteps in the Past- ISBN 978-0-244-25919-8 This is history turned into a gripping novel. All historical facts are true.

Jane finds herself whisked back in time to 1842, after seeing a ghostly figure running away from the Ash Hall nursing home where she works.

She finds herself working for Job Meigh, the entrepreneur pottery master who built Ash Hall. He was a violent Victorian, but a great philanthropist and a magistrate. He, and industrialist pottery and mine owners had grown rich from the labours of their workers, who were driven to starvation when their pay was repeatedly cut. The Chartists wanted to get the People's Charter approved by Parliament to offer the people representation in Parliament and the vote. This was rejected, resulting in the violent Pottery Riots.

Jane has to discover why she has been sent back into the past and how to get back, and gets involved with the riots – which lead her into life- threatening danger. She also has to find out who the ghostly figure was.

Footsteps in the Past – The Secret – ISBN 978-0-355-63374-2 The Secret takes the main characters 39 years on from the Pottery Riots of 1842. There is a mining disaster in Bucknall, Stoke, in which Jane and John's son is involved. While nursing John back to health, after his attempt to rescue their son, Jane reminisces what has happened since they met.

Her stories unravel while desperately awaiting news if their son is still alive or not. All historical facts are true.

The Day the Sun Disappeared, 27 Nov 1944

Footsteps in the Past – John's Story –
ISBN 978-1-716-16818-127
This tells John's story from his youth in the countryside village of Hanley in the 1820s through its industrialisation. It tells John's poignant story of his life, loves and losses in the background of the traumatic times and struggles of people fighting for their rights, representation in Parliament and the vote, which lead to the Pottery Riots of 1842. It also tells of the Cholera Pandemic of 1832 similar to Covid today) and his time in the workhouse.

Munford-Gunn – ISBN 97985-322-313-68
This is a dramatic and thrilling true adventure story following two families of pioneers trying to get to Utah, America to escape prejudice for their beliefs. They meet other prejudice along the way, this time against Africans and First Nation Indians. The book is based on true-life reports.

The families make the life-threatening journey by sailing ship (taking six weeks in those days to cross the Atlantic) then join ox-drawn wagon trains, walking beside these across the 1,300 miles of searing hot plains, dragging the wagons through rivers and perilously hauling them up and over the mountains to get to Salt Lake City. Many die along the way of starvation, dehydration and disease.

The two families meet up. Ann Munford marries George Gunn, only to have to set out immediately to clear land and build settlements – that is until the Black Hawk Wars start.

Review: "What a nightmare. I had to keep reminding myself to breathe. Going to make a cup of tea to get over the trauma. The description is brilliant. I felt I was right there with them."

The Day the Sun Disappeared, 27 Nov 1944

The Barlaston Murderer – Leslie Green
ISBN 979875449770

This is the story of the brutal murder of Mrs Mary Maud Wiltshaw, n 16th July 1952, at her home – going by the name of 'Estoril' on Station Road, Barlaston, Stoke-on-Trent.

Leslie Green, former chauffeur of the Wiltshaws, was hanged for the murder on 23rd December 1952, but right up to the moment of the noose going around his neck, he denied carrying out the murder, saying he was elsewhere – asleep on a park bench. I was intrigued by this – did he do the murder or not? Yes, you can say that he was a loser, a thief, and that drink played a part in the attack – possibly. I was also intrigued by the fact that he presented himself to the police station of his own accord. Now, why would he do that, if he had committed the murder? Also, there was a later deathbed confession that was not investigated.

This book sets out the actual police investigations and trial that led to his sentence of hanging, taken from newspapers at the time. However, I wanted to give another possible side of the story, that could conceivably have had a bearing on Leslie Green's state of mind at the time – a mind that, from his early childhood and mistreatment, had manifested itself into loss of memory – when he experienced a sense of 'loss of time' - when another personality took over.

Please note that this is a completely fictitious notion but seemed to fit the bill. None of the history of Leslie Green before the trial, apart from his prosecutions, is factual or could be verified, despite meticulous investigations.

The Rough Clouse Murder – ISBN 9 799306 60830 6
This is a true crime for 1886 in Stoke on Trent. John Daniel shot his brother, William , dead, after a quarrel concerning John's wife. William is a nasty drunk, who has lost his business and his home and comes back to live at his father's farm, which John is managing, but William hates John's wife.

I was given this story by someone who actually lived in the house and noticed paranormal activity.

A new family move in and start to refurbish the old farmhouse. Dave gets electrocuted and his personality starts to change - drinking heavily and becoming nasty. Has he been infiltrated by the spirit of William? A real life psychic medium is called in to investigate.

Printed in Great Britain
by Amazon